THE volumes of the University of Michigan Studies and Publications are published by authority of the Board of Regents under the direction of the University of Michigan Press. The contributors are chiefly, but not exclusively, members of the faculties or graduates of the University. The expense is borne in part by gifts, in part by appropriations of the Board of Regents. A list of volumes already published or in preparation is given at the end of this volume.

Volumes may be obtained by ordering from the Librarian, University of Michigan, Ann Arbor, Michigan.

University of Michigan Studies

HUMANISTIC SERIES

VOLUME XXXVII

COINS FROM SELEUCIA ON THE TIGRIS

COINS FROM SELEUCIA ON THE TIGRIS

BY

ROBERT HARBOLD McDOWELL

ANN ARBOR
UNIVERSITY OF MICHIGAN PRESS
1935

Set up and printed,
August, 1935

PRINTED IN THE UNITED STATES OF AMERICA
BY THE PLIMPTON PRESS • NORWOOD • MASS.

Paperback ISBN : 978-0-472-75170-9

C. S. B.

TO WHOSE EVER-WILLING
AND CAPABLE ASSISTANCE
THIS VOLUME OWES MUCH

PREFACE

THE coins included in this volume were found on the site of Seleucia on the Tigris in connection with the excavations conducted there during the seasons 1927/28 to 1931/32 by Professor Leroy Waterman under the auspices of the University of Michigan, the Toledo Museum of Art, and, for the last two seasons, the Cleveland Museum of Art.[1]

The total of the coins found amounts to more than thirty thousand. The majority came from the surface débris over the whole extent of the mounds and represent all the principal levels of occupation of the site. During each period in antiquity represented, coins of earlier occupations were brought to what was then the surface through the excavation of subsurface structures such as wells and foundation walls. The objects thus carried along to the latest level of occupation were finally exposed on the present surface as a result of the erosive action of wind and water. It is readily to be seen, therefore, that surface coins, especially when recovered in large numbers, contribute largely in their own way to the study of an ancient site.

Slightly more than one half of the coins included in the volume came from definite provenances — rooms, streets, and burials of the areas excavated. In the catalogs the provenances of the coins have been indicated only in the case of certain of the more important caches. The relation of the coins to the architectural features of the site must be reserved for a separate study. A further limitation in the scope of the volume has been the exclusion of the relatively few Roman and Characenian pieces and the fairly numerous examples of the Sassanian, Mongol, and Arab coinages.

The greater part of the coins from Seleucia are in a poor state of preservation. This appears to have been due to the nature and quantity of the salts with which the earth and débris

[1] Details regarding the site and the excavations may be found in Dr. N. C. Debevoise's *Parthian Pottery from Seleucia on the Tigris*, pp. 6–11, and the author's *Stamped and Inscribed Objects from Seleucia on the Tigris*, p. vii. Both these volumes are in this series.

of the site have been impregnated. In order to provide the some two thousand six hundred specimens which are described in the catalogs, nearly ten thousand coins were treated and cleaned. Silver coins were placed in a weak solution of hot formic acid. The greater part of the bronze coins were passed through an electrolytic process; the others were treated in a solution of caustic soda and Rochelle salts. In this connection the writer wishes to express his appreciation to Dr. Henry W. Nichols, Associate Curator in the Field Museum of Natural History, for his counsel and suggestions in connection with the installation of the electrolytic baths. As a check on the technique used locally, Mr. Newell and Mr. Noe of the American Numismatic Society kindly undertook the treatment of a representative lot of the bronze coins from Seleucia and obtained results approximately similar. The generally poor condition of the coins has limited the number of plates which accompany the catalogs. The preparation of plates from casts of the coins did not prove satisfactory. Mr. George Swain, to whom the photographs are due, obtained the best results possible under the circumstances by coating each coin with a light film of uniform color.

The writer wishes to express his appreciation to the members of the Institute of Archaeological Research of the University of Michigan, under whose direction this volume has been prepared, and to the Executive Board of the Graduate School, under whose auspices it has been published. In particular Dr. A. E. R. Boak, chairman of the Department of History, and Dr. Leroy Waterman, head of the Department of Oriental Languages and Literature and director of the excavations at Seleucia, have given the writer the benefit of generous counsel and aid. In addition, real benefit has been derived from frequent discussions with Dr. Wilhelmina van Ingen of the University of Michigan, who is now engaged upon the publication of the figurines from Seleucia. The editors of the Graduate School Publications have been unstinted in their coöperation towards the preparation of the volume.

It is a matter of great regret to the writer that he was unable to place before Mr. E. T. Newell proofs of the manuscript until shortly before its publication. In spite of this handicap the volume owes much to his always generous counsel and wide experience. Owing, however, to the conditions, it has been necessary to incorporate certain of Mr. Newell's suggestions as special notes without making, in some instances, the corresponding alteration in the text which the suggestion warranted. Mr. Newell also very kindly placed at the disposition of the writer the manuscript of a study of the Parthian coinage which is to appear in Mr. Arthur Upton Pope's forthcoming *A Survey of Persian Art and Archaeology.*

To Professor A. T. Olmstead of the Oriental Institute, the University of Chicago, the writer is indebted for stimulating suggestions and for illuminating discussions of the background of Parthian history. Throughout the period of the preparation of the manuscript numerous discussions with Dr. N. C. Debevoise of the Oriental Institute have been of invaluable assistance. Dr. Debevoise generously permitted the writer frequent access to the notes and manuscript of his forthcoming *A Political History of Parthia*, to be published by the University of Chicago.

The completion of this volume would have been impossible without the loyal coöperation of capable assistants in the preparation of the coins. The greater part of the weighing and measuring of the coins was carried out by Mr. Charles P. Spicer, Jr., A.M., who aided also in their cleaning. Dr. Louise Shier of the University of Michigan shared in the weighing and measuring and aided in the filing of the coins. The principal burden of the cleaning and filing of the coins during more than two years fell on Miss Catharine S. Bunnell, A.M., who gave to this work a particularly fine enthusiasm and adeptness. With equal capacity Miss Bunnell carried out the preliminary identification of a large proportion of the Parthian coins. To my wife, Olga R. McDowell, I am indebted for extensive assistance in the proofreading and for the reorganization of the coin files upon the completion of the volume.

R. H. McD.

CONTENTS

PLATES

(The plates are to be found at the end of the book)

BIBLIOGRAPHY

Babelon, E., Les Rois de Syrie, d'Arménie et de Commagène. Paris, 1890.

—— See under Morgan, J. de.

Bellinger, A. R., "The Coins," The Excavations at Dura-Europos, Preliminary Report of Third Season of Work, November 1929—March 1930 (ed. P. V. C. Bauer, M. I. Rostovtzeff, and A. R. Bellinger). New Haven, 1932, pp. 139–160.

—— "The Coins," The Excavations at Dura-Europos, Preliminary Report of Fourth Season of Work, October 1930—March 1931 (ed. P. V. C. Bauer, M. I. Rostovtzeff, and A. R. Bellinger). New Haven, 1933, pp. 259–282.

Bouché-Leclercq, A., Histoire de Séleucides. Paris, 1914.

Dayet, Marcel, "Un Tétradrachme arsacide inédit," Aretheuse, 1 (1925), 63–65.

Debevoise, N. C., A Political History of Parthia (to be published shortly by the University of Chicago Press).

Dieudonné, A., "La Mission de Suse," Revue numismatique, 4e série, 32 (1929), 27–34.

Fuÿe, A. de la, "Les Monnaies de l'Elymaïde," Revue numismatique, 4e série, 22 (1919), 45–83.

Gardner, P., The Parthian Coinage. London, 1877.

—— Catalogue of Greek Coins, The Seleucid Kings of Syria. London, 1878.

—— Catalogue of Coins in the British Museum: Thessaly to Aetolia. London, 1883.

Grose, S., Catalogue of the McClean Collection of Greek Coins. Cambridge, 1929.

Gutschmid, A. von, Geschichte Irans und seiner Nachbarländer. Tübingen, 1888.

Hill, G. F., Catalogue of the Greek Coins of Arabia, Mesopotamia and Persia. London, 1922.

—— "A Hoard of Coins from Nineveh," The Numismatic Chronicle, Fifth series, 11 (1931), 160–170.

Imhoof-Blumer, F., Monnaies grecques. Paris and Leipzig, 1883.

Johnson, Jotham, Dura Studies (Thesis, University of Pennsylvania). Philadelphia, 1932.

Jordan, J., Uruk-Warka, nach den Ausgrabungen durch die deutsche Orient-Gesellschaft. Leipzig, 1928.

Legrain, L., "Coins from Nippur," The Museum Journal, University of Pennsylvania, 15 (1924), 70–76.

LINDSAY, J., A View of the History and Coinage of the Parthians. Cork, 1852.

LONGDEN, R. P., "Notes on the Parthian Campaign of Trajan," The Journal of Roman Studies, 21 (1931), 1–35.

LONGPÉRIER, A. DE, Mémoires sur la chronologie et l'iconographie des rois parthes arsacides. Paris, 1853.

McDOWELL, R. H., "The Excavations at Seleucia on the Tigris," Papers of the Michigan Academy of Science, Arts and Letters, 18 (1932), 101–119.

—— Stamped and Inscribed Objects from Seleucia on the Tigris. Ann Arbor, 1935.

MARKOFF, A., Catalogue des monnaies arsacides. St. Petersburg, 1889.

MINNS, E. H., "Parchments of the Parthian Period from Avroman in Kurdistan," The Journal of Hellenic Studies, 35 (1915), 22–65.

MORGAN, J. DE, Numismatique de la Perse Antique. Paris, 1927. (This is Volume III, Part 1, in Traité des monnaies grecques et romaines, ed. E. Babelon.)

NEWELL, E. T., The Seleucid Mint at Antioch. New York, 1918.

—— "A Parthian Hoard," The Numismatic Chronicle, Fifth series, 4 (1924), 141–180.

—— Mithradates of Parthia and Hyspaosines of Characene: A Numismatic Palimpsest, Numismatic Notes and Monographs, No. 26. New York, 1925.

—— The Fifth Dura Hoard, *ibid.*, No. 58. New York, 1933.

—— "The Coins" (in Mr. A. U. Pope's forthcoming Survey of Persian Art and Archaeology).

PETROWICZ, A. RITTER VON, Arsaciden-Münzen. Vienna, 1904.

PROKESCH-OSTEN, M. LE COMPTE, Les Monnaies des rois parthes. Paris, 1874–1875.

RAWLINSON, G., The Sixth Great Oriental Monarchy. London, 1873.

ROGERS, E., "New Seleucid Coin Types," The Numismatic Chronicle, Fifth series, 1 (1921), 26–36.

ROSTOVTZEFF, M. I., "Syria and the East," The Cambridge Ancient History, VII, 155–196.

—— AND WELLES, C. B., "A Parchment Contract of Loan from Dura-Europos on the Euphrates," Yale Classical Studies, 2 (1930), 1–78.

STRECK, M., "Seleukeia," Pauly-Wissowa Real Encyclopädie der classischen Altertumswissenschaft, Zweite Reihe, Vol. II.

TARN, W., "Parthia," The Cambridge Ancient History, IX, 574–613.

VAN INGEN, WILHELMINA, Figurines from Seleucia on the Tigris (a forthcoming volume in this series).

WROTH, W., Catalogue of the Coins of Parthia. London, 1903.

PART I

COINS OF THE SELEUCID PERIOD

CHAPTER I

CATALOG OF COINS

THE serial numbers of the catalog refer to the successive type groups; the figures in parentheses, to the number of examples of the group which have been studied. Under the heading "Monogram" the serial numbers are those of Plate I, on which have been reproduced all monograms and groups of initials of both the Seleucid and the Parthian periods. To facilitate reference to them all occurrences of each monogram and of each group of initials have been listed on the plate. Published coins have been cited by the names of authors; the full titles are given in the Bibliography on page xiii. In order to maintain the clarity of the catalog for purposes of rapid comparison, all notes dealing with individual groups or coins have been brought together in the next chapter. Each note bears the serial number of the type group to which it is related and in the catalog is cited by the page number only. In the plates the catalog numbers of the coins are retained. The weight and the greatest diameter of each specimen of a group have been recorded in the order of the weight of the coins. In only a few instances has an effort been made to distinguish the various denominations of the bronze coins.

On pages 44–47 a table will be found which lists the type groups of the Seleucid period and gives the total number of groups and of coins for each reign.

ALEXANDER THE GREAT[1]

(Prior to 321 B.C.)

1 Æ (2)

Obv.: Zeus, half-draped, seated l. on a throne without a back. The r. hand rests on a scepter in front, the l. hand, on the throne.

Rev.: A lion advancing l., the tail raised.

Legend: None occurs.

[1] The two coins of Alexander, although strictly speaking not of the Seleucid period, in a practical sense, form a part of this series.

Monograms: Obv., beneath throne, on the larger coin, No. 1, on the smaller, obscured; rev., beneath lion, on the larger, No. 2, on the smaller, No. 3.

The adjustment of the dies is normal. There is a border of dots on obverse and reverse.

Cf. Hill, 181–191, Nos. 3–60; XX, 16, to XXII, 17. See Pl. II and discussion, p. 28.

gr. : 14.81 1.33
mm. : 23.60 12.4

SELEUCUS I

As Satrap (prior to 311 B.C.)

2 Æ (1)

Obv.: A head r. male, wearing an elephant-scalp headdress.

Rev.: To the r., the head of a horse; to the l., an anchor, inverted.

Legend: Through the center of the field, down ΑΛΕΞΑΝΔΡΟΥ.

Monogram: In the field l., No. 4.

The adjustment of the dies is ↑ →. No border can be distinguished. The edge is straight.

Cf. Babelon, v, Fig. 5. See Pl. II and discussion, p. 28.

gr. : 2.37
mm. : 12.5

As King (311–280 B.C.)

3 Ꭱ (1)

Obv.: Head of Hercules r., without beard, wearing a lion-skin headdress.

Rev.: Zeus seated l. on a throne with a high back. The outstretched r. arm holds an eagle; the l. rests on a long scepter, behind.

Legend: Obscure traces in the field r. and in the exergue.

Symbol: In the field l., an inverted anchor.

The adjustment of the dies is normal. No border can be distinguished.

Babelon, 2, No. 6; I, 4. See discussion, p. 29.

gr. : 17.41
mm. : 27.00

4 AR (1)

Obv.: As on No. 3.

Rev.: As on No. 3 except that the throne has no back.

Legend: Obscure traces in the field r. The exergue is off flan.

Monogram: None can be distinguished.

The adjustment of the dies is ↑ →. No border can be distinguished. The coin is silver-plated over a bronze core.

Babelon, 2, Nos. 4, 8; I, 2, 5. See discussion, p. 29.

gr. : 12.63
mm. : 24.60

5 Æ (1)

Obv.: Head of Zeus r., laureate.

Rev.: Athena standing r. in a chariot drawn by four elephants and brandishing a thunderbolt in the r. hand.

Legend: l., obscure, ex. [ΣΕΛ]ΕΥΚΟΥ.

Monogram: None can be distinguished, perhaps owing to the condition of the coin.

Symbol: In the field r., an anchor.

The adjustment of the dies is ↑ →. No border can be distinguished.

Babelon, 11, Nos. 72–73; III, 2. See discussion, p. 29.

gr. : 3.00
mm. : 15.5

6 Æ (2)

Obv.: Heads of the Dioscuri ¾ l.

Rev.: Nike standing l., crowning a trophy. The l. hand holds a palm over the shoulder.

Legend: r. ΒΑΣΙΛΕΩΣ, l. ΣΕΛΕΥΚΟΥ.

Monogram: In the field center, No. 5.

Symbol: At the feet of Nike, a boar's head.

The adjustment of the dies is normal. There is a border of continuous fillet. The edges are straight.

Cf. Babelon, 8, No. 47. See discussion, p. 29.

gr. : 3.64 1.17
mm. : 17.4 17.9

7 Æ (1)

Obv.: Head of Apollo ¾ l., laureate.

Rev.: The head of a bull ¾ r.

Legend: Entirely obscured.

Monogram: None can be distinguished, perhaps owing to the condition of the coin.

The adjustment of the dies is ↑ →. There is a border of continuous fillet. The edge is straight.

Babelon, 9, No. 52; II, 6.

gr. : 5.46
mm. : 18.3

8 Æ (1)

Obv.: Head of Apollo r., laureate. Rev.: The head of a bull facing front.

Legend: r. [B]ΑΣΙΛΕΩ[Σ], l. [Σ]ΕΛΕΥ[ΚΟΥ].

Monogram: None can be distinguished, perhaps owing to the condition of the coin.

The adjustment of the dies is ↑ →. No border can be distinguished. The edge is straight.

Pl. II. See discussion, p. 29.

gr. : 5.83
mm. : 19.2

9 Æ (16)

Obv.: The head of a horse r., with horns. Rev.: An anchor, upright.

Legend: r. ΒΑΣΙΛΕΩΣ, l. ΣΕΛΕΥΚΟΥ.

Monogram: In the field r., No. 6. This can be distinguished on five coins of various sizes. On the rest this portion of the field has been obscured or is off flan.

The adjustments of the dies are ↑ ↑, ↑ ↗, ↑ ↖, ↑ ↙. There is a border of dots. The edges are straight.

Babelon, 10, Nos. 59, 62; II, 13, 16. See discussion, p. 29.

gr. :	7.73	4.00	3.86	3.85	3.40	3.13	3.01	2.77	2.72	2.57	2.56
mm. :	26.0	16.4	16.7	16.5	16.5	17.0	16.1	15.6	15.8	16.8	15.0
	2.45	2.45	2.41	2.12	2.08						
	16.3	15.5	15.0	15.5	16.1						

10 Æ (6)

Obv.: Bust of Seleucus facing slightly off front. The head is surmounted by horns. Rev.: A horseman r., in the act of hurling a javelin at a prostrate foe.

Legend: Above ΒΑΣΙΛΕΩΣ, below ΣΕΛΕΥΚΟΥ.

Monograms: In the field l., No. 7, r., on some coins, No. 8, on the others, an obscure monogram.

The adjustments of the dies are ↑ ↑, ↑ ↗, ↑ →. There is a border of continuous fillet. The edges are straight.

Babelon, 10, No. 63; II, 17. See discussion, p. 30.

gr. :	7.45	4.04	3.99	3.73	3.28	3.18
mm. :	22.6	17.9	18.0	17.8	17.2	17.7

11 Æ (13)

Obv.: Head of Apollo r., laureate. Rev.: A humped bull r., with head lowered.

Legend: Above ΒΑΣΙΛΕΩΣ, below ΣΕΛΕΥΚΟΥ.

Monograms and symbols: In denomination *(a)* on one coin occur No. 9 and No. 10; on two, an anchor; on four, a star and a sphere; on one, all details have been obscured. In denomination *(b)* on one coin appears K; on the second, a star and a sphere; on the third, all details have been obscured. The two coins of denomination *(c)* are in a very obscure condition, and no monogram or symbol can be distinguished.

The adjustments of the dies vary extensively without relation to the denomination. There is a border of dots. The edges are straight.

Babelon, 13, No. 86; III, 8. See discussion, p. 30.

The coins appear to belong to three denominations.

gr. :	*(a)*	5.60	5.48	5.46	5.46	4.97	4.61	3.84	2.82	*(b)* 3.08	2.49
mm. :		19.3	19.0	18.9	19.0	18.6	19.0	19.0	18.6	15.3	14.7

1.84	*(c)*	0.97	0.68
15.1		10.9	11.3

12 Æ (5)

Obv.: Head of Apollo $\frac{3}{4}$ l., laureate. Rev.: Nike standing l., holding a wreath through the royal name.

Legend: r. ΒΑΣΙΛΕΩΣ, l. ΣΕΛΕΥΚΟΥ.

Monograms: In the field l., on one coin, No. 11; on a second, No. 7. On the rest this portion of the field has been obscured or is off flan.

The adjustments of the dies vary extensively. There is a border of dots. The edges are straight.

Pl. II. See discussion, p. 30.

gr. :	3.58	3.13	2.86	2.40	1.41
mm. :	16.6	14.0	15.0	14.2	13.6

13 Æ (1)

Obv.: An obscure head ¾ l., partly off flan. The representation is probably of Apollo, possibly of Medusa.

Rev.: A draped figure, female (?), standing ¾ r. The head is largely off flan. The l. arm is raised in front, the hand off flan. The r. arm extends backward as though in the act of hurling an object; the hand is off flan. The type probably represents Athena.

Legend: r. off flan, l. [ΣΕ]ΛΕΥΚΟΥ.

Monogram: None can be distinguished, perhaps owing to the condition of the coin.

Symbol: In the field l., an inverted anchor.

The adjustment of the dies is normal. No border can be distinguished. The edge is straight.

Pl. II (rev. only). See discussion, p. 30.

gr. : 3.52
mm. : 14.8

14 Æ (2)

Obv.: Head of Apollo ¾ l., laureate.

Rev.: A tripod.

Legend: r. ΒΑΣΙΛΕΩΣ, l. ΣΕΛΕΥΚΟΥ.

Monogram: None can be distinguished, perhaps owing to the condition of the coins.

The adjustments of the dies are ↑ ↑, ↑ →. No border can be distinguished. The edges are straight.

See discussion, p. 30.

gr. : 1.55 1.34
mm. : 11.4 11.6

ANTIOCHUS I

(280–261 B.C.)

15 Æ (1)

Obv.: Head of Antiochus r., diademed.

Rev.: Apollo, nude, seated l. on an omphalos. The r. hand, advanced, holds an arrow diagonally down; the l. rests on a grounded bow.

Legend: Entirely obscured.

Monogram: None can be distinguished, perhaps owing to the condition of the coin.

The adjustment of the dies is ↑ →. No border can be distinguished. The edge is straight.

Babelon, 20, No. 146; IV, 17. See discussion, p. 30.

gr. : 1.50
mm. : 15.0

16 Æ (17)

Obv.: Head of Apollo r., laureate.

Rev.: Athena standing r., in her upraised r. hand a thunderbolt; in her l., a shield held advanced diagonally. The ends of a folded chlamys hang from the two elbows.

(*a*) Legend: r. ΒΑΣΙΛΕΩΣ, l. ΑΝΤΙΟΧΟΥ.

Monograms: In the field l., No. 12, r., No. 13.

gr.	: 6.62	6.53	5.62	5.54
mm.	: 17.0	19.0	17.4	17.9

(*b*) Legend: r. ΒΑ, l. ΑΝ.

Monograms: On two coins l., No. 12, r., No. 13; on two l., No. 12, r., No. 14; on one, No. 15.

gr.	: 3.25	2.80	2.65	2.63	2.05
mm.	: 15.2	14.7	14.9	15.3	14.5

(*c*) Legend: As under (*a*).

Monograms: On one coin l., No. 16, r., No. 17; on two only No. 16 can be distinguished; on two none can be distinguished, owing to wear.

gr.	: 3.35	2.95	2.33	2.00	1.86
mm.	: 15.4	15.6	14.1	15.5	14.9

(*d*) Legend: As under (*a*).

Monogram: None can be distinguished, perhaps owing to wear.

gr.	: 1.67	1.41	1.22
mm.	: 13.3	12.5	12.8

The adjustments of the dies vary widely without regard to denomination or monograms. There is a border of dots. The edges are straight. The coins appear to comprise three denominations.

Cf. Babelon, 21, Nos. 151–152; V, 1. See discussion, p. 31.

17 Æ (1)

Obv.: Head of Apollo ¾ l., laureate. Rev.: As on No. 16.

Legend: r., obscure, l. Α[ΝΤΙΟΧΟΥ].

Monograms: In the field l. and r., obscured.

The adjustment of the dies is normal. No border can be distinguished. The edge is straight.

See discussion, p. 31.

gr. : 2.34
mm. : 14.0

18 Æ (3)

Obv.: As on No. 16.

Rev.: Athena standing r. as on No. 16, except that the shield is held advanced in a horizontal position.

Legend: r. ΒΑΣΙΛΕΩΣ, l., obscure.

Monograms: In the field l., No. 16, r., No. 17. They can be distinguished on two coins; on the third these portions of the field have been obscured.

The adjustment of the dies is normal. There is a border of dots. The edges are straight.

Cf. Babelon, 13, Nos. 80–85. See Pl. II (rev. only) and discussion, p. 31.

gr. : 2.41 1.10 0.90
mm. : 15.0 11.4 13.5

19 Æ (2)

Obv.: Head of Apollo r., laureate.

Rev.: Athena standing l. The r. hand grasps an upright spear; a grounded shield rests against the knees.

Legend: r. ΒΑΣΙΛΕΩΣ, l. ΑΝΤΙΟΧΟΥ.

Monogram: In the field r., No. 7.

The adjustment of the dies is ↑ ↙. No border can be distinguished. The edges are straight.

Babelon, 21, No. 156; V, 3. See discussion, p. 31.

gr. : 7.90 1.75
mm. : 19.2 12.3

20 Æ (13)

Obv.: Bust of Apollo ¾ r., laureate.

Rev.: Nike standing r., erecting a trophy.

Legend: r. ΒΑΣΙΛΕΩΣ, l. ΑΝΤΙΟΧΟΥ.

Monograms: On two coins in the field l., No. 17; on one of these in the field r., No. 18; on the other this portion of the field is off flan. On two coins in the field l., No. 19; on both the r. side of the field has been obscured. On four coins in the field r., No. 13; on two of these in the field l., No. 20; on the other two this portion of the field is off flan. On the remaining five coins no monograms can be distinguished, presumably owing to their condition.

The adjustments of the dies vary widely without relation to monograms or size. There is a border of dots. The edges are straight.

Babelon, 23–24, Nos. 177–180; V, 10–11. See discussion, p. 31.

gr. :	3.85	3.83	3.46	3.34	3.25	3.04	2.52	1.85	1.74	1.52	1.30
mm. :	17.0	17.0	16.7	16.0	16.8	16.5	16.5	13.0	14.4	16.0	14.0
	1.15	0.91									
	12.5	11.2									

21 Æ (14)

Obv.: Head of Apollo ¾ r., laureate. Rev.: A tripod.

Legend: r. ΒΑΣΙΛΕΩΣ, l. ΑΝΤΙΟΧΟΥ.

Monogram: In the field l., on four coins, No. 21. On the rest this portion of the field has been obscured or is off flan.

The adjustment of the dies is normal. No border can be distinguished. The edges have been flattened.

Babelon, 24, No. 181; V, 12. See discussion, p. 31.

gr. :	4.17	3.26	3.17	3.00	2.95	2.51	2.46	2.44	2.39	2.21	1.91
mm. :	17.5	14.8	15.0	14.9	16.2	14.1	14.6	16.2	13.6	15.5	14.3
	1.87	1.85	1.73								
	14.0	13.6	14.3								

22 Æ (4)

Obv.: Head of Athena ¾ l.

Rev.: Apollo seated r. on an omphalos, clad in a chiton. A cithara rests on the knees, held by the l. hand. *The r. arm is dropped at the side.*

Legend: r. ΒΑΣΙΛΕΩΣ, l. ΑΝΤΙΟΧΟΥ.

Monograms: On one coin in the field r., No. 7; in the field l., an obscure monogram, comprising in part X. On the rest both sides of the field have been obscured.

The adjustments of the dies are ↑ ↑, ↑ →. No border can be distinguished. The heaviest coin has a beveled edge; the edges of the rest are straight.

Cf. Babelon, 24, Nos. 186–187; V, 15. See discussion, p. 31.

gr. :	4.30	3.41	1.02	0.58
mm. :	16.4	16.7	13.0	11.1

23 Æ (9)

Obv.: Head of Athena ¾ r. Rev.: As on No. 22.

Legend: As on No. 22.

Monogram: None can be distinguished, perhaps owing to the condition of the coin.

The adjustments of the dies are ↑ ↑, ↑ ↓. No border can be distinguished. The edges are beveled with the exception of that of the lightest coin, which is straight.

See discussion, p. 31.

gr.	: 4.25	3.66	3.62	3.57	3.37	3.16	3.14	2.30	1.89
mm.	: 16.9	16.0	17.7	16.5	15.2	16.0	16.8	16.7	14.9

24 Æ (5)

Obv.: Head of Athena r. Rev.: Apollo, nude, standing l. The r. hand, advanced, holds an arrow diagonally down; the l. rests on a grounded bow.

Legend: r. ΒΑΣΙΛΕΩΣ, l. ΑΝΤΙΟΧΟΥ.

Monograms: On one coin in the field r., No. 22, l., an obscure monogram. On the rest both sides of the field have been obscured.

The adjustments of the dies are normal on the three small coins; on the two large, ↑→, ↑ ↓. There is a border of dots. The edges are straight.

Babelon, 25, No. 188; V, 16. See discussion, p. 32.

gr.	: 4.21	3.91	1.58	1.37	1.00
mm.	: 19.5	20.8	13.5	12.9	12.3

25 Æ (7)

Obv.: Head of Apollo ¾ l., laureate. Rev.: As on No. 24.

Legend: As on No. 24.

Monogram: None can be distinguished, perhaps owing to the condition of the coins.

The adjustments of the dies vary widely. There is a border of dots. Both beveled and straight edges occur.

Pl. II. See discussion, p. 32.

gr.	: 2.65	2.51	2.46	2.25	2.19	1.86	1.49
mm.	: 14.5	14.1	14.0	14.3	13.9	14.3	12.5

26 Æ (2)

Obv.: Head of Apollo ¾ r.

Rev.: A quiver, apparently alone.

Legend: r., obscure, l. ANTIO[XOΥ].

Monogram: None can be distinguished, perhaps owing to the condition of the coins.

The adjustments of the dies are ↑ ↑, ↑ ↗. No border can be distinguished. The edges are beveled.

See discussion, p. 32.

gr. : 3.02 2.54
mm. : 15.0 14.6

27 Æ (4)

Obv.: A head ¾ r., male, with mustache and beard. The form of the headdress cannot be determined. It appears to be intended to represent Zeus.

Rev.: A figure standing r. male, nude, probably Apollo. The r. hand is held over a tripod in front and clasps a short shaft, possibly an arrow. Behind the shoulder is an obscure object which suggests a quiver. The form of the headdress cannot be determined.

Legend: r. ΒΑΣΙΛΕΩΣ, l. ANTIOXOΥ.

Monogram: On one coin in the field l., No. 23. On the rest the sides of the field have been obscured or are off flan.

The adjustment of the dies is normal. There is a border of dots. The edges are slightly beveled.

Pl. II. See discussion, p. 32.

gr. : 4.84 3.10 3.01 2.90
mm. : 16.8 16.3 16.0 16.5

ANTIOCHUS II

(261–246 B.C.)

28 Æ (8)

Obv.: Head of Apollo r., laureate.

Rev.: Apollo nude, seated l. on an omphalos. The r. hand, advanced, holds an arrow diagonally down; the l. rests on a grounded bow.

Legend: r. ΒΑΣΙΛΕΩΣ, l. ANTIOXOΥ.

Monogram: On two coins in the field r., No. 24. On three coins appear traces of what is probably the same monogram. On the rest this portion of the field is entirely off flan.

The adjustments of the dies are ↑ ↑, ↑ ↓, ↑ ↖. There is a border of dots. The edges are straight.

Babelon, 32, Nos. 239–242; VI, 17. See discussion, p. 33.

gr. : 3.10 2.93 2.90 2.65 2.65 2.61 2.09 2.01
mm. : 15.3 15.1 15.0 15.0 14.8 13.6 14.0 15.0

SELEUCUS II

(246–226 B.C.)

29 Æ (1)

Obv.: Head of Seleucus r., diademed. The presence or absence of a beard cannot be determined.

Rev.: Apollo nude, standing l., leaning the l. elbow on a tripod. The r. hand, advanced, holds an arrow diagonally down.

Legend: r. ΒΑΣΙΛ[ΕΩΣ], l., obscure.

Monogram: None can be distinguished, perhaps owing to the condition of the coin.

The adjustment of the dies is ↑ ↗. No border can be distinguished.

Babelon, 33–35, Nos. 248–260, VII, 4, 6. See discussion, p. 33.

gr. : 13.01
mm. : 27.90

30 Æ (1)

Obv.: Head of Seleucus r., diademed; slight whiskers, no mustache.

Rev.: Nike standing l., the top of the r. wing showing over the r. shoulder. The r. hand, advanced, holds a wreath *through* the royal name. A palm rests along the l. arm.

Legend: r. [ΒΑ]ΣΙΛΕΩΣ, l. ΣΕΛΕΥΚΟΥ.

Monograms: In the field l., No. 25, r., an incomplete monogram, probably No. 26.

The adjustment of the dies is ↑ →. No border can be distinguished. The edge is beveled.

Pl. II. See discussion, p. 33.

gr. : 5.24
mm. : 19.6.

31 Æ (18)

Obv.: Head of Seleucus r., diademed, apparently clean-shaven.

Rev.: Apollo nude, standing l. The r. hand, advanced, holds an arrow diagonally down; the l. rests on a grounded bow.

Legend: r. ΒΑΣΙΛΕΩΣ, l. ΣΕΛΕΥΚΟΥ.

Monograms: On two coins, one large and the other small, in the field l., No. 26, r., No. 27. The one or the other can be distinguished on three additional coins. Traces of monograms can be discerned on the majority of the group, and it is probable that the entire group bore these two monograms.

The adjustment of the dies is normal. A border of dots can be distinguished on two of the smaller coins. The edges are straight.

Cf. Gardner, 16, Nos. 12–13; VI, 3. See Pl. II and discussion, p. 34.

gr. : 10.6	9.46	9.41	8.94	8.89	8.84	8.49	8.34	8.13	7.22	7.18
mm. : 22.6	21.2	22.0	21.2	22.0	22.0	20.7	22.2	21.9	21.0	21.5
4.90	4.45	4.79	4.42	4.26	4.14	3.56				
20.7	17.5	17.4	17.3	17.3	19.8	16.7				

ANTIOCHUS III

(223–187 B.C.)

32 Æ (4)

Obv.: Head of Antiochus r., diademed. The features are very youthful.

Rev.: Nike standing l. The r. hand, advanced, holds a wreath in front of the body.

Legend: r. ΒΑΣΙΛΕΩΣ, l. ΑΝΤΙΟΧΟΥ.

Monogram: On two coins in the field r., No. 28. On the rest this portion of the field has been obscured.

The adjustment of the dies is normal. There is a border of dots. The edges are straight.

See discussion, p. 34.

gr. : 3.67	2.78*	2.09	1.35
mm. : 17.1	16.7	13.4	15.3

* Broken

33 Æ (2)

Obv.: Head of Antiochus r., diademed. The features are youthful but more developed than those in the portrait of No. 32.

Rev.: Apollo, fully draped, standing ¾ r. The l. arm holds a cithara to the breast. The r. arm is dropped, the hand holding a plectrum (?).

Legend: r. ΒΑΣΙΛΕΩΣ, l. ΑΝΤΙΟΧΟΥ.

Monogram: In the field l., No. 28.

The adjustment of the dies is normal. There is a border of dots. The edges appear somewhat flattened.

Pl. II. See discussion, p. 34.

gr. : 5.43 5.25
mm. : 21.9 21.0

34 Æ (2)

Obv.: Head of Apollo r., laureate, the hair done in a knot.

Rev.: Nike standing l., the r. hand holding a wreath over the royal name. The l. hand is dropped at the side. Above the l. shoulder protrudes a palm, presumably held in the l. hand.

Legend: r. ΒΑΣΙΛΕΩΣ, l. ΑΝΤΙΟΧΟΥ.

Monograms: In the field r., No. 28, l., obscure.

The adjustment of the dies is normal. There is a border of dots. The edges are slightly beveled.

Rogers, 28, No. 3. See Pl. II and discussion, p. 35.

gr. : 8.21 7.84
mm. : 21.7 20.7

35 Æ (10)

Obv.: Bust of Artemis r., the hair done in a knot and bound with a diadem or a double fillet. Behind the shoulder protrude the bow and quiver.

Rev.: Apollo nude, standing r., holding in both hands a lyre or a cithara.

Legend: r. ΒΑΣΙΛΕΩΣ, l. ΑΝΤΙΟΧΟΥ.

Monogram: On five coins in the field l., No. 28. On the rest this portion of the field has been obscured or is off flan.

The adjustment of the dies is normal on nine coins; on the tenth, ↑ →. There is a border of dots. The edges are more or less beveled.

See discussion, p. 35.

gr.	: 3.12	2.53	2.27	2.06	1.99	1.76	1.69	1.67	1.64	1.41
mm.	: 13.9	13.7	14.0	12.9	14.4	13.1	13.6	12.8	13.4	12.6

36 Æ (2)

Obv.: Head of Apollo r., laureate.

Rev.: Apollo nude, standing l. The r. hand, advanced, holds an arrow diagonally down; the l. rests on a grounded bow.

Legend: r. ΒΑΣΙΛΕΩΣ, l. ΑΝΤΙΟΧΟΥ.

Monograms: On one coin in the field r., No. 28; on the other in the field l., No. 7. On each the opposite side of the field is off flan.

The adjustment of the dies is normal. There is a border of dots. The edges are slightly beveled.

Babelon, 54–55, Nos. 405–414; X, 6–7. See discussion, p. 35.

gr. : 2.38 2.37
mm. : 14.3 18.9

37 Æ (1)

Obv.: Head of Apollo r., laureate. The arrangement of the hair is obscure.

Rev.: A female figure standing l., clad in a tunic with girdle and, perhaps, high boots. The r. hand, advanced, holds what apparently is a long torch. The l. hand is dropped at the side. This appears to be a representation of Artemis.

Legend: r. [ΒΑ]ΣΙΛ[ΕΩΣ], l. ΑΝΤΙΟΧΟΥ.

Monogram: In the field l., somewhat obscure, No. 7.

The adjustment of the dies is normal. There is a border of dots. The edge is slightly beveled.

See discussion, p. 36.

gr. : 2.44
mm. : 14.6

38 Æ (9)

Obv.: Head of Apollo r., laureate, the hair arranged in curls on the neck.

Rev.: An elephant *advancing* r., with tusks and lowered trunk.

Legend: Above ΒΑΣΙΛΕΩΣ, below ΑΝΤΙΟΧΟΥ.

Monogram: On five coins in the field l., No. 29. On the rest this portion of the field is off flan or has been obscured.

The adjustment of the dies is normal. No border can be distinguished. The edges are somewhat beveled.

Rogers, 29, No. 5. See Pl. III and discussion, p. 36.

gr. :	4.94	4.07	4.04	3.86	3.65	3.63	3.26	3.18	3.08
mm. :	17.2	17.3	15.9	16.1	16.0	16.6	15.5	15.0	16.4

39 Æ (5)

Obv.: A male bust facing front, the head turned ¾ r. and covered by a kausia-like headdress. It appears to be a portrait, presumably of Antiochus. The features are not distinct.

Rev.: An elephant *standing* r. The tusks are short. The trunk is lowered with the tip slightly upturned.

Legend: Above ΒΑΣΙΛΕΩΣ, below ΑΝΤΙΟΧΟΥ.

Monogram: On one coin in the field l., No. 29. In the same relative position on a second coin there is an obscure monogram which appears to be similar. On the rest this portion of the field has been obscured.

The adjustments of the dies are ↑ ↑, ↑ →, ↑ ↖. No border can be distinguished. The edges are slightly beveled.

Pl. III. See discussion, p. 36.

gr.	: 2.88	2.88	2.55	2.18	2.14
mm.	: 14.7	14.2	13.7	14.3	14.5

40 Æ (2)

Obv.: A male head ¾ r., covered by a kausia-like headdress. Details of the features have been obscured; very possibly the representation is of Antiochus.

Rev.: A figure standing r., apparently male, draped in a long cloak. On the head is what seems to be a flat, turban-like headdress; this may be an elaborate arrangement of the hair. The face is clean-shaven. The r. arm is outlined under the cloak and appears to be held to the breast. The l. arm does not show. There is no suggestion of an object in front of the figure.

Legend: r. ΒΑΣ[ΙΛΕΩΣ], l. ΑΝΤΙΟ[ΧΟΥ].

Monogram: In the field l. on one coin, No. 29, on the other, an obscure monogram, perhaps the same.

The adjustment of the dies is normal. There is a border of dots. The edges are slightly beveled.

Pl. III. See discussion, p. 37.

gr.	: 3.89	2.59
mm.	: 17.4	16.9

41 Æ (1)

Obv.: A head r., obscure and partly off flan. There are traces that suggest a diadem.

Rev.: The head of an elephant l., with tusks and elevated trunk. Behind, a tripod.

Legend: Above ΒΑΣΙΛΕΩΣ; below ΑΝ[ΤΙΟΧΟΥ].

Monogram: None can be distinguished, perhaps owing to the condition of the coin.

The adjustment of the dies is normal. There is a border of dots. The edge is straight. The coin is of thick fabric.

Cf. Babelon, 56, Nos. 424–428; X, 12. See discussion, p. 38.

gr. : 3.14
mm. : 12.6

42 Æ (1)

Obv.: Head of Antiochus r., diademed.

Rev.: A mare standing l., suckling a foal.

Legend: Above ΒΑΣΙΛΕΩΣ, below ΑΝΤΙ[ΟΧΟΥ].

Monogram: In the field l., obscure.

The adjustment of the dies is ↑ ↖. No border can be distinguished. The edge is straight.

Babelon, 58, Nos. 446–448; XI, 3. See discussion, p. 38.

gr. : 8.20
mm. : 24.3

SELEUCUS IV

(187–175 B.C.)

43 Æ (1)

Obv.: Head of Apollo r., laureate, the hair done in a knot.

Rev.: Apollo nude, standing l., the l. arm resting on a tripod behind. The r. hand, advanced, holds an arrow diagonally down.

Legend: r. ΒΑΣΙΛΕΩΣ, l. [ΣΕ]ΛΕΥΚ[ΟΥ].

Monograms: In the field l., No. 30; on the obverse behind, No. 31.

The adjustment of the dies is normal. There is a border of dots. The edge is serrated.

Babelon, 63–64, Nos. 479–491; XI, 16. See discussion, p. 38.

gr. : 6.60
mm. : 21.5

ANTIOCHUS IV

(175–164 B.C.)

44 Æ (43)

Obv.: Head of Antiochus r., radiate.

Rev.: Tyche seated l. on a throne with a high back. The r. hand, advanced, holds a Nike, l., with a wreath. *The l. hand is dropped at the side.* In front of the feet stands a bird, l., with a long beak.

Legend: r. ΒΑΣΙΛΕΩΣ, l. ΑΝΤΙΟΧΟΥ.

Monogram: None occurs.

Symbols of denomination: On the obverse, behind, on three of the coins grouped under (*a*) $\frac{\mathrm{B}}{\mathrm{X}}$; on nine of the coins under (*b*) $\frac{\mathrm{A}}{\mathrm{X}}$. On the rest this portion of the obverse is off flan or has been obscured.

The adjustment of the dies is normal. A fillet border occurs on the obverse and a border of dots on the reverse. The edges are beveled.

Babelon, 71–72, Nos. 548–555; XIII, 1–3. See discussion, p. 38.

gr. :	(*a*)	8.77	8.34	8.18	7.67	7.18	6.99	5.94		(*b*)	4.40	4.10
mm. :		20.0	20.3	21.6	20.3	20.4	19.0	19.3			16.4	15.6
	4.09	3.88	3.80	3.51	3.47	3.41	3.32	3.30	3.26	3.19	2.91	2.80
	17.0	15.7	15.5	15.9	17.0	15.4	16.3	15.2	16.8	14.9	15.4	15.3
	2.72	2.65	2.58	2.56	2.55	2.52	2.52	2.49	2.35	2.34	2.21	2.11
	15.7	14.0	14.6	16.5	15.0	14.4	15.7	14.9	15.6	15.0	13.8	13.8
	2.08	1.93	1.91	1.79	1.76	1.50	1.38	1.38	1.27	1.20		
	15.3	14.8	14.3	13.0	15.6	13.4	14.5	11.1	12.0	12.9		

45 Æ (1)

Obv.: Head of Antiochus r., radiate.

Rev.: Zeus standing l. half-draped, on his head a wreath. The r. hand, advanced, holds a thunderbolt; the l. grasps a long scepter. At the feet stands a bird, l., the form of which cannot be determined.

Legend: r. two lines, obscure, l. ΘΕΟΥ[ΕΠΙΦ]ΑΝΟΥ[Σ].

Monogram: In the field l., reading down, the initials No. 32.

The adjustment of the dies is normal. No border can be distinguished. The edge is straight.

Babelon, 72, Nos. 559–563; XIII, 5. See discussion, p. 39.

gr. : 5.12
mm. : 19.7

46 Æ (12)

Obv.: Head of Apollo $\frac{3}{4}$ r., laureate, the hair arranged in curls on the neck.

Rev.: Tyche standing l., on the head a kalathos, in the l. arm a cornucopiae. The r. arm appears to extend through the letters of the royal name. It is not clear whether an object is held in this hand.

Legend: r. ΒΑΣΙΛΕΩΣ, l. ΑΝΤΙΟΧΟΥ.

Monogram: On four coins in the field l., No. 33. On the rest this portion of the field is off flan or has been obscured.

The adjustment of the dies is normal. There is a border of dots on both obverse and reverse. The edges are slightly beveled.

Pl. III. See discussion, p. 39.

gr.	: 3.15	2.85	2.52	2.52	2.52	2.51	2.46	2.27	2.18	2.06	2.01	1.87
mm.	: 15.0	14.0	15.5	14.1	15.8	15.4	15.5	15.3	15.8	15.1	14.4	14.3

DEMETRIUS I

(162–150 B.C.)

47 Æ (5)

Obv.: Head of Helios ¾ l.

Rev.: Artemis standing r., clad in a tunic. The arrangement of the hair cannot be distinguished. The l. hand, advanced, holds a bow; the r. is raised behind the shoulder, having just released an arrow.

Legend: r. ΒΑΣΙΛΕΩΣ, l. ΔΗΜΗΤΡΙΟΥ.

The adjustment of the dies is normal. No border can be distinguished. The edges are beveled.

Imhoof-Blumer, 435, No. 109. Imhoof-Blumer assigns this type to the second Demetrius. See Pl. III and discussion, p. 39.

gr.	: 4.17	3.79	3.75	3.74	3.09
mm.	: 16.6	16.5	16.0	16.7	16.9

48 Æ (1)

Obv.: Head of Artemis r., diademed. Behind the shoulders, a bow and quiver.

Rev.: A quiver and bow, upright.

Legend: r. ΒΑΣΙΛ[ΕΩΣ], l. [ΔΗ]ΜΗΤΡΙ[ΟΥ].

The adjustment of the dies is normal. No border can be distinguished. The edge is serrated.

Babelon, 92–93, Nos. 726–729; XVI, 5. See discussion, p. 40.

gr. : 7.15
mm. : 20.5

49 Æ (14)

Obv.: The busts of Demetrius and the queen r., jugate.

Rev.: Nike standing l., the r. hand extending a wreath over the royal name.

Legend: r. ΒΑΣΙΛΕΩΣ, l. ΔΗΜΗΤΡΙΟΥ.

The adjustment of the dies is normal. No border can be distinguished. The edges are beveled.

Babelon, 101, No. 791; XVII, 7. See discussion, p. 40.

gr. :	5.78	5.17	5.02	4.96	4.86	4.72	4.44	4.24	4.01	3.76	3.70
mm. :	17.8	18.3	17.1	17.9	18.2	18.2	17.8	17.3	16.7	16.9	17.2
	3.19	2.34	1.74								
	16.2	16.6	15.6								

50 Æ (3)

Obv.: Head of Demetrius r., diademed.

Rev.: Apollo nude, seated l. on an omphalos. The r. hand, advanced, holds an arrow diagonally down; the l. rests on a grounded bow.

Legend: r. ΒΑΣΙΛΕΩΣ, l. ΔΗΜΗΤΡΙΟΥ, ex. ΣΩΤΗΡΟΣ.

The adjustment of the dies is normal. There is a border of continuous fillet. The edges are serrated.

Cf. Babelon, 94, No. 737; XVI, 11. See discussion, p. 40.

gr. :	5.20	4.61	3.90
mm. :	18.0	16.6	16.7

51 Æ (6)

Obv.: Head of Demetrius r., diademed.

Rev.: A cornucopiae, upright.

Legend: r. ΒΑΣΙΛΕΩΣ, l. ΔΗΜΗΤΡΙΟΥ.

The adjustment of the dies is normal. No border can be distinguished. The edges are beveled.

Pl. III. See discussion, p. 40.

gr. :	3.33	3.22	2.99	2.79	2.65	2.10
mm. :	16.7	18.0	16.6	16.4	17.7	16.1

52 Æ (5)

Obv.: Head of Helios ¾ l.

Rev.: As on No. 51.

Legend: r. ΒΑΣΙΛΕΩΣ, l. ΔΗΜΗΤΡΙΟΥ.

The adjustment of the dies is normal. No border can be distinguished. The edges are beveled.

Pl. III. See discussion, p. 40.

gr. :	3.44	3.25	3.12	2.96	2.74
mm. :	16.5	17.7	16.7	16.5	17.3

53 Æ (7)

Obv.: Head of Demetrius r., radiate. The characteristic forelock is shown.

Rev.: Tyche seated l. on a throne without a back. The head appears to be bare, the hair done in a knot. In the l. arm is a cornucopiae. The r. arm is extended over the lap toward the royal name. No object can be distinguished in the hand.

Legend: r. ΒΑΣΙΛΕΩΣ, l. ΔΗΜΗΤΡΙΟΥ.

The adjustment of the dies is normal. There is a border of dots. The edges are slightly beveled.

Pl. III. See discussion, p. 41.

gr.	: 3.76	3.62	3.46	3.38	3.34	3.25	2.37*
mm.	: 17.0	16.5	16.5	17.0	16.6	16.6	17.4

* Broken

54 Æ (3)

Obv.: Head of Demetrius r., diademed. The forelock is shown.

Rev.: Tyche standing l., the head bare and the hair done in a knot. In the l. arm is a cornucopiae. The r. hand is dropped in front, and it cannot be determined whether it grasps an object.

Legend: r. ΒΑΣΙΛΕΩΣ, l. ΔΗΜΗΤ[ΡΙΟΥ].

The adjustment of the dies is normal. There is a border of dots. The edges are slightly beveled.

Pl. III. See discussion, p. 41.

gr.	: 1.88	1.83	1.30
mm.	: 14.8	14.2	13.9

55 Æ (17)

Obv.: Bust of Apollo ¾ l., apparently laureate.

Rev.: Tyche standing l. On the head is a kalathos, in the l. arm a cornucopiae. The l. elbow rests on a short column. The r. arm is dropped in front with the hand extended toward the royal name. It cannot be determined whether an object is held in this hand.

Legend: r. ΒΑΣΙΛΕΩΣ, l. ΔΗΜΗΤΡΙΟΥ.

The adjustment of the dies is normal. There is a border of dots. The edges are beveled.

Pl. III. See discussion, p. 41.

gr.	: 6.19*	4.81	4.49	4.45	4.36	4.10	3.93	3.91	3.81	3.47	3.35
mm.	: 17.6	17.4	16.8	17.0	16.8	18.3	17.0	18.0	16.9	17.5	17.9
	3.07	3.04	2.97	2.92	2.54†	2.19					
	16.9	17.6	17.2	16.6	16.9	16.7					

* Very thick † Broken

ALEXANDER BALA

(152–144 B.C.[2])

56 Æ (1)

Obv.: Heads of Cleopatra Thea and Alexander r., jugate, with that of the queen in the foreground.

Rev.: Nike standing l., the r. hand extending a wreath over the royal name. Further details have been obscured.

Legend: Entirely obscured.

The adjustment of the dies is normal. There is a border of dots. The edge is slightly beveled.

Pl. III. See discussion, p. 41.

gr. : 2.31
mm. : 14.7

57 Æ (6)

Obv.: Head of Alexander r., wearing a helmet.

Rev.: Nike standing l., apparently as above. In the field l. an upright branch can be distinguished. It cannot be determined whether a palm is held in the l. hand.

Legend: r., obscure, l., on one coin ΑΛΕ[ΞΑΝΔΡΟΥ].

The adjustment of the dies is normal. There is a border of dots. The edges are flattened.

Babelon, 108–110, Nos. 853–865; XVIII, 1. See discussion, p. 42.

gr.	: 2.40	2.38	2.36*	2.36	2.00	1.42
mm.	: 16.0	15.3	15.5	16.3	16.7	15.9

* Broken

[2] The exact duration of this reign in Seleucia is not known.

58 Æ (2)

Obv.: Heads of Cleopatra and Alexander r., jugate, with that of the queen in the foreground.

Rev.: Apollo nude, standing l. The hair is done in a knot. The r. hand, advanced, holds an arrow diagonally down; the l. rests on a grounded bow.

Legend: Entirely obscure.

The adjustment of the dies is normal. No border can be distinguished. The edges are slightly beveled.

Pl. III. See discussion, p. 42.

gr. : 4.33 2.65
mm. : 16.9 16.3

59 Æ (1)

Obv.: Head of Alexander r., represented as Hercules with a lion-skin headdress.

Rev.: As on No. 58.

Legend: r. ΒΑΣΙΛΕΩΣ, l. ΑΛΕΞ[ΑΝΔΡΟΥ].

The adjustment of the dies is normal. There is a border of dots. The edge is slightly beveled.

Babelon, 104–105, Nos. 810–824; XVII, 14. See discussion, p. 42, under Nos. 58–59.

gr. : 5.81
mm. : 18.7

60 Æ (2)

Obv.: Head of Alexander r., diademed.

Rev.: Zeus half-draped, seated l. on a throne without a back. The r. hand, advanced, holds a Nike who extends a wreath r.; the l. hand rests on a long scepter.

Legend: r. ΒΑΣΙΛΕΩΣ, l. ΑΛΕΞΑΝΔ[ΡΟΥ].

The adjustment of the dies is normal. There is a border of dots. The edges are beveled.

Pl. III. See discussion, p. 42.

gr. : 2.97 2.73
mm. : 16.2 16.9

DEMETRIUS II

First Reign (146–140/39 B.C.[3])

61 Æ (8)

Obv.: Head of Demetrius, r., wearing an elephant-scalp headdress.

Rev.: Athena in high-crested helmet seated l. The r. hand, in front, grasps a spear which slants back over the r. shoulder. The l. hand rests on a grounded shield at the side.

Legend: r. ΒΑΣΙΛΕΩΣ, l. ΔΗΜΗΤΡΙΟΥ.

The adjustment of the dies is normal. There is a border of dots. The edges are beveled.

Pl. IV. See discussion, p. 42.

gr.	: 3.80	3.49	3.45	3.30	3.30	2.41	1.77*	0.81*
mm.	: 16.9	16.5	16.5	16.3	15.6	17.8	14.6	13.8

* Incomplete

62 Æ (3)

Obv.: Head of Demetrius r., wearing an elephant-scalp headdress.

Rev.: Athena in high-crested helmet standing l. The r. hand, in front, grasps an upright spear; the l. rests on a grounded shield at the side.

Legend: r., 1st [Β]ΑΣΙΛ[ΕΩΣ], 2nd ΔΗΜΗ[ΤΡΙΟΥ],
l., obscure [ΦΙΛΑΔΕΛΦΟΥ ΝΙΚΑΤΟΡΟΣ].

The adjustments of the dies are ↑ ↑, ↑ ↗. No border can be distinguished. The edges are slightly beveled.

Gardner, 61, No. 27; XVIII, 9. See discussion, p. 42.

gr.	: 4.04	3.30	2.22
mm.	: 16.0	16.8	16.4

63 Æ (4)

Obv.: Head of Demetrius r., diademed.

Rev.: Nike standing l. The r. arm is advanced through the legend, the hand off flan. The l. hand is dropped at the side.

Legend: r., 1st ΒΑΣΙΛΕΩΣ, 2nd ΔΗΜΗΤΡΙΟΥ,
l., 1st ΦΙΛΑΔΕΛΦΟΥ, 2nd ΝΙΚΑΤΟΡΟΣ.

[3] It is very possible that Demetrius effectively controlled Seleucia only between 141/40 and 140/39 B.C.

The adjustment of the dies is normal. No border can be distinguished. The edges are slightly beveled.

Cf. Babelon, 121, No. 942; XIX, 9. See discussion, p. 42.

gr. : 3.88 3.03 2.60 2.06 *
mm. : 15.9 15.7 15.6 16.7

* Broken

SECOND REIGN (?) (130–125 B.C.)

64 Æ (1)

Obv.: Female head r., the hair done in a knot and surmounted by a kalathos.

Rev.: A cornucopiae, upright, from which fall streamers.

Legend: r. ΒΑΣΙΛ[ΕΩΣ], l. ΔΗΜΗΤ[ΡΙΟΥ].

The adjustment of the dies is normal. No border can be distinguished. The edge is beveled.

Cf. Babelon, 161, Nos. 1249, 1250; XXII, 21. See Pl. IV and discussion, p. 43.

gr. : 3.07
mm. : 13.9

SECOND REIGN

65 Æ (1)

Obv.: Entirely obscure.

Rev.: Zeus seated l. on a throne with a high back. The r. hand, advanced, holds a Nike r.; the l. rests on a long scepter. All other details have been obscured.

Legend: r., 1st [Β]ΑΣΙ[ΛΕΩΣ], 2nd [Δ]ΗΜΗΤΡΙΟ[Υ], l., obscure and off flan.

The adjustment of the dies cannot be determined. No border can be distinguished. The edge is straight.

See discussion, p. 43.

gr. : 10.8
mm. : 23.6

CHAPTER II

NOTES ON THE COINS

This chapter is devoted to discussions regarding the individual type groups, the inclusion of which in the catalog would have detracted from its ready use for reference. The serial numbers correspond to those in the catalog.

ALEXANDER THE GREAT

1. The two examples of this type group representing two different denominations are the only coins found at Seleucia which bear the types of Alexander but lack the symbols characteristic of Seleucus. They cannot well be dated later than the opening years of the first governorship of Seleucus; very possibly they antedate 321 B.C. They differ both in details of execution and in the form of the monograms from those published in Hill. On one of the latter appears a monogram similar to Seleucia monogram No. 1, except that it lacks the encircling omega (cxlviii, No. 13).

SELEUCUS I AS SATRAP

2. The coin in Babelon has a similar obverse type. On the reverse, however, it shows the anchor not inverted and apparently unaccompanied by the horse's head. In this connection should be noted the clay model of a coin found at Seleucia which bears the types and the name of Alexander and a symbol of Seleucus.[1] The assignment of coins which bear the name of Alexander to the second governorship of Seleucus, that is, after 311 B.C., would require the assumption that at this period Seleucus lacked the personal power to inspire confidence in his coinage. The facts oppose such an assumption. Seleucus returned to Babylonia in the spring of 311 practically unaccompanied. Through his personal popularity with the army and the populace within a few months he had defeated two armies of Antigonus and had inaugurated a successful campaign into Iran. This was clearly a personal venture and in no sense a

[1] R. H. McDowell, *Stamped and Inscribed Objects from Seleucia on the Tigris*, p. 243, No. 1a(1).

defense of the rights of Alexander's heirs. It is reported that the natives of Babylonia hailed him as king immediately upon his arrival in 311.[2] On these grounds the coin and the clay model have been assigned to the period of the first governorship, from 321/20 to 315/14 B.C. The imitation of coins of Alexander by his successors to a fairly late period is an admitted fact, but this was practiced in areas where the instability of the *de facto* government or the backward character of the population required it. Neither of these conditions prevailed in Babylonia.

The initials on this coin are those which appear in monogram on type No. 20 (monogram No. 19) of the reign of Antiochus I. It is possible, but not likely, that a single mint official is indicated.

SELEUCUS I AS KING

3. The legend on the coin from Seleucia undoubtedly comprised the title as well as the royal name. The coin in Babelon bears monograms which do not occur on coins from Seleucia of the same general period.

4. The coins cited are similar in type, showing the throne without a back, but they are both drachmae. One bears the name of Seleucus alone, the other the name with the royal title. The form of the legend on the coin from Seleucia cannot be determined nor, consequently, its exact chronological position. The monograms on the coins in Babelon do not occur on coins from Seleucia of the same general period.

5. The royal title occurs in the field left, but obscured. The first of the coins cited bears a monogram which appears on a coin of Antiochus I from Seleucia, type No. 16, monogram No. 14.

6. Babelon describes a silver coin of Seleucus which bears not only similar types but the same symbol and monogram which occur on the coins from Seleucia (8, No. 46). The character of these adjuncts on the bronze coin cited is not clear.

8. The coin is assigned to the first Seleucus because the motif of the reverse types is most characteristic of this reign, and because of the obvious relationship of this type group to that preceding, No. 7.

9. The coin in Babelon appears to lack a monogram. With

[2] M. I. Rostovtzeff, "Syria and the East," *The Cambridge Ancient History*, VII, 166–167.

the exception of the specimen weighing 7.73 gr., the coins of this group are of a single denomination. They represent the largest group of the coins of Seleucus I found at Seleucia.

10. The coin cited shows a monogram in the left field only, similar to that occupying the corresponding position on the coins from Seleucia. The coins of the group appear to comprise two denominations.

11. The kappa which occurs in the field of one of these coins may be one element of an obscured monogram, perhaps No. 6. The coin in Babelon shows the symbol, a star and a sphere. It appears that in the case of this type group, at least, the symbols and monograms possessed a coördinate value, that is, both represented mint officials. If this is so, it must be admitted that the anchor, although a symbol representative of the dynasty, might distinguish an individual official. This type comprises the second largest group of coins of this reign found at Seleucia.

12. This combination of types appears to be new. The obverse type is more characteristic of the coinages of the first two Seleucid kings than of those of their successors. The reverse type is in a general way similar to that on a coin of Seleucus I published by Babelon (14, No. 97). On this coin the wreath is held over rather than through the royal name, and Nike holds a palm in the left hand. The attribution of the group to Seleucus I is further supported by the form of the second monogram, which is reproduced on another group of this reign, type No. 10. [Mr. E. T. Newell informs me that the collection of Dr. Edgar Rogers contains examples of this type. See Preface, p. viii.]

13. The assignment of this coin to Seleucus I is based on the style of the obverse type and on the character of the symbol. After the reign of Antiochus I only a few coins show the obverse head in frontal position, and the anchor is not employed as a symbol by the later kings who bore the name Seleucus.

14. The coins are in a very obscure condition. The general similarity of this combination of types to that found on an issue of Antiochus I, and the frontality of the obverse head, justify the assignment of this group to Seleucus I.

ANTIOCHUS I

15. The coin cited bears monograms which do not occur on coins from Seleucia of the same general period.

16. The coins in Babelon show two of the monograms which occur on the group from Seleucia, Nos. 12 and 13. The intentional abbreviation of the legend in subgroup (*b*) is analogous to the use of the first four letters of the words of the legend on other issues of Antiochus I (Babelon, 20, Nos. 147–149; 22, No. 165; 25, No. 190).

17. The close relationship of this variety to the preceding group requires no discussion. It appears to have been characteristic of the Seleucia mint to emit successive issues distinguished only by a change in the style of the obverse type, such as from the profile to the frontal position.

18. The obverse type of this group is that of No. 16. The reverse differs from that of Nos. 16 and 17 only in the position of the shield, held horizontally rather than diagonally. The types of this group, however, differ from those of an issue of Seleucus I only in the presence of the folded chlamys (Babelon, 13, Nos. 80–85). The illegibility of the royal name, therefore, makes the attribution of the group somewhat doubtful. The presence of the chlamys appears to be more significant than the variation in the position of the shield.

19. The coin cited bears monograms which do not appear on coins from Seleucia of the same general period.

20. The coins in Babelon show only one monogram; this is not found on coins from Seleucia of this period. Monogram No. 18 is composed of the characters which comprise monogram No. 14 on type No. 16. The characters of monogram No. 19 appear as initials on type No. 2. There appears to be no relationship between the variations in size within the group and the change of monograms.

21. No monogram appears on the coin cited.

22. On the reverse of the coins in Babelon the right hand of Apollo rests on the lap. One of the coins cited bears in the field right monogram No. 7, as on the coins from Seleucia. In the field left occurs a monogram which does not appear on coins from Seleucia of this general period. One of the elements in this monogram is the letter X. It is possible, therefore, that the obscure monogram on the coins from Seleucia is similar.

23. This group is distinguished from the preceding one only by the variation in the execution of the obverse, the change in the position of the head from left to right. This may be the

result of an error on the part of the engraver. It is equally possible, however, that the two groups furnish another illustration of the apparent practice at the Seleucia mint of retaining a common reverse type on two successive issues, while varying the execution of the obverse.

24. The coin cited shows only one monogram, obscure.

25. The attribution of this group to the first Antiochus is supported by the close relationship of the reverse type to that of the preceding group and by the style of the obverse which is characteristic of the first two Seleucid reigns. The two groups illustrate again the tendency noted under No. 23. The substitution of the head facing partly front for that in profile emphasizes the strength of this technique in engraving at the Seleucia mint. This condition is discussed further on pages 47–48. It should be noted that one of the coins of group No. 25, weighing 2.46 gr., is of very crude execution (see Pl. II).

26. The assignment of these coins to Antiochus I is based on two factors. The representation of the head of Apollo facing partly front is characteristic only of this and the preceding reign. A quiver, accompanied by a bow, forms the reverse type of another issue of Antiochus (Babelon, 25, Nos. 189–190). The representation of a quiver without the associated bow is unusual. Since the coins from Seleucia are in a very obscure condition, it is not impossible that a bow was intended to be shown as a second element in the design of the reverse.

27. The types of this group are new and of an unusual interest. The obverse shows a definite relationship to the heads of Zeus executed in profile on early Seleucid coins. It is distinctly unlike the portrayals of Zeus on coins of Antiochus IV and his successors. Some of the representations of Zeus on early Seleucid issues appear to possess the features of Seleucus I, that is, they portray an assimilation of Seleucus to Zeus.[3] The frontal position of the obverse head on the coins under consideration makes difficult a comparison with portraits of Seleucus in profile. They appear, however, to possess certain elements in common, and it is possible that the obverse type represents the deified Nikator.

The reverse type has been obscured on all the specimens. In the absence of evidence to the contrary the nudity of the figure and the presence of the tripod require an attribution to Apollo.

[3] McDowell, *op. cit.*, pp. 209–212.

If the object held in the hand is an arrow, the identification is of course strengthened; the type becomes a modification of the common motif of Apollo leaning on the tripod and holding an arrow. The object behind the shoulder is very obscure. If a quiver, it introduces an unusual element in the motif.

The single appearance of the monogram in an obscured condition is unfortunate. It may represent one of the two alternatives grouped as monogram No. 11 of the reign of Seleucus I, or monogram No. 21 of the reign of Antiochus I. On the other hand, it may be similar to monogram No. 29, which occurs repeatedly on coins of Antiochus III. Should this be the case it would not justify an assignment of the group to the third Antiochus. A representation of Zeus as an obverse type in this reign is unknown, and representations of Apollo appear but rarely on the reverse types. Though frontality of the obverse type occurs on coins of Antiochus III, it is rare (type groups Nos. 38 and 39). Of prime significance is the character of the execution of the obverse, which links these coins to the early issues in the name of Antiochus I. The group may well be assigned to the opening years of this reign.

ANTIOCHUS II

28. The coins cited in this group bear a monogram which appears at Seleucia on an issue of Seleucus II, type No. 30, monogram No. 25. Repeated examination of the group under consideration, as well as of the corresponding reproduction in Babelon, suggests strongly that the obverse type portrays not Apollo but Antiochus Theos as Apollo. In view of the consolidation of the observance of the royal cult during this reign such a concept would not be unnatural.

SELEUCUS II

29. This is the latest Seleucid silver coin that has been found at Seleucia. Among the monograms appearing on the coins cited are three which occur on contemporary coins from Seleucia, monograms Nos. 7 and 13 on type groups Nos. 19, 22, 16, and 20 of the reign of Antiochus I, and monogram No. 25 on type group No. 30 of the current reign.

30. The attribution of this coin to Seleucus II is determined by the portrait of the obverse. Babelon has published a bronze

coin of this reign with a reverse generally similar but on the obverse an Athena head (37, No. 273). The first monogram on the coin from Seleucia, No. 25, occurs on a silver coin of Seleucus II and on a bronze coin of the reign of Antiochus II (Gardner, 16, No. 5; Babelon, 32, No. 239).

31. The coins published by Gardner appear to be entirely similar in types except that the king is described as wearing slight whiskers. There is no suggestion of a beard on the obverse type of the coins from Seleucia. The second monogram on the coins, No. 27, occurs on the specimens cited, where it is associated with a monogram which does not appear on coins from Seleucia of the same general period.

ANTIOCHUS III

32. The attribution to Antiochus III is required by the portrait of the obverse. Babelon has published coins of this king with types superficially similar (57, Nos. 438–439). The portrait on these coins, however, is that of a mature man, and the reverse has as adjunct the head of a horse. There appears to be no relationship between these coins and the group from Seleucia. The monogram which occurs on the group is common to the four succeeding issues of Antiochus at Seleucia.

The chronological position of this issue within the reign is determined by the relation of the portrait to that on the next group, No. 33. In both issues the king is represented as youthful, but the features portrayed on the second are definitely more mature. The comparison is rendered legitimate by the facts that the two groups were the product of one mint and cannot be widely separated in time. Though engravers might increase the age of their royal subjects when the latter were very young, as a point of state policy, the contrary may not well be assumed. It should be noted further that the young Antiochus was resident in Seleucia at the time of his elevation to the throne.[4] It will be shown below that type groups Nos. 33 and 34 preceded the revolt of Molon. Group No. 32 must have been issued, therefore, within a few months after the accession of Antiochus.

33. The details of the portrait require the attribution to Antiochus III. The monogram is that which occurs on the

[4] M. Streck, "Seleukeia," Pauly-Wissowa, *Real-Encyclopädie des classischen Altertumswissenschaft*, Zweite Reihe, Vol. II.

coins of the preceding group and on those of the three groups which follow. The reverse type appears to be entirely similar to that of a coin of Molon (Babelon, 60, No. 457). Though a usurper might well continue the coin types of his predecessor, it is highly improbable that a type instituted by a rebel would appear shortly afterward on the legitimate coinage. The conditions require, therefore, that the issue under consideration be assigned to the period prior to the revolt of Molon.

34. The coin cited shows in the field left $\overset{\Omega}{\mathrm{P}}$. The reverse type is closely similar to that of an issue of Molon (Babelon, 60, No. 458). It is reasonable to assume, therefore, that the coins under consideration were issued for Antiochus shortly before the capture of Seleucia by Molon. The latter retained the types for an issue in a smaller denomination. It is possible that the reverse type on the issue of Antiochus commemorated an initial repulse of the rebel army before the city. The suggestion is supported by the fact that type groups Nos. 33 and 34, although issued at about the same time, are of a single denomination.

The monogram which occurs on the group is common also to groups Nos. 32, 33, 35, and 36. To judge by an examination of the plate in Babelon, the monogram on the corresponding issue of Molon is similar. Babelon, however, gives it as an eta inclosing an inverted alpha. This form appears on another coin of Molon (Babelon, 60, No. 457).

35. The obverse type of this group is closely related to that on an issue of Seleucus IV (Babelon, 65, No. 501). The reverse appears to be new to the Seleucid coinage. It is a modification of that found on No. 33 which, as has been shown, was imitated by Molon. The modification may have been due to this circumstance. The continuation on the coins of this group of the monogram which characterizes the earliest issues of Antiochus requires the assignment of the group to the first half of the reign. It is the heaviest issue of Antiochus found at Seleucia.

36. This issue appears to be the latest in the series distinguished by monogram No. 28. It is accompanied here by a monogram which occurs alone on the succeeding issue of Antiochus, No. 37. The coins cited in the catalog are entirely similar in type but bear monograms which do not occur at Seleucia in this general period.

37. The attribution of this coin to Antiochus III depends partly on the form of the monogram which is that of group No. 36. However, this monogram occurs also on coins of Antiochus I, type groups Nos. 19 and 22. The decisive factor lies in the motif of the reverse. Representations of Artemis as obverse type appear as early as the reign of Seleucus II, but on the reverse only with the reigns of Antiochus III and his successors. Coins with types generally similar to those of this group were issued for Antiochus by the Aetolian League.[5] The group from Seleucia, however, must be placed at an earlier point in the reign. The monogram which characterizes the group occurs on the preceding group associated with the monogram which is common to the earliest issues of the reign. The three succeeding issues, which bear a new monogram, appear on the basis of the character of their reverse types to belong to the period of the campaign of Antiochus to the Upper Satrapies and India, prior to his conflicts with Rome.

38. The attribution of this issue and of No. 39 presents some difficulties. Though the use of the elephant as a reverse type is more characteristic of the third than of the first Antiochus, it occurs on the earlier coins with sufficient frequency to warrant consideration. Further, the monogram found on this group may occur also on coins of Antiochus I, type group No. 27. The attribution to Antiochus III is based principally on the fact that the monogram characterizes type groups Nos. 39 and 40, which possess elements foreign to the period of Antiochus I but germane to that with which we are now concerned.

The reverse type of the group differs from the elephant motif found on bronze coins of Antiochus published by Babelon, but is rather similar to that on the silver (52, Nos. 394, 395). After No. 35 this appears to be the heaviest issue of Antiochus III at Seleucia.

39. The monogram on this issue relates it to group No. 38 above and to No. 40 below. The reverse type differs from that of No. 38 in that the elephant is pictured as standing rather than advancing and has short tusks and the trunk curled upward near the extremity. In these respects the group is more closely related than is No. 38 to the bronze coins with generally similar reverse types published by Babelon. The obverse, however,

[5] P. Gardner, *Catalogue of Coins in the British Museum: Thessaly to Aetolia*, Pl. XXVII, No. 5.

presents features which are new to the Seleucid coinage. The frontality of the obverse head should normally associate the coins with the reigns of Seleucus I and Antiochus I. But at Seleucia this technique in coin engraving persisted throughout the Seleucid period.[6] It is the character of the headdress on the obverse that appears to require the assignment of the group to Antiochus III. On Bactrian coins the king is frequently portrayed wearing a kausia or a helmet shaped like a kausia.[7] From Seleucia we have impressions of seals of Timarchus which show a similar form of headdress, probably the result of Bactrian influence.[8] On no other official monuments of the Seleucid Empire or its successor states is this style of headdress pictured, although it appears on scattered coins from other parts of the Hellenistic world. The kausia was of course a common Macedonian feature, yet it appears to have gained an especial significance in Bactria. It is difficult to associate Antiochus I with these conditions, but in view of his lengthy stay in the Upper Satrapies, as well as the chronological factor, they do apply to the third Antiochus. As none of the other Antiochi of the Seleucid line were in any particular sense associated with the Upper Satrapies or India, both the obverse and the reverse of the group would be foreign to their coin types.

The reverse type of this as of the preceding group may reasonably be assigned to the period of the Indian campaign of Antiochus or shortly thereafter.[9] The representation of Antiochus wearing the kausia must be linked to some incident of the campaign, but its exact significance cannot be determined. Antiochus may have adopted a practice already followed by the Bactrian princes; it is equally possible that the use of the kausia by the Great King set a style that was imitated and retained by the Bactrian dynasty.

40. The monogram of this group is that of the two preceding groups. The relationship of the obverse to that of No. 39 is evident. In the absence of specimens in good condition it must

[6] See below, pp. 47–48.

[7] S. Grose, *Catalogue of the McClean Collection of Greek Coins,* III, 408–411, Nos. 9689, 9692, 9703, 9705.

[8] McDowell, *op. cit.,* pp. 46, 67, 214–220. The new coin types of Antiochus III had not come to light when the study of the impressions was made. They do not alter, however, the conclusions reached in the passages cited, since the features portrayed on the impressions are definitely not those of Antiochus.

[9] Babelon, lxxviii.

be presumed that both portraits represent the features of Antiochus III. I am unable to explain the exact significance of the reverse type. So far as the condition of the coins permits of observation it may be suggested that the motif represents a religious act in an Oriental cult. It is definitely foreign to the body of known Seleucid coin types. As in the case of the obverse, the reverse type can best be explained on the assumption that it was inspired by some incident of the campaign of Antiochus in the Upper Satrapies. Figurines found at Selucia show an arrangement of the hair which produces a turban-like effect.[10]

41. The reverse type of this single coin appears to be entirely similar to that of the coins cited. Although it is possible that the obverse shows a female head veiled, as on the coins in Babelon, so far as the condition of the piece permits of judgment the details suggest a portrait of Antiochus. The thick fabric is unusual, as is the form of the omega in the royal title (see p. 244, No. 16). The coin may have been struck in a mint farther to the east. In the absence of a monogram it is difficult to assign the issue to a particular period in the reign. The character of the reverse suggests that it belongs to the campaign coinage or to that which immediately succeeded the campaign.

42. The monograms on the coins of this type published by Babelon and Imhoof-Blumer do not occur on coins from Selucia of this general period. The character of the reverse suggests that the issue originated in a mint farther to the north or the east.

SELEUCUS IV

43. This is the sole coin of this reign found at Seleucia. The monograms on the coins cited in Babelon do not occur on coins from Seleucia of this general period. It should be noted, however, that the obverse of one of the coins is stated to bear a monogram, an alpha inclosing a beta. Actually this may be monogram No. 31, the epsilon having become obscured on the specimen examined by Babelon.

ANTIOCHUS IV

44. It should be noted that Babelon describes the Tyche of the reverse type as holding a long scepter in the left hand. The

[10] See *Figurines from Seleucia on the Tigris*, a forthcoming volume in this series by Dr. Wilhelmina van Ingen.

scepter does not form a part of the design on the coins from Seleucia, and I fail to distinguish it on the plates in Babelon.

45. The coins cited show initials and a monogram which do not occur on coins from Seleucia of this general period.

46. The attribution of this issue presents some difficulties. Representation of an obverse head in a frontal position is most characteristic of the first two Seleucid reigns, but this style does occur in the reigns of Antiochus III and Demetrius I.[11] The concept of Tyche, the city-goddess, first appears as a Seleucid coin type in the reign of Antiochus IV. In view of these facts an attribution of the group to the first or the second Antiochus would be entirely uncalled for, and an assignment to Antiochus III as opposed to Antiochus IV would require further direct evidence in support of the contention. Actually the extant direct evidence supports the latest date. The coins from Seleucia issued prior to the reign of Antiochus IV show a border only on the obverse. On the coins of type group No. 44 of this reign the obverse bears a border of continuous fillet, the reverse a border of dots. On the coins of the issue under consideration a border of dots can be observed on both obverse and reverse, a characteristic of coins of later periods.

DEMETRIUS I

47. The attribution of this group to the first rather than to the second Demetrius is warranted by the character of both obverse and reverse types. Two other issues bearing the name Demetrius, Nos. 52 and 55, have the obverse head executed in the frontal position. In the case of the former the reverse type is that of group No. 51 which bears on the obverse the portrait of Demetrius I. The motif of the obverse of the group under consideration cannot well be divorced from the frequent recurrence of Apollo and Artemis concepts on the coins of this king, nor from his adoption of the title of Soter. Although popular tradition attributed this title to the gratitude of certain elements in Babylonia toward Demetrius for his defeat of Timarchus,[12] it is more probable that from the moment of his accession Demetrius sought to assimilate himself to Apollo the ancestor of the Seleucid line. The political basis for this course may well have been the fact that Antiochus IV, who had assumed the throne which

[11] See pp. 47–48. [12] Appian, *Syriaca*, xi.47; Justin, xxxiv.35.

rightfully belonged to Demetrius upon the death of Seleucus IV, had sought to assimilate himself to Zeus.

The reverse type of the group under consideration appears to be entirely similar to that of a coin of Timarchus (Gardner, 50, No. 1). Since it cannot be assumed that the legitimate dynasty would imitate a type adopted by a rebel, the group must be assigned to the beginning of the reign of Demetrius, prior to the revolt.

48. In view of the facts that the queen of Demetrius is represented with him on one issue, No. 49, and that Demetrius himself was assimilated to Apollo, it is very possible that the motif of Artemis on coins of this reign refers to an assimilation in the royal cult of the queen to this goddess, the sister of Apollo. The relationship between the types of this group and the reverse type of the preceding group, and the fact that they are of different denominations, suggest that the two issues may be contemporary.

49. On the coin cited Nike is shown holding a palm in the left hand. This feature cannot be distinguished on the coins from Seleucia, but this may be due to their obscure condition. The jugate heads of Demetrius and his queen appear on a silver coin on which the types of Demetrius have been struck over those of Timarchus (Gardner, 50, No. 20). It is reasonable, therefore, to assign the bronze issue under consideration to the period immediately after the close of the revolt.

50. The coin in Babelon has similar types and legend, but is of a larger denomination and lacks the serrated edge. The title Soter occurs on the coin cited above, on which the types of Demetrius have been struck over those of Timarchus (Gardner, 50, No. 20). Groups Nos. 50 and 49 should be, therefore, approximately contemporary.

51. The attribution of these coins to the first Demetrius is based on the portrait of the obverse. It is very similar to that on a silver coin of Demetrius which has as reverse type a cornucopiae of slightly different form (Babelon, 96, No. 753). The motif of the reverse may be connected with the characteristic Tyche motifs of this reign.

52. The group is assigned to Demetrius I because the reverse type is that of the preceding group and because both the style and the fabric of the two issues are similar. The two groups, Nos.

51 and 52, exemplify a procedure characteristic of the Seleucia mint during the early Seleucid period, the retention in a new issue of the reverse type of a preceding issue, together with a change in the position of the obverse head from the profile to the frontal.[13] The obverse type of the group is closely similar to that of No. 47. In neither instance does the condition of the coins permit of a determination whether Helios is represented with the features of Demetrius. In any case the recurrence of the motif was intended to emphasize the relationship of the king to Apollo.

53. The portrait of the obverse is definitely that of Demetrius I. The association of the radiate headdress with the portrait has not hitherto been noted on coins of this reign. Its occurrence strengthens the suggestion that the facing head of Helios on two other issues of Demetrius, Nos. 47 and 52, is in fact a portrait of Demetrius as Apollo.

54. The assignment of the group to Demetrius I is, of course, required by the character of the portrait on the obverse. It constitutes the only issue of small bronze at Seleucia during this reign.

55. The attribution of this group to the first Demetrius is based on the motifs of the two types. The cults of Apollo and of the City-Goddess are closely related to the coinage of this reign and they influence only slightly that of Demetrius II. The reverse type presents a variation of the Tyche motif which is new to the Seleucid coinage. The group constitutes the largest issue of the reign of Demetrius I.

ALEXANDER BALA

56. Babelon has published a coin of Alexander with a similar obverse and on the reverse a likeness of Nike in a different pose (119, No. 928 *bis*). Although the details have been obscured, the reverse of the coin under consideration appears to be similar to that of the succeeding group, No. 57, which bears on the obverse a portrait of Alexander alone. Likewise type groups Nos. 58 and 59 have a common reverse; on the obverse in the one case is the portrait of the king and queen, in the other, that of the king alone. I suggest that those issues of Alexander which bear the portrait of Cleopatra Thea alongside that of the king should be assigned to the opening years of the reign, while this interloper

[13] See pp. 48–49.

in the Seleucid line was yet dependent upon the prestige and the power of Egypt. The hostility displayed by Ptolemy Philometor toward Alexander before the close of his short reign cannot have arisen overnight. It may well have been instigated by an early readiness on the part of his son-in-law to forget the basis of his rise to the throne.

57. Although the coins are in an obscure condition they appear to be entirely similar to the examples cited. As has been stated the reverse type seems in turn to be similar to that of the preceding group, No. 56.

58. The obverse type of this group is that of No. 56, and as in the case of that issue the group is assigned to the early years of the reign. The reverse type is that of the succeeding group, No. 59.

59. The coin from Seleucia appears to be entirely similar to those cited. The relationship of type groups Nos. 58 and 59 through their common reverse type is discussed under No. 56 above.

60. The types of this bronze issue are found on a gold coin of Alexander published by Babelon (101–102, No. 793; XVII, 9).

DEMETRIUS II (FIRST REIGN)

61. The obverse and reverse types of this group relate it closely to the group just below, No. 62, which must be assigned to the second Demetrius on the basis of the legend. The character of the types, especially that of the obverse, reminiscent as it is of Alexander the Great and his conquest of India, suggests that the two issues were minted either just prior to or during the early, successful phases of the campaign of Demetrius to Babylonia and beyond. In the absence of direct evidence to the contrary, the issue under consideration, with its simple legend, must be assumed to predate group No. 62, which bears in addition the titles Nikator and Philadelphos.

62. The attribution to Demetrius II, first made by Gardner, is required by the form of the legend which is characteristic of the coinage of this reign and does not occur on that of Demetrius I.

63. On the reverse of this group the Nike presumably holds a wreath through the royal name. On the coin cited the wreath is held over the name, and the legend lacks the title Philadelphos.

The question may be raised as to the conditions under which Demetrius assumed the title Nikator. If it was inspired by a specific victory does it refer to the defeat of Tryphon or to the initial successes of Demetrius over the Parthians? It is difficult to assume that once this, and the title of Philadelphos, had been adopted they were omitted from subsequent coin issues. The obverse type common to groups Nos. 61 and 62, with its suggestion of the exploits of Alexander the Great, supports an assumption that these coins were issued in connection with the campaign in the east. Since one of these issues includes in its legend the title Nikator whereas the other lacks it, if the line of reasoning pursued is justified, one must assume that the title was adopted as a result of events in the east rather than in Syria. On the basis of this argument group No. 63, which bears in addition to the title the reverse motif of Nike, cannot have been issued prior to groups Nos. 61 and 62, and probably immediately followed the second of these.

DEMETRIUS II (SECOND REIGN?)

64. The coins in Babelon differ slightly from our specimen in the details of the reverse type, and one of them bears the date 126/25 B.C. (by the Macedonian calendar). The coin from Seleucia does not appear to have been intended to show a date. In the absence of further examples I have assumed that it was carried by chance into Parthian territory from Syria. It is not impossible, however, that the coin represents a local issue of the first reign of Demetrius II, the types of which were later copied by one of the western mints.

DEMETRIUS II (SECOND REIGN)

65. The character of the reverse of this single specimen requires its assignment to the second reign of Demetrius. Its size differs greatly from that of Seleucid issues struck at Seleucia; in this respect it is related to types issued in Syria and to an autonomous issue of Seleucia struck during the reign of Mithradates I (p. 94, No. 126). Nos. 64 and 65 comprise the sole examples of Seleucid coins apparently struck after the capture of Seleucia by the Parthians which have as yet been recovered from the excavations.

CHAPTER III

CONCLUSION

The coins of the Seleucid period which have been described in the preceding chapters total three hundred and forty-seven and represent a number of new types, combinations of types, and varieties. They have been discussed individually in Chapter II; certain general characteristics, however, warrant further observations. The table which follows is intended to show the character of the types and the proportions in which the coins of each type group and each reign occur. The numbers in parentheses at the left indicate the total of the type groups of each reign, the silver and the bronze being figured separately. The figures in column at the right give the total number of coins of each group, those in parentheses the total for each reign, the two metals again being classified independently.

ALEXANDER THE GREAT (prior to 321 B.C.)

Æ (1)	Zeus seated l.	Lion advancing l.	2	(2)

SELEUCUS I AS SATRAP (prior to 311 B.C.)

Æ (1)	Head of Alexander r.	Horse's head and anchor.	1	(1)

SELEUCUS I AS KING (311–280 B.C.)

Æ	Head of Hercules r.	Zeus seated l.	1	
Æ	Head of Hercules r.	Zeus seated l.	1	
Æ (3)	Head of Zeus r.	Athena in chariot r.	1	(3)
Æ	Heads of the Dioscuri ¾ l.	Nike crowning trophy l.	2	
Æ	Head of Apollo ¾ l.	Head of a bull ¾ r.	1	
Æ	Head of Apollo r.	Head of a bull front.	1	
Æ	Head of a horse r.	Anchor	16	
Æ	Bust of Seleucus front	Horseman in combat r.	6	
Æ	Head of Apollo r.	Humped bull r.	13	
Æ	Head of Apollo ¾ l.	Nike and wreath l.	5	
Æ	Obscure head ¾ l.	Athena (?) ¾ r.	1	
Æ (9)	Head of Apollo ¾ l.	Tripod	2	(47)

ANTIOCHUS I (280–261 B.C.)

Æ	Head of Antiochus r.	Apollo on omphalos l.	1	
Æ	Head of Apollo r.	Athena Alkis r.	17	
Æ	Head of Apollo ¾ l.	Athena Alkis r.	1	
Æ	Head of Apollo r.	Athena Alkis r.	3	
Æ	Head of Apollo r.	Athena Promachos l.	2	
Æ	Bust of Apollo ¾ r.	Nike and trophy r.	13	
Æ	Head of Apollo ¾ r.	Tripod	14	
Æ	Head of Athena ¾ l.	Apollo Citharoedos r.	4	
Æ	Head of Athena ¾ r.	Apollo Citharoedos r.	9	
Æ	Head of Athena r.	Apollo l.	5	
Æ	Head of Apollo ¾ l.	Apollo l.	7	
Æ	Head of Apollo ¾ r.	Quiver	2	
Æ (13)	Head of Zeus ¾ r.	Apollo (?) r.	4	(82)

ANTIOCHUS II (261–246 B.C.)

Æ (1)	Head of Apollo r.	Apollo on omphalos l.	8	(8)

SELEUCUS II (246–226 B.C.)

AR (1)	Head of Seleucus r.	Apollo l., tripod	1	(1)
Æ	Head of Seleucus r.	Nike and wreath l.	1	
Æ (2)	Head of Seleucus r.	Apollo l.	18	(19)

SELEUCUS III (226–223 B.C.)

No coins of this reign have been found.

ANTIOCHUS III (223–187 B.C.)

Æ	Head of Antiochus r.	Nike and wreath l.	4	
Æ	Head of Antiochus r.	Apollo Citharoedos ¾ r.	2	
Æ	Head of Apollo r.	Nike, wreath and palm l.	2	
Æ	Bust of Artemis r.	Apollo Citharoedos nude r.	10	
Æ	Head of Apollo r.	Apollo l.	2	
Æ	Head of Apollo r.	Artemis l.	1	
Æ	Head of Apollo r.	Elephant advancing r.	9	
Æ	Bust of Antiochus (?) ¾ r.	Elephant r.	5	
Æ	Head of Antiochus (?) ¾ r.	Unidentified figure r.	2	
Æ	Head of Antiochus (?) r.	Head of an elephant l.	1	
Æ (11)	Head of Antiochus r.	Mare and foal l.	1	(39)

SELEUCUS IV (187–175 B.C.)

Æ (1)	Head of Apollo r.	Apollo l., tripod	1	(1)

ANTIOCHUS IV (175–164 B.C.)

Æ	Head of Antiochus r.	Tyche Nikephoros seated l.	43
Æ	Head of Antiochus r.	Zeus l.	1
Æ (3)	Head of Apollo ¾ r.	Tyche l.	12 (56)

ANTIOCHUS V (164–162 B.C.)

No coins of this reign have been found.

DEMETRIUS I (162–150 B.C.)

Æ	Head of Helios ¾ l.	Artemis r.	5
Æ	Head of Artemis r.	Quiver and bow	1
Æ	Busts of Demetrius and queen r.	Nike and wreath l.	14
Æ	Head of Demetrius r.	Apollo on omphalos l.	3
Æ	Head of Demetrius r.	Cornucopiae	6
Æ	Head of Helios ¾ l.	Cornucopiae	5
Æ	Head of Demetrius r.	Tyche seated l.	7
Æ	Head of Demetrius r.	Tyche l.	3
Æ (9)	Bust of Apollo ¾ l.	Tyche l., column	17 (61)

TIMARCHUS (161–160 B.C.)

No coins of this reign have been found.

ALEXANDER BALA (152–144 B.C.)

Æ	Heads of Cleopatra and Alexander r.	Nike and wreath l.	1
Æ	Head of Alexander r.	Nike and branch l.	6
Æ	Heads of Cleopatra and Alexander r.	Apollo l.	2
Æ	Head of Alexander as Hercules r.	Apollo l.	1
Æ (5)	Head of Alexander r.	Zeus seated l.	2 (12)

DEMETRIUS II (first reign 146–140/39 B.C.[1])

Æ	Head of Demetrius as Alexander the Great r.	Athena seated l.	8

[1] It is entirely possible that Demetrius effectively controlled Seleucia only from 141/40 to 140/39 B.C.

Æ	Head of Demetrius as Alexander the Great r.	Athena l.	3
Æ (3)	Head of Demetrius r.	Nike l.	4 (15)

DEMETRIUS II (second reign ? 130–125 B.C.)

Æ (1)	Female head r.	Cornucopiae	1 (1)

DEMETRIUS II (second reign)

Æ (1)	Obscured	Zeus Nikephoros seated l.	1 (1)

The greater number of these coins must be presumed to have been struck at the mint in Seleucia. Evidence is lacking concerning the few examples of the silver coinage. In respect to the bronze, however, it must be borne in mind that coins of this metal would have been transported from one mint area to another only by chance and in very small quantities. Only by an odd chance do examples of such comparatively rare migrant coins find their way into the hands of the excavator of an ancient site. I assume without hesitation, therefore, that type groups represented by more than one specimen were struck at Seleucia. I would tentatively assume that single bronze coins are examples of local issues unless specific characteristics are hostile to the assumption. Of the seventeen coins that fall within this classification only four appear to possess characteristics which require their assignment to mints other than Seleucia. Two coins of Demetrius II, Nos. 64 and 65, one of which is certainly, the other probably, of the second reign, presumably were brought to Seleucia after the occupation of the city by the Parthians. On the basis of their fabric and design groups Nos. 41 and 42 of the reign of Antiochus III must be attributed to mints of Iran, No. 42 perhaps to that at Ecbatana, No. 41 to some center farther to the east. [Mr. E. T. Newell informs me that types similar to those of the single coins Nos. 43, 45, 48, and 59 and of the group No. 57 occur on coins which almost certainly should be assigned to the Antioch mint. See Preface, p. viii.]

Special attention should be paid to the frequent recurrence on the coins from Seleucia of frontality as a technique in the engraving of the obverse types. Of the fifty-seven types or varieties of bronze struck during the period from the opening of the reign of Seleucus I as king through the first reign of Demetrius II — the presumable limits within which the Seleucid mint at Seleucia functioned — twenty, or just over thirty-five per cent, are characterized by this technique. For the reign of Seleucus I the proportion of its occurrence amounts to sixty-six and two-thirds per cent; for that of Antiochus I, just over sixty-one per cent; for the reigns of Antiochus IV and Demetrius I, thirty-three and one-third per cent; and for that of Antiochus III, a little more than eighteen per cent. So far as I have knowledge the technique is employed on only three Seleucid bronze types which have not, as yet, been found at Seleucia.[2] In view of the frequency of its occurrence at Seleucia it is very possible that this style, as applied to coin engraving in the Seleucid Empire, was limited to the Babylonian mint. Its very occasional use in the west outside the empire was certainly imitative. The technique was employed at intervals in the Parthian and Sassanian coinage; some of these later coins were struck at Seleucia, but for the determination of the mints, whether Parthian or Sassanian, responsible for the others, one must await further studies. Whatever the primary source from which the technique in engraving was derived, it must be sought east of the Euphrates, and there is nothing to suggest that Seleucia (with Ctesiphon)[3] was not the center in which it developed and survived. The appearance of this style in other forms of art has been noted at Seleucia and at Dura-Europos.[4]

It is interesting to remark that of the twenty occurrences of frontality on the coins from Seleucia, fourteen represent Apollo or Helios, one the Dioscuri, one Athena, one either Zeus or the Nikator as Zeus, one Seleucus I wearing the horns of divinity, and two Antiochus III as a mortal. The examples on Seleucid coins not found at Seleucia portray Apollo and Athena.

It will be observed that a number of successive issues bear the same reverse type, but on the obverse show either a common type executed in different positions or two distinct types. The first group is constituted by Nos. 16 and 17 and Nos. 22 and 23

[2] One of Seleucus I (Babelon, II, 7), one of Antiochus I (*ibid.*, V, 14), and one of Demetrius I (Rogers, 31, No. 8).

[3] It is to be presumed that after the occupation by the Sassanians the mint was located in Ctesiphon.

[4] This statement applies in particular to terra-cotta figures. A volume on the figurines from Seleucia will be published by Dr. Wilhelmina van Ingen (see p. 38, note 10). Dr. van Ingen has called to my attention various examples of frontality as it has been observed in connection with the material from Dura.

of the reign of Antiochus I; the second group by Nos. 24 and 25 of the same reign; Nos. 51 and 52 of the reign of Demetrius I; and Nos. 56 and 57 and Nos. 58 and 59 of the reign of Alexander Bala. Further examples of the retention of a single reverse for two different obverse types have been noted by Dr. Edgar Rogers,[5] the English numismatist. On these coins the royal portrait of the obverse is discarded in favor of the representation of a deity, or vice versa. On the coins from Seleucia this is true of but one pair, Nos. 51 and 52, which shows on the one the head of Demetrius I, on the other that of Helios. In the two pairs of the reign of Alexander Bala the shift is explained by the political situation which marked the period.[6] In no instance can the changes have been intended to indicate distinctions in denominations, nor is there evidence to suggest that the individuals of a pair were struck at different mints. It is interesting to note that aside from the two pairs of the reign of Alexander Bala, the changes in the obverse type are accompanied by a shift in the position of the head from a profile to a frontal pose.

Throughout the series of Seleucid coins no uniformity is to be remarked in the form of the edges of the flans. Frequently considerable variation exists within a single type group. This carelessness as to finish will be found also in the series of autonomous coins of Seleucia. It is particularly interesting that the serrated edge occurs on but three type groups, No. 43 of Seleucus IV and Nos. 48 and 50 of Demetrius I. Nothing in the nature of a mint mark can be discerned on the coins from Seleucia, but owing to the general lack of examples of the silver coinage little significance may be attached to the fact.[7] Monograms (or initials having a similar value) were apparently intended to be shown on all issues until the reign of Antiochus IV. Of the three type groups of this reign represented in our series, one, No. 44, lacks any indication of a monogram or its equivalent. Beginning with the next reign, that of Demetrius I, no monogram or inital appears on any of the coins, notwithstanding that on contemporary coins such as those published by Babelon, presumably of Syrian mints, they are of frequent occurrence.

[5] "New Seleucid Coin Types," *The Numismatic Chronicle*, Fifth series, 1 (1921), p. 30.

[6] See p. 41, under note 56.

[7] Mr. E. T. Newell has noted that the mint of Antioch in the Seleucid period employed no mint marks, whereas the coins of secondary mints, such as Tyre, generally showed them. (*The Seleucid Mint of Antioch*, pp. 3–4.)

In view of the fact that the greater part of the excavations at Seleucia has been conducted in Parthian rather than Seleucid levels of occupation,[8] no comparison can be made between the totals of the coins of the two periods. The three hundred and forty-seven examples of the earlier coinage which have been cataloged do constitute, however, a body of material sufficiently comprehensive to permit of observations on the proportions which obtain between the issues of the successive Seleucid reigns.

Of the six silver coins five belong either to the period of Alexander the Great or to the early portion of the reign of Seleucus I. In this connection there should be noted clay models of Seleucid tetradrachms which have been found at Seleucia.[9] There is no indication that these objects were used as currency; indeed, the purpose they served is obscure. In view of these facts only limited conclusions can be drawn from the evidence which they may afford. A certain value, however, attaches to the fact that the originals for these models were tetradrachms which undoubtedly were actually in circulation in Seleucia. Of the nineteen examples sixteen are models of tetradrachms of Seleucus I, Antiochus I, and Seleucus, the elder son of Antiochus I, and comprise eleven issues. The remaining three represent the reigns of Antiochus III, Antiochus IV, and Timarchus. These proportions, to the extent of their value, thus support the coins in suggesting that the extensive minting of silver by Alexander the Great was continued by his immediate successors in the east, and that, thereafter, the issue of this metal was relatively light.

No coins have been recovered for the reigns of Seleucus III or Antiochus V, or of the rebels Molon and Timarchus. It is very possible that the mint was inactive during the few years covered by the first two of these reigns. Molon presumably employed only the mint at Ecbatana. That no coins of Timarchus have been found is more difficult to comprehend and may possess a certain significance. In addition to the model of a tetradrachm referred to above, impressions of official seals of Timarchus have been recovered at Seleucia.[10] They appear to have belonged to the period just prior to the outbreak of open rebellion. These facts are discussed below on pages 55–56.

[8] See Preface, p. vii.

[9] McDowell, *Stamped and Inscribed Objects from Seleucia on the Tigris*, pp. 241–250.

[10] *Ibid.*, p. 46, Nos. IA30(1) and IA30(2).

The ten Seleucid reigns represented in the catalog display a marked difference in the rate of issue of bronze currency at Seleucia. This is illustrated by the table below. Owing to the probability that they were never in circulation at Seleucia, the last two coins assigned to Demetrius II in the catalog have not been included in the table.

King	*Length of reign*	*Coins*	*Average rate of issue per year*
Seleucus I	31	47	1.51
Antiochus I	19	82	4.26
Antiochus II	15	8	0.53
Seleucus II	20	19	0.95
Antiochus III	36	39	1.08
Seleucus IV	12	1	0.08
Antiochus IV	11	56	5.09
Demetrius I	12	61	5.08
Alexander Bala	6	12	2.00
Demetrius II	4	15	3.75

Without overstressing the value of these proportions certain general conclusions may reasonably be drawn from them. The fifty-year period covered by the first two reigns shows an average rate of issue of 2.58 coins per year. The apparent great increase in the rate during the second reign should be somewhat reduced if, as is possible, certain issues of Antiochus were struck during the lifetime of his father. From the accession of Antiochus II to the death of Seleucus IV there was an elapsed period of eighty-six years, just over one half of the total period of Seleucid rule in Babylonia. For this interval we get an average rate of issue of 0.78 coins per year. There followed twenty-five years covered by the reigns of Antiochus IV, Antiochus V, and Demetrius I, during which minting reached and maintained a peak with an average rate of 4.68 coins per year. We do not know, of course, the exact year in which the administration of Alexander Bala succeeded that of Demetrius I in Seleucia. Either ten or eleven years may be allowed, therefore, as the period during which Alexander and Demetrius II controlled the mint. Depending upon the figure employed, the rate for this period is either 2.7 or 2.45 coins per year.

It is perhaps needless to remark that in an ancient society, unused to banking and to commercial paper as we understand the terms, the effective volume of currency very definitely reflected the prosperity of the community. Furthermore, the bronze currency possessed greater significance as a medium of exchange; it represented greater purchasing power than does our copper coinage today and it maintained a much higher ratio to the total volume of currency. With these conditions in mind it is reasonable to state that in an ancient society the rate of issue of the bronze coinage was normally responsive to two demands: the necessity for the replacement of the currency in circulation, owing either to a change of government or to wear and loss, and the need for an increase in the volume of the coinage to meet an increase in the population or in commercial activity and, possibly, capital wealth. It should be noted, also, that in order to affect appreciably the rate of issue of bronze — the local medium of exchange — as opposed to tetradrachms — extensively employed in interregional trade — any increase in commercial activity or in prosperity must have been one which applied primarily to the mass of the population rather than to a small group in the community, such as the merchants in the transit trade.

To some extent the changes in the rate of issue at Seleucia, as suggested by the proportions in which our coins occur, were due to the institution of the new Seleucid currency by Seleucus I, the adequacy of which may possibly have obviated the necessity for the striking of new issues during subsequent reigns until the original coinage was dissipated in use. This explanation, however, is only partially satisfactory. An indicated increase in the rate of issue amounting to six times that which had prevailed over almost ninety years — notwithstanding the limited character of our basic figures — must have been due in part to other factors. The evidence suggests strongly that during the reigns of Antiochus IV and Demetrius I, from about 175 to 150 B.C., Seleucia enjoyed a significant increase either in population or in the general level of prosperity, or in both. It is natural and probably reasonable to connect this with the well-known efforts of Antiochus IV to preserve the unity of the empire through his encouragement and subsidy of the Hellenized urban elements. That the sharp rise in the rate of issue was maintained for a quarter of a century and that the subsequent decrease during the remainder of the Seleucid period appears to have been moderate, in spite of the political disturbances which marked those years, suggest again the general character as well as the solidity of the changes which had taken place. It is interesting, and very likely significant in the light of the ease with which the Parthians were allowed to occupy Babylonia, that Seleucia appears to have entered upon an era of economic growth and prosperity while at the same time in Syria the dynasty was frittering away the strength and destroying the tradition of loyalty which might have enabled them to hold together their empire in the east.

Although full benefit of the numismatic material from Seleucia cannot be enjoyed until further excavation will have revealed more of the Seleucid levels of occupation, the coins of the Seleucid period serve to throw some light upon other contemporary political events. Nothing definite can be added to the little which is already known regarding the date for the foundation of Seleucia. The presence of coins of Alexander the Great and of Seleucus as satrap, together with the wide variety in the types of Seleucus as king, is inconclusive as evidence, but, of course, favors the conclusion that the city was founded considerably earlier than 300 B.C., the date frequently suggested. On grounds which cannot be discussed within the limits of this work I have assumed that Seleucia was in existence as capital and mint city very shortly after the return of Seleucus to Babylonia in 311 B.C.[11] The rise in the rate of issue of bronze under Antiochus I supports the conclusion that the initial large increase in population brought to the new capital took place during this reign.[12]

It is very possible that a definite relationship existed between the number of distinct types and varieties struck for each king in proportion to the years of the reign and the degree of personal interest displayed by the king toward the community in which the coins were intended to circulate. While practical motives governed the volume of the currency, the king's pleasure must frequently have dictated not only the nature of the designs but the frequency with which the designs were altered. This

[11] Reference can be made to a former study by the author which covers in part the evidence favoring an earlier date for the foundation of Seleucia: "The Excavations at Seleucia on the Tigris," *Papers of the Michigan Academy of Science, Arts and Letters*, 18 (1932), 107–109.

[12] Cf. McDowell, as cited in note 11.

tendency, apparently, is illustrated by the coins from Seleucia. Those of the Seleucidae who are known to have spent some time in the east and who were personally interested in that portion of the empire — Seleucus I, Antiochus I, Antiochus III, Demetrius I, and Demetrius II — are represented by coinages rich in the variety of design displayed by obverse and reverse types. During the Parthian period a somewhat similar relationship may be noted. In both the Seleucid and the Parthian periods this tendency can be remarked within given reigns, the issues of which, through their types, can be related to particular episodes in which the king played a personal part.

The numerous issues struck at Seleucia for Antiochus III illustrate the tendency. Type group No. 32 must have been struck immediately after his accession, Nos. 33 and 34 prior to the revolt of Molon, and Nos. 35–37 shortly thereafter. Nos. 38–40 belong to the period of the great campaign to the east, as does No. 41, a specimen of some Iranian mint.[13] This campaign brought to a close the first half of the reign of Antiochus. His accession found the young king beyond the Euphrates, probably with his headquarters at Seleucia; here he placed himself during his reorganization of the administration after the revolt of Molon, and from this stronghold as a base was conducted the campaign in Iran. During the second half of his reign Antiochus was exclusively involved in the west until shortly before his death, and to this period at best one issue of the Seleucia mint might be assigned, No. 42. As the relation of this group to the local mint is in fact doubtful, it is very possible that no bronze was struck for Antiochus at Seleucia during the final eighteen years of his reign.

The coins of Demetrius I struck at Seleucia have some bearing upon the circumstances attendant upon the revolt of Timarchus. At least one and probably two issues had been struck before the revolt became overt in this area.[14] The adherents of Demetrius appear to have succeeded in securing Seleucia from the party of Antiochus V very shortly after the *coup d'état* of Demetrius had been inaugurated in Syria, if not simultaneously with that event. This circumstance and the rapid rise thereafter of the independent movement of Timarchus suggest that certain groups in

[13] See pp. 34–38.

[14] See pp. 39–40, under Nos. 47 and 48.

Seleucia and Babylonia which were dominant at the moment were moved by no strong loyalty toward the memory of Antiochus IV. One may legitimately inquire whether this condition was not brought about in part by the policies to which this ruler had been devoted. The extremely powerful Jewish communities in Babylonia must have been incensed by his conduct in respect to Jerusalem, and his efforts to re-create Babylon as an active Hellenized center must undoubtedly have offended not only conservative Babylonians but also the elements in Seleucia which had profited largely from the supremacy of the latter city and which for the most part controlled its government.

The recovery of issues of Demetrius I struck immediately prior to and after the revolt and the absence of coins of Timarchus, together with the fact that impressions of official seals have been found at Seleucia which belong to the inception rather than the culmination of the revolt,[15] suggest that the overt rebellion in the city covered a very short period, during which his currency failed to pass into general circulation. The evidence requires the conclusion that Seleucia and, probably, Babylonia were not focal points of the movement which Timarchus represented. It has been suggested elsewhere by the writer that this movement had for its purpose the restriction of Parthian expansion through the replacement of the disintegrating Seleucid Empire by a more compact and vigorous state on the western borders of Iran which would coöperate more closely toward this end with the Bactrian state in the east.[16] The source from which Timarchus drew his principal strength appears to have been Media, and it is reasonable to assume that his coinage was issued from Ecbatana rather than from Seleucia or Babylon. The maintenance of order in the great cities and along the trade routes was essential to the survival of the Greek commercial aristocracy of Seleucia and Iran. The absorption of the Seleucid kings in western politics and the consequent weakening of their control over the East placed a severe strain on the traditional loyalty of the Greeks in those regions. It is probable that the promise of their support rather than a nationalistic awakening among the Iranians and Babylonians constituted the preponderant force

[15] See p. 50.

[16] McDowell, *Stamped and Inscribed Objects from Seleucia on the Tigris*, pp. 218–220.

behind Timarchus. The rapid collapse of the separatist movement denoted only that the natives remained indifferent and that the Greeks of Seleucia saw in the audacity and vigor of the young Demetrius the basis of an effective revival of the empire. Disappointment with the subsequent failure of Demetrius and the degeneration of the intradynastic strife into a series of brawls, together with the continued prosperity of Seleucia, as suggested in an earlier paragraph, may be presumed to have swung the Greek aristocratic party toward that alliance with the Parthian military power which characterized the later history of the city.[17]

The coins of Demetrius II struck at Seleucia contribute nothing to a more exact determination of the date at which Seleucid rule in that city finally ceased to be effective. They possess, however, a definite historical interest. The representation of the young king wearing an elephant-scalp headdress was certainly intended to call to mind the conquest of the east by Alexander the Great. An impression of the seal of a royal steward at Seleucia reproduces the same motif.[18] The implication of this style is that in his campaign beyond the Euphrates Demetrius sought more than recruits and treasure with which to retain the surviving Seleucid territories in the east and to carry on the war in Syria; he appears to have had visions of restoring the Seleucid Empire to the limits it had attained in the early reigns. The initial victories of the young king over the armies of Mithradates I, fresh from their conquest of Bactria, Media, and the powerful tribal groups of Iran, and the fact that the Parthian was obliged to resort to a trick in order to defeat him,[19] demonstrate real military ability on the part of Demetrius. The short reign of his brother Antiochus revealed an even superior capacity for organization.[20] The successful course of subsequent Parthian history proves the absence of any effective nationalistic spirit in the East prior to the rise of the Sassanian renaissance. The majority groups within all classes of the population in Babylonia and Iran rejected the Seleucid line in favor of the equally alien Arsacids only because of the continued vigor and military power of the latter. It is fascinating, therefore, to ponder over the changes in

[17] See below, pp. 216–221.

[18] McDowell, *op. cit.*, p. 68, No. IIA1s(1).

[19] Justin, xxxvi.1.4; xxxvi.1.5; xxxviii.9.2.

[20] E. R. Bevan, *The House of Seleucus*, II, 242.

the history of the Near East which might well have resulted if Demetrius and his brother had succeeded in reëstablishing the Seleucid Empire east of the Euphrates.

We possess no direct evidence as to the course of events in Seleucia after 146 B.C., when Demetrius II first launched his attack on Alexander Bala, and prior to the first occupation of Babylonia by Mithradates I in 141 B.C.[21] Seleucia probably fell with the rest of Babylonia, but the evidence is not positive. Demetrius recovered Babylonia late in 141 or early in 140 B.C. and was finally defeated and taken prisoner late in 140 or early in 139 B.C.[22] It is this period of the campaign, comprising at the most a year and a half, to which must be assigned the three issues of the first reign of Demetrius which have been recovered at Seleucia.[23] Although the absence of coinage struck in the name of Demetrius does not prove that his administration was not recognized at Seleucia during the preceding five years, it does suggest strongly that these years constituted an interregnum, during which Seleucia lay outside the area effectively controlled by any aspirant to paramount power. The interval was of prime importance to the people of Seleucia. Both to the east and to the west fundamental political changes were taking place which would obviously affect the future course of the city. Sister cities in Syria were being torn by the factional strife which had been encouraged by the dynastic struggle. The hostility of Rome toward the Seleucid kingdom was becoming more marked, but there was as yet no clear indication that Rome herself intended to guarantee order and the security of commerce in western Asia. The Greek cities on the Iranian plateau were becoming accustomed to Parthian rule. The new power was clearly not so barbarous as might have been expected; rather, the Arsacids had rapidly proved themselves tolerant in their relations with the newly subjected peoples. Of particular importance to Seleucia, the great trade route to Central Asia, India, and China for the larger part of its course lay securely under Parthian control. The opportunity to examine the situation dispassionately, unbiased by the actual presence of one or the other of the rival forces, served the city well. The initial onset of the Parthians

[21] W. Tarn, "Parthia," *The Cambridge Ancient History*, IX, 580.

[22] *Ibid.*

[23] See p. 42 under No. 63.

and the counterstroke of Demetrius were accepted with equal passivity, but by 140/39 B.C. Seleucia was striking silver and bronze for Mithradates I in consummation of an alliance the value of which to each party subsequent Parthian history amply proves.[24]

[24] The evidence afforded by the early coinage of the Parthian period as to the relationship between Seleucia and the Parthian dynasty is discussed on pages 201–216.

PART II

COINS OF THE PARTHIAN PERIOD

CHAPTER IV

CATALOG OF COINS

THE coins of the Parthian period fall into two divisions, the royal coinage and the autonomous coinage of Seleucia. The general arrangement of the catalog is that employed for the coins of the Seleucid period (see p. 3). In the legends no attempt has been made to reproduce those peculiarities in the formation of the Greek letters which characterize certain periods. All changes in form, however, have been described in the "Notes on the Coins," to which references are made in the catalog. The peculiarities have been reproduced on page 244. The dates have been calculated by the Babylonian calendar, and it has been assumed that by the year 46/47 A.D. an extra month had been intercalated in the Greek cycle. The general problem of the calendar has been treated on pages 147–153. As in the case of the Seleucid coins, all discussion of the individual type groups and coins has been reserved for the next chapter. A discussion of the historical evidence afforded by the coins of the Parthian period will be found in subsequent chapters. On pages 183–200 will be found a table of all coins of the Parthian period which are considered to have been struck at the mint of Seleucia.

The serial numbers are continuous from Part I.

1. THE ROYAL COINAGE

PERIOD OF MITHRADATES I

(171–138/37 B.C.)

66 Æ (1)

Obv.: Bust of the king r., diademed; long beard. The hair is represented in a very naturalistic manner.

Rev.: The beardless Hercules standing ¾ l. The club is held in the l. arm. The r. hand, in front, grasps an obscure object.

Legend: r., 1st, obscure
2nd [Μ]ΕΓΑΛ[ΟΥ]

l., 1st [Α]ΡΣΑΚ[ΟΥ]
2nd [ΦΙΛΕΛΛΗ]ΝΟΣ

Monogram: None can be distinguished, perhaps owing to the condition of the coin.

Date: None can be distinguished.

Wroth, 12–15, Nos. 48–50, 55–56, 58–60; III, 7. See discussion, p. 112.

gr. : 13.4
mm. : 27.0

ARTABANUS I

(128/27–124/23 B.C.)

67 Æ (1)

Obv.: Bust of the king r., diademed; medium, pointed beard; increased formalism in the treatment of the hair on the head. Border of continuous fillet.

Rev.: Tyche seated l. on a throne without a back. The head is bare, the hair done in a knot. In the l. arm is a cornucopiae; the r. hand, advanced, holds a Nike who extends a wreath toward Tyche.

Legend: r. [Β]ΑΣΙΛΕΩΣ, l. ΑΡΣΑΚΟΥ.

Monograms: In the ex., No. 34, No. 33.

Date: None appears to occur.

Wroth, 20, note 1. See Pl. IV and discussion, p. 112.

gr. : 11.05
mm. : 31.00

MITHRADATES II

(123/22–91/90 B.C.)

68 Æ (2)

Obv.: Bust of the king l., diademed; long beard; formal treatment of the hair. Border of dots.

Rev.: Arsaces seated r. on an omphalos. The r. hand, advanced, grasps a bow; from behind the l. side protrudes a sword. In the field r. is an upright palm.

Legend: l., up ΒΑΣΙΛΕΩΣ above [Μ]ΕΓΑΛΟΥ
r. ΑΡΣΑΚΟΥ ex. ΕΠΙΦΑΝΟΥΣ

Monogram: In the ex., 2nd No. 35.

Date: None occurs.

Wroth, 24, Nos. 1–3; VI, 1–2. See discussion, p. 112.

gr. : 14.94 12.99
mm. : 28.70 27.30

ORODES II

(57–38/37 B.C.)

69 Æ (1)

Obv.: Bust of the king l., diademed; hair in three waves; close beard. Border of dots.

Rev.: The king seated r. on a throne with a high back, receiving the hand of Tyche kneeling l. Tyche wears a turreted headdress and holds a scepter in the l. arm.

Legend: Above, 1st ΒΑΣΙΛΕΩΣ
2nd ΒΑΣΙΛΕΩΝ
l., 1st [Ε]ΠΙΦΑΝΟΥΣ
2nd [ΦΙ]ΛΕΛΛΗΝΟ[Σ]

r., 1st ΑΡΣΑΚΟΥ
2nd ΕΥΕΡΓΕΤΟΥ
ex., 1st (inverted) ΔΙΚΑΙΟΥ

Monogram: In the field center, No. 36.

Date: Of the year, does not appear to occur; of the month, in the ex., 2nd [·]Α.

Wroth, 72, No. 31; XIV, 11. See discussion, p. 112.

gr. : 12.70
mm. : 29.50

70 Æ (1)

Obv.: Bust of the king l., diademed; hair in three waves; close beard. Border of dots.

Rev.: The king seated l. on a throne with a high back. The head is uncovered and bears the diadem. The r. hand, advanced, holds a Nike who extends a wreath toward the king. The l. hand rests on a long scepter. The pose is that of Zeus Nikephoros.

Legend: Above, 1st ΒΑΣΙΛΕΩΣ
2nd ΒΑΣΙΛΕΩΝ
l., 1st ΕΠΙΦΑΝΟΥΣ
2nd [Φ]ΙΛΕΛΛΗΝΟΣ

r., 1st ΑΡΣΑΚΟΥ
2nd ΕΥΕΡΓΕΤΟΥ
ex., 1st (inverted) ΔΙΚΑΙΟΥ

Monogram: None occurs.

Date: None can be distinguished.

Wroth, 73, No. 34; XV, 1. See discussion, p. 113.

gr. : 12.06
mm. : 29.40

PHRAATES IV

(38/37–2/1 B.C.)

71 Æ (1)

Obv.: Bust of the king l., diademed; hair in four formal rows; short beard; no star on the tunic. Border of dots.

Rev.: The king seated r. on a throne with a high back, receiving a palm from Tyche standing l. Tyche wears a kalathos and carries a cornucopiae in the l. arm. The presence or absence of a pellet cannot be determined.

Legend: Largely obscured; l., 1st [ΕΠΙ]ΦΑΝΟΥ[Σ], ex., 1st (inverted) ΔΙΚΑΙΟΥ.

Monogram: None occurs.

Date: In the field center ϛΠΣ, 26/25 B.C.; in the ex., 2nd ΥΠΕΡ[ΒΕΡΕΤΑΙΟΥ], the 6th month.

Wroth, 103, No. 20; XIX, 5. See discussion, p. 113.

gr. : 8.72
mm. : 27.6

72 Æ (1)

Obv.: Bust of the king l., diademed; hair in four formal rows; short beard; no evidence of a star on the tunic. Border of dots.

Rev.: The king seated r. on a throne without a back, receiving a diadem from Tyche standing l. Tyche wears a kalathos and carries a cornucopiae in the l. arm.

Legend: Above, 1st [Β]ΑΣΙΛΕΩΣ
2nd ΒΑΣΙΛΕΩΝ
l., 1st [Ε]ΠΙΦΑΝΟΥΣ
2nd [ΦΙΛΕ]ΛΛΗΝ[ΟΣ]
r., 1st ΑΡΣΑΚΟΥ
2nd ΕΥΕΡΓΕΤΟΥ
ex., 1st (inverted) ΔΙΚΑΙΟΥ

Monogram: None occurs.

Date: In the ex., 2nd ϛΠΣ, 26/25 B.C.; ΑΠΕΛ[ΛΑΙΟΥ], the 8th month.

Wroth, 103, No. 21; XIX, 6. See discussion, p. 113.

gr. : 9.96
mm. : 30.7

73 Æ (3)

Obv.: Bust of the king l., diademed; hair in four formal rows; short beard. The presence or absence of a star on the tunic cannot be determined. Border of dots.

Rev.: The king seated r. on a throne with a high back, receiving a palm from Tyche standing l. Tyche wears a kalathos and carries a cornucopiae in the l. arm. In the field center, a pellet.

Legend: Above, 1st ΒΑΣΙΛΕΩ[Σ]
2nd ΒΑΣΙΛΕΩΝ
l., 1st ΕΠΙΦΑΝΟΥΣ
2nd [ΦΙ]ΛΕΛΛΗΝΟ[Σ]
r., 1st ΑΡΣΑΚΟΥ
2nd ΕΥΕΡΓΕΤΟΥ
ex., 1st (inverted) ΔΙΚΑΙΟΥ

Monogram: None occurs.

Date: Beneath the throne, on two coins ΖΠΣ, 25/24 B.C.; on the third, obscure. In the ex., 2nd ΠΑΑΝ (ΠΑΝΗΜΟΥ), the 3rd month, ΔΙΟΥ, the 7th month; on the third coin, month obscure.

Wroth, 104, No. 26; XIX, 7. See discussion, p. 113.

gr. : 14.49 9.36 9.05
mm. : 28.00 30.1 30.4

74 Æ (2)

Obv.: Bust of the king l., diademed; hair in four formal rows; medium, pointed beard. No border can be distinguished.

Rev.: The king seated l. on a throne without a back. The r. hand, advanced, grasps a bow; the l. rests on a long scepter behind.

Legend: Above, 1st [Β]ΑΣΙΛΕΩ[Σ]
2nd ΒΑΣΙΛΕΩ[Ν]
l., 1st [Ε]ΠΙΦΑΝΟΥΣ
2nd [ΦΙΛ]ΕΛΛΗΝ[ΟΣ]
r., 1st ΑΡΣΑΚΟΥ
2nd ΕΥΕΡΓΕΤΟΥ
ex., 1st (inverted) ΔΙΚΑΙΟΥ

Monograms: In the field l., No. 37; on one of the coins, between the legs of the throne, No. 38.

Date: Of the year, none; of the month in the ex., 2nd ΑΡΤΕΜΙ[ΣΙΟΥ], the 1st month.

Wroth, 108, Nos. 52–54; XX, 2. See discussion, p. 113.

gr. : 9.79 7.25
mm. : 28.3 27.3

75 Æ (1)

Obv.: As on No. 74. Border of dots.

Rev.: The king seated r. on a throne without a back, receiving a palm from Tyche standing l. Tyche wears a kalathos and carries a long scepter in the l. arm.

Legend: Above, 1st ΒΑΣΙΛΕΩΣ
2nd ΒΑΣΙΛΕΩΝ
l., 1st ΕΠΙΦΑΝΟ[ΥΣ]
2nd off flan
r., 1st ΑΡΣΑΚΟ[Υ]
2nd ΕΥΕΡΓΕ[ΤΟΥ]
ex., 1st (inverted) ΔΙΚΑΙΟ[Υ]

Monogram: In the field, none; between the legs of the king Α; between the legs of the throne, No. 39.

Date: Of the year, none; in the ex., 2nd, the month off flan.

Wroth, 109, Nos. 55–56, XX, 3. See discussion, p. 114.

gr. : 12.14
mm. : 28.10

PHRAATACES (PHRAATES V)

(2/1 B.C.–4/5 A.D.)

76 Æ (5)

Obv.: Bust of the king l., diademed; hair in three rows; short beard; apparently no star on the tunic; in front of the head a Nike r., with a wreath. The field behind the head is off flan. No border can be distinguished.

Rev.: Arsaces seated r. on a throne with a back. The r. hand, advanced, grasps a bow.

Legend: Above, 1st ΒΑΣΙΛΕ[ΩΣ]
2nd ΒΑΣΙΛΕΩ[Ν]
l., 1st ΕΠΙΦΑΝΟΥ[Σ]
2nd ΦΙΛΕΛΛΗΝ[ΟΣ]

r., 1st ΑΡΣΑ[ΚΟΥ]
2nd ΕΥΕΡΓΕ[ΤΟΥ]
ex., 1st (inverted) [Δ]ΙΚΑΙ[ΟΥ]

Monogram: None occurs. Beneath the throne on one coin, two pellets; on another, one pellet.

Date: In the field r., down ΑΙΤ, 1 B.C.–1 A.D. In the ex., 2nd, the month off flan.

Wroth, 137, Nos. 5–8; XXIII, 11. See discussion, p. 114.

gr.	: 11.60	11.39	9.83	8.70	6.01
mm.	: 26.50	27.70	27.70	28.60	25.40

77 Æ (1)

Obv.: Bust of the king l., diademed; hair in five rows, which are indicated by dots rather than lines; short, pointed beard. In front of the head is a Nike with a crown flying r.; behind the head are traces, perhaps of a second Nike. Border of dots.

Rev.: As on No. 76, except that there appears to be no back to the throne.

Legend: As on No. 76, except that the first line of legend in the exergue is not inverted.

Monogram: None occurs.

Date: In the field r., horizontally ΔΙΤ, 3/4 A.D.; in the ex., 2nd, the month obscure.

De Morgan, 286, No. 191; XVI, 40. See Pl. IV and discussion, p. 114.

gr. : 10.35
mm. : 26.90

78 Æ (1)

Obv.: Bust of the king l., diademed; hair in two natural rows; medium, curly beard. In front a Nike with a crown flying r. No border can be distinguished.

Rev.: Bust of the queen r., wearing tiara and diadem. In front, obscure, a Nike flying l.

Legend: Illegible traces can be distinguished on the obverse and the reverse.

Monogram: None can be distinguished.

Date: Obverse behind the shoulders ΔIT, 3/4 A.D. No month date can be distinguished.

Petrowicz, 102, No. 16; XV, 9.

gr. : 12.0
mm. : 26.7

79 Æ (1)

Obv.: Bust of the king l. The fillets of the diadem fall from the top of the head. Short beard; necklace and V-necked tunic. In front and behind Nikes fly to crown the king.

Rev.: Tyche seated l.; turreted headdress. The r. hand, advanced, grasps a palm; the l. falls at the side.

Legend: None can be distinguished.

Monogram: In the field r., No. 40.

Date: None can be distinguished.

Cf. Wroth, 139, Nos. 19–20. See discussion, p. 114.

gr. : 1.36
mm. : 14.5

ARTABANUS II

(11/12–40/41 A.D.)

80 Æ (2)

Obv.: Bust of the king l., diademed; hair in four formal rows; medium, squared beard. No border can be distinguished.

Rev.: The king seated r. on a throne with a low back, receiving a palm from Tyche standing facing front. Tyche wears a kalathos and carries a cornucopiae in the l. arm.

Legend: Above, 1st ΒΑΣΙ[ΛΕΩΣ] 2nd ΒΑΣΙΛΕ[ΩΝ]
l., 1st ΕΠΙΦΑΝΟ[ΥΣ] 2nd [Φ]ΙΛΕΛΛΗ[ΝΟΣ]
r., 1st [ΑΡΣ]ΑΚΟ[Υ] 2nd [Ε]ΥΕΡΓΕΤΟ[Υ]
ex., 1st (inverted) ΔΙΚΑΙΟΥ

Monogram: None occurs.

Date: In the field r., down ΒΚΤ, 11/12 A.D. No month date can be distinguished.

Wroth, 146, No. 1; XXV, 1. See discussion, p. 115.

gr. : 12.48 12.26
mm. : 25.60 29.30

81 Æ (1)

Obv.: Bust of the king l., diademed; hair in two less formal rows; medium, squared beard. Border of dots.

Rev.: As on No. 80.

Legend: So far as visible, as on No. 80.

Monogram: None occurs.

Date: Of the year, does not appear; in the field r., down, the month date, obscure.

Wroth, 146, Nos. 4–7. Cf. Petrowicz, 105–106, Nos. 2–4. See discussion, p. 115.

gr. : 10.77
mm. : 28.00

82 Æ (10)

Obv.: Bust of the king l., diademed; hair in three less formal rows; medium, squared beard. Border of dots.

Rev.: The king seated l. on a throne with a low back, receiving a palm from Tyche standing r. Between the two a male figure kneeling r. offers a diadem to the king. The distinctive headdress of Tyche appears to be lacking.

Legend: Above ΒΑΣΙΛΕΩΝ
ex. (inverted) [Ε]ΥΕΡΓΕΤΟ[Υ]
r. ΒΑΣΙΛΕΩ[Σ?]
l. (up) ΑΡΣΑΚΟΥ

Monogram: None occurs

Date: In the field center ΔΛΤ, 23/24 A.D. On some specimens this date appears also on the obverse at the l., up. In the exergue, 2nd, the month date is off flan on all of the coins.

Wroth, 147–148, Nos. 11–19; XXV, 3. See discussion, p. 115.

gr.	: 12.81	12.49	11.16	11.05	10.30	9.98	9.47	9.43	7.78	7.19
mm.	: 25.40	27.90	26.10	28.80	26.10	26.9	25.8	24.6	25.0	26.3

83 AR (2)

Obv.: Bust of the king facing front, diademed; hair falling in less formal rows; short, squared beard. No border can be distinguished.

Rev.: The king mounted on a horse standing l., receiving a palm from Tyche standing r. The headdress of Tyche and the object held in the l. arm are off flan.

Legend: Above [B]ΑΣΙΛΕΩ[Σ] r. ΑΡΣΑΚ[ΟΥ]
ex. (inverted) ΔΙΚ[ΑΙΟΥ] l. obscure.

Monogram: Beneath the horse apparently a simple A. Possibly other details have been obscured.

Date: In the field center Τ, r., down ΛΗ, 27/28 A.D. No month date appears to occur.

Wroth, 148–149, Nos. 20–32; XXV, 5–6. See discussion, p. 116.

gr.	: 9.21	5.80
mm.	: 26.3	25.6

84 Æ (10)

Obv.: Bust of the king l., diademed; hair falling in two or in three less formal rows; medium beard; V-necked tunic. The diadem has a long fillet falling from the top of the head.

Rev.: Bust of Tyche r., draped; turreted headdress.

Monogram: None can be distinguished.

Date: In the obverse field l., up (2) ΕΛΤ, 24/25 A.D.; (4) ϚΛΤ, 25/26 A.D.; (1) ΖΛΤ, 26/27 A.D.; (3) obscure dates.

There is a border of dots on obverse and reverse. The edges are flattened.

Pl. IV (obv. only). See discussion, p. 116.

gr.	: 1.76	1.36	1.29	1.29	1.22	1.16	0.98	0.94	0.90	0.81
mm.	: 14.2	14.9	14.1	12.2	12.3	13.9	14.6	12.8	12.5	15.1

85 Æ (1)

Obv.: Bust of the king l., badly obscured in front; hair in three rows. A fillet of the diadem hangs from the top of the head; V-necked tunic.

Rev.: The king seated l. on a throne. The r. hand, advanced, holds a Nike r.; the l. rests on a long scepter behind. All details of the head have been obscured. The figure is draped, probably wearing loose trousers and tunic.

Monogram: None can be distinguished.

Date: In the obverse field l., down ϚΛΤ, 25/26 A.D.

There is a border of dots on the obverse. The edge is flattened.

See discussion, p. 116.

gr. : 0.93
mm. : 12.6

86 Æ (9)

Obv.: Bust of the king facing front, diademed; the hair in waves at the sides; medium beard, V-necked tunic.

Rev.: Bust of Tyche r., draped; turreted headdress.

Monogram: None can be distinguished.

Date: In the reverse field r., up (1) probably ΜΤ, 29/30 A.D.; (1) probably ΑΜΤ, 30/31 A.D.; (7) dates off flan.

No border can be distinguished. The flans were definitely too small for the dies. The edges are curved rather than flattened.

Pl. IV. See discussion, p. 116.

gr. :	1.57	1.40	1.28	1.13	1.07	0.90	0.87	0.87	0.65
mm. :	10.8	10.8	9.90	10.1	10.2	9.50	10.7	10.4	9.40

VARDANES I

(40/41–45 A.D.)

87 Ꭱ (6)

Obv.: Bust of the king l., diademed; hair in four formal rows; short beard. On one coin a star appears on the tunic. Border of dots.

Rev.: The king seated r. on a throne with a back, receiving a palm from Tyche standing l. The head of Tyche appears to be bare; a cornucopiae is held in the l. arm.

Legend: Above, 1st ΒΑΣΙΛΕΩ[Σ]
2nd ΒΑΣΙΛΕΩ[Ν]
l., 1st ΕΠΙΦΑΝΟΥΣ
2nd [Φ]ΙΛΕΛΛΗΝ[ΟΣ]

r., 1st ΑΡΣΑΚ[ΟΥ]
2nd ΕΥΕΡΓΕΤΟ[Υ]
ex., 1st (inverted) ΔΙΚΑΙΟΥ

Monogram: None can be distinguished.

Date: In the field center (1) ΓΝΤ, 42/43 A.D.; (2) ΔΝΤ, 43/44 A.D.; (2) ΕΝΤ, 44/45 A.D.; (1) an obscure date. In the ex., 2nd, a month date can be distinguished on only one coin, of 44/45 A.D., ΟΛΩΟΥ, the 4th. On the rest this portion of the field is off flan or has been obscured.

Wroth, 153–156, Nos. 1–23; XXVI, 1. See Pl. IV (rev. only) and discussion, p. 117.

gr. : 12.12 11.98 10.21 9.63 9.16 7.91
mm. : 27.60 25.40 26.40 27.9 25.2 27.8

88 Æ (4)

Obv.: Bust of the king r., diademed; hair falling in waving natural lines; medium beard; V-necked tunic.

Rev.: A female head r., veiled. On each coin the top of the head is off flan. It is possible that a kalathos is worn.

Legend: In the reverse field l., down]ΟΥ. This is visible on one coin; on the others this portion of the field is off flan.

Monogram: None occurs.

Date: In the obverse field r., down ΔΝΤ, 43/44 A.D.

The adjustment of the dies is normal on three coins; on the fourth ↑ ↓. There is a border of dots on obverse and reverse. The edges are approximately straight. The metal is of unusual color and texture. The engraving of both types is of unusual excellence.

Pl. IV. See discussion, p. 117.

gr. : 0.94 0.73 0.48* 0.30*
mm. : 11.6 8.20 9.80 10.5

* Broken

89 Æ (94)

Obv.: Bust of the king l., diademed; hair in three formal rows; short beard.

Rev.: A figure completely draped seated r. on a circular seat with a back shaped to represent the neck and head of a swan. The head of the figure is probably bare, although on all coins the top is largely off flan. The r. hand lies along the lap, the hand grasping a short upright scepter or staff. The l. arm, under the folds of the robe, is raised toward the face.

Legend: In the reverse field r., down ΒΟΥΛΗ.

Symbol: On two coins (small) on the reverse, behind, Α. On a number, of varying size, it is clear that no symbol occurs. On the majority of the coins this portion of the field is off flan.

Date: In the obverse field l., down (10) ΔΝΤ, 43/44 A.D.; (5) ΕΝΤ, 44/45 A.D.; (13) ϚΝΤ, 45/46 A.D.; (66) dates obscure or off flan.

The adjustment of the dies is normal on ninety coins; four have ↑ ↓. There is a border of dots on obverse and reverse. The edges are straight.

Wroth, 157–158, Nos. 37–39; XXVI, 6–8. See Pl. IV (rev. only) and discussion, p. 117.

gr. :	3.68	3.64	3.49	3.47	3.47	3.41	3.37	3.23	3.16	3.02	3.00
mm. :	14.4	13.9	13.3	15.8	15.3	16.4	14.5	13.3	15.0	15.1	15.0
	3.00	2.99	2.94	2.93	2.90	2.87	2.84	2.67	2.66	2.65	2.57
	14.9	15.7	15.0	14.3	15.6	13.5	15.0	16.4	14.0	13.7	15.9
	2.31	2.20	1.96	1.74	1.71	1.62	1.61	1.58	1.57	1.51	1.47
	16.1	14.0	12.5	13.1	12.9	12.6	12.9	12.2	13.0	12.9	11.9
	1.43	1.42	1.41	1.38	1.33	1.31	1.31	1.29	1.27	1.25	1.23
	14.0	11.1	12.8	12.6	12.3	12.4	12.1	11.8	12.4	11.9	12.5
	1.23	1.22	1.20	1.20	1.20	1.18	1.16	1.16	1.16	1.15	1.15
	11.4	13.0	12.6	12.4	11.7	14.1	14.0	12.2	12.2	12.9	12.8
	1.15	1.14	1.11	1.10	1.09	1.09	1.08	1.08	1.05	1.03	1.02
	12.7	11.7	12.2	12.8	12.8	11.8	12.8	11.9	10.7	12.1	12.0
	1.01	1.00	1.00	1.00	0.99	0.98	0.98	0.98	0.97	0.96	0.94
	12.5	15.0	12.7	12.5	10.2	13.0	12.6	10.8	12.3	13.7	12.9
	0.94	0.94	0.94	0.93	0.93	0.90	0.88	0.88	0.87	0.81	0.80
	12.3	12.2	12.0	12.8	11.3	12.7	12.5	11.9	12.7	12.5	12.2
	0.79	0.79	0.78	0.74	0.69	0.69					
	12.0	11.7	13.2	13.0	12.7	9.80					

GOTARZES II

(44–51/52 A.D.)

90 Æ (1)

Obv.: Bust of the king l., diademed; hair in four formal rows; long beard; V-necked tunic on which appear K and a star. No border can be distinguished.

Rev.: The king seated r. on a throne with a back, receiving a diadem from Tyche standing l. The headdress of Tyche has been obscured; in the l. arm is a cornucopiae.

Legend: Above, 1st, off flan
2nd ΒΑΣΙΛΕΩΝ
l., 1st [Ε]ΠΙΦΑΝΟΥ[Σ]
2nd [ΦΙΛ]ΕΛΛΗΝ[ΟΣ]

r., 1st ΑΡΣΑ[ΚΟΥ]
2nd ΕΥΕΡΓΕ[ΤΟΥ]
ex., 1st (inverted) ΔΙΚΑΙΟΥ

Monogram: None can be distinguished.

Date: In the field center HNT, 47/48 A.D.; in the ex., 2nd ΞΑΝΔ[ΙΚΟΥ], the 1st month (see pp. 151–153 for intercalary change at this period).

Wroth, 163, Nos. 12–20; XXVI, 12. See Pl. IV (rev. only) and discussion, p. 118.

gr. : 8.06
mm. : 29.9

91 Æ (1)

Obv.: Bust of the king l., diademed; hair in vertical lines; long beard; other details obscure.

Rev.: A figure, three-quarters length, standing r. and holding a palm. The figure is draped. All other details have been obscured.

Symbol: In the reverse field r. A.

Date: None occurs.

There is a border of dots on obverse and reverse. The edge is straight.

Wroth, 170, Nos. 78–88; XXVII, 13–14. See discussion, p. 119.

gr. : 1.34
mm. : 11.6

92 Æ (45)

Obv.: Bust of the king l., diademed; hair in three formal rows; long beard. The diadem has a loop at the back; the fillets show only below the hair.

Rev.: Bust of Tyche r., draped; turreted headdress. A single fillet hangs from beneath the knot of the hair.

Monogram: In the reverse field l., No. 41. This can be distinguished on twenty-one coins of both years. On the rest this portion of the field has been obscured or is off flan.

Date: In the obverse field l., down (19) ZNT, 46/47 A.D.; (8) HNT, 47/48 A.D.; (18) obscure dates. On the coins for the year 46/47 month dates occur in the reverse field r., (5) ΞA, Xandikos, the 1st month; (1) AP, Artemisios, the 2nd month; (1) ΔA, Daisios, the 3rd month; (2) ΠA, Panemos, the 4th month; (1) OΛΩ, Loos, the 5th month; (3) ΓOP, Gorpiaios, the 6th month; (2) ΥΠΕ, Hyperberetaios, the 7th month; (4) month obscure. On some coins of the first year, the zeta of the date is found reversed. The months are arranged according to Johnson's intercalation.

There is a border of dots on obverse and reverse. The edges are straight.

Pl. IV. See discussions, pp. 119 and 152–153.

gr. : 46/47 A.D.:	Xandikos	3.12	3.10	3.03	2.54	2.08
mm. :		14.5	15.3	15.5	13.8	13.0
	Artemisios	2.20				
		13.3				
	Daisios	2.77				
		14.5				
	Panemos	2.98	2.78			
		12.8	13.3			
	Loos	3.35				
		14.4				
	Gorpiaios	2.45*	2.44	2.41		
		14.5	14.4	14.4		
	Hyperberetaios	2.48	2.13			
		14.0	13.7			
	Month obscure	3.28	2.84	2.41	2.18	
		14.5	14.5	12.0	13.5	
47/48 A.D.:		2.87	2.19	1.79		
		14.6	14.4	14.0		

* Broken

gr. :	1.76	1.70	1.53	1.18	0.87	Year obscure:		2.85	2.61	2.56	2.48
mm. :	13.4	12.7	15.0	13.7	12.7			14.0	14.5	13.7	14.7
	2.18	2.17	2.15	2.03	1.90	1.89	1.69	1.68	1.64	1.62	1.59
	13.5	13.3	16.1	13.8	13.0	14.2	13.6	15.0	14.0	13.4	14.1
	1.53	1.47	1.25								
	14.0	14.2	12.4								

VOLAGASES I

51–80 A.D.

93 Æ (1)

Obv.: Bust of the king facing front with the head turned l., diademed; hair in four formal rows; short beard. No border can be distinguished.

Rev.: The king seated l. on a throne without a back, receiving a diadem from Tyche standing r. Tyche wears a turreted headdress.

Legend: Above, 1st [B]ΑΣΙΛΕΩ[Σ]
2nd ΒΑΣΙΛΕΩΝ
l., 1st ΕΠΙΦΑ[ΝΟΥΣ]
2nd [ΦΙ]ΛΕΛΛ[ΗΝΟΣ]

r., 1st ΑΡΣΑ[ΚΟΥ]
2nd ΕΥΕΡΓΕ[ΤΟΥ]
ex., 1st (inverted) ΔΙΚΑ[ΙΟΥ]

Monogram: None occurs.

Date: In the field center ΕΞΤ, 54/55 A.D.; in the ex., 2nd, the month date, off flan.

Wroth, 178–180, Nos. 1–14; XXVIII, 12.

gr. : 13.21
mm. : 25.50

94 Æ (1)

Obv.: Bust of the king l., diademed; helmet with hooked appendages; hair in two rows; short beard. Border of dots.

Rev.: The king seated l. on a throne with a back, receiving a large diadem from Tyche standing r. The king wears a helmet and rests the l. hand on a sword. Tyche holds a scepter in the l. hand. The back of the throne has a crosspiece.

Legend: Above, 1st [B]ΑΣΙΛ[ΕΩΣ]
2nd Β[ΑΣ]ΙΛΕ[ΩΝ]
l., 1st ΕΠΙΦΑΝ[ΟΥΣ]
2nd [ΦΙΛ]ΕΛΛ[ΗΝΟΣ]

r., 1st [Α]ΡΣΑ[ΚΟΥ]
2nd ΟΛΑΓΑ[ΣΟΥ]
ex., 1st ΔΙΚΑΙΟΥ

Symbol: In the obverse field r. A.

Date: In the field center ϚT, 79/80 A.D.; in the ex., 2nd, the month date, off flan.

Wroth, 209–210, Nos. 1–7; XXXII, 6–7. Wroth assigns this coin to a "first" reign of Volagases II. See discussion, pp. 119–121.

gr. : 9.60
mm. : 26.6

95 Æ (6)

Obv.: Bust of the king, l., diadamed; hair in three formal rows; short beard; necklace, V-necked tunic.

Rev.: Bust of Tyche r., draped; turreted headdress.

Monogram: In the reverse field r., No. 42.

Date: In the obverse field l., down ΠT, 69/70 A.D.

There is a border of dots on the obverse and reverse. The edges are slightly beveled.

Pl. IV. See discussion, p. 121.

gr.	1.14	1.12	1.08	0.99	0.94	0.88
mm.	11.7	10.9	10.8	12.3	12.1	11.4

96 Æ (66)

Obv.: Bust of the king l., diademed; similar in style to No. 95.

Rev.: Nike standing l., holding in the outstretched r. hand a wreath from which fall two short fillets. The l. arm is dropped at the side.

Monogram: In the reverse field l., No. 43. This can be distinguished on thirty-three coins of all the years represented in the group. On the rest this portion of the field is off flan or has been obscured.

Date: In the obverse field l., down (6) ΠT, 69/70 A.D.; (3) AΠT, 70/71 A.D.; (1) ΓΠT, 72/73 A.D.; (3) ΔΠT, 73/74 A.D.; (1) ϛΠT, 75/76 A.D.; (1) HΠT, 77/78 A.D.; (1) ΘΠT, 78/79 A.D.; (4) either AΠT or ΔΠT; (14) [ ]ΠT; (32) obscure dates. The first numeral of ΘΠT is partly off flan. It does not appear possible to complete it except as theta. However, since this is the latest date in the series, the reading is classed as tentative.

The adjustments of the dies vary widely. There is a border of dots on obverse and reverse. The edges are somewhat flattened.

Pl. IV. See discussion, p. 121.

gr.	1.66	1.40	1.29	1.29	1.27	1.21	1.21	1.18	1.17	1.15	1.13
mm.	12.2	11.3	11.0	10.9	10.8	11.8	11.6	10.8	13.0	11.2	11.5
	1.13	1.12	1.11	1.11	1.11	1.10	1.09	1.08	1.08	1.07	1.06
	11.4	10.7	11.4	10.9	10.5	13.2	11.1	12.0	11.5	10.8	11.2

gr.	: 1.06	1.05	1.03	1.01	1.00	1.00	0.98	0.96	0.96	0.95	0.95
mm.	: 11.0	11.1	10.4	11.0	12.4	10.0	11.2	10.9	10.5	10.9	10.3
	0.94	0.94	0.92	0.92	0.90	0.89	0.89	0.88	0.85	0.84	0.84
	12.0	9.90	11.1	11.3	10.2	11.1	11.0	11.4	9.90	11.9	10.5
	0.83	0.83	0.83	0.83	0.82	0.82	0.79	0.78	0.78	0.78	0.76
	11.8	11.5	10.8	10.4	11.1	10.0	11.2	11.6	11.5	10.6	11.2
	0.73	0.73	0.71	0.66	0.65	0.58	0.55	0.52	0.52	0.48	0.34
	11.4	9.90	11.0	10.6	8.90	9.70	10.5	11.5	9.50	9.20	10.0

97 Æ (1)

Obv.: Bust of the king l., diademed; high helmet with squared flaps; rather short beard. The presence or absence of hooked appendages on the helmet cannot be determined.

Rev.: An eagle with wings outstretched standing facing front with head turned l.

Monogram: None can be distinguished.

Date: In the obverse field l., down HΠT, 77/78 A.D.

No border can be distinguished. The edge is slightly beveled.

Pl. IV. See discussion, p. 122.

gr. : 1.07
mm. : 11.5

PACORUS II

(78–115/16 A.D.)

98 AR (1)

Obv.: Bust of the king l., diademed; hair in four formal rows; clean-shaven. Border of continuous fillet.

Rev.: The king seated l. on a throne with a high back, receiving a diadem from Tyche standing r. Tyche holds a scepter in the l. hand. The back of the throne has a cross-piece.

Legend: Above, 1st, off flan
2nd [B]ΑΣΙΛΕΩΝ
l., 1st ΕΠΙΦΑΝ[ΟΥΣ]
2nd, off flan
r., 1st [ΑΡΣ]ΑΚ[ΟΥ]
2nd ΠΑΚΟΡ[ΟΥ]
ex., 1st ΔΙΚΑΙΟΥ

Symbol: In the obverse field r. Γ.

Date: In the field center ϞΤ, 79/80 A.D.; in the ex., 2nd ΑΥΔΝ[ΑΙΟΥ], the 10th month.

Wroth, 193–194, Nos. 1–13; XXX, 1–2. See discussion, p. 122.

gr. : 11.8
mm. : 28.2

99 Æ (1)

Obv.: Head of the king l., diademed; hair in three formal rows; clean-shaven; necklace. The shoulders and tunic are not shown.

Rev.: A bust r., male. The head is bare but the top is off flan. No traces of diadem or wreath can be discerned around the head, but behind the head are traces of what appear to be fillets. There is a short curly beard. Only the top of the shoulders is shown and there is no drapery. The features and the execution are Greek rather than Oriental.

Monogram: None occurs.

Date: In the obverse field l., up AϘT, 80/81 A.D.

There is a border of dots on the obverse only. The edge is beveled.

Pl. V. See discussion, p. 122.

gr. : 1.31
mm. : 11.5

100 Æ (44)

Obv.: Bust of the king l., diademed; hair in three formal rows; slight beard. The fillets of the diadem hang from a loop at the top of the head.

Rev.: Bust of Tyche r., draped; turreted headdress.

Symbol: In the reverse field r. A. This can be distinguished on thirty coins of both years. On one coin of the year 83/84 there appears to have been no symbol intended. On the rest this portion of the field is off flan.

Date: In the obverse field l., down (13) ΔϘT, 83/84 A.D.; (6) EϘT, 84/85 A.D.; (3) [ ]ϘT; (22) the date off flan or entirely obscured.

There is a border of dots on obverse and reverse. The edges are straight.

Wroth, 198–199, Nos. 37–44; XXX, 11–12. Cf. Petrowicz, 147, Nos. 15, 18. See discussion, p. 122.

gr. :	3.99	3.94	3.70	3.69	3.58	3.46	3.44	3.38	3.37	3.24	3.18
mm. :	14.8	14.8	15.3	14.7	16.1	15.0	16.9	14.8	14.2	15.7	14.4
	3.16	3.16	3.15	3.15	3.13	3.11	3.09	3.08	3.07	3.00	2.99
	16.6	15.1	14.3	14.2	15.0	14.8	14.0	14.5	14.4	13.8	18.5
	2.97	2.96	2.87	2.84	2.84	2.81	2.81	2.70	2.67	2.59	2.46
	15.4	14.9	15.6	17.5	13.7	14.9	14.2	14.3	13.5	14.9	15.0
	2.42	2.41	2.35	2.23	2.13	2.06	2.00	1.87	1.56	1.41	1.39
	15.2	14.8	13.7	16.0	13.6	13.8	14.6	16.7	14.7	12.9	14.7

101 Æ (9)

Obv.: Bust of the king l., diademed; helmet or other headdress with perpendicular stripes and short, straight flaps; hair in two less formal rows; short beard; probably necklace and V-necked tunic.

Rev.: Head of Tyche r.; turreted headdress.

Symbol: In the reverse field r., a palm branch. This can be distinguished on seven coins; on two this portion of the field is off flan.

Date: In the reverse field l., down ϚKΥ, 115/16 A.D. This can be distinguished on six coins; on three this portion of the field is off flan.

There is a border of dots on obverse and reverse. The edges are straight.

Cf. Wroth, 202, No. 52 and note 1. See Pl. V and discussion, p. 123.

gr. :	1.16	1.05	1.01	0.99	0.98	0.96	0.86	0.71	0.69
mm. :	11.9	10.6	12.7	10.8	12.0	10.4	11.7	10.7	10.8

OSROES

(109/10–128/29 A.D.)

102 Æ (39)

Obv.: Bust of the king l., diademed; hair in bunches; long beard.

Rev.: Bust of Tyche r., draped; turreted headdress.

Symbol: In the reverse field l. Λ. This can be discerned on twenty-one coins; on the rest this portion of the field is off flan.

Date: In the reverse field r., up (2) ΔKΥ, 113/14 A.D.; (1) EKΥ, 114/15 A.D.; (11) HKΥ, 117/18 A.D.; (9) ΘKΥ, 118/19 A.D.; (3) ΛΥ, 119/20 A.D.; (13) the date incomplete or off flan.

There is a border of dots on obverse and reverse. The edges are approximately straight.

Wroth, 205–206, Nos. 8–17; XXXI, 10–14. See discussion, p. 123.

gr. :	7.77	6.81	4.48	4.34	4.32	4.29	4.28	4.18	4.13	4.10	4.09
mm. :	22.9	19.2	16.4	16.9	17.8	16.8	17.4	16.9	16.8	15.9	16.9
	4.06	4.00	3.99	3.98	3.95	3.84	3.74	3.74	3.62	3.60	3.48
	17.6	16.4	17.3	16.2	16.4	17.3	17.3	11.7	17.3	17.0	16.4
	3.48	3.36	3.35	3.35	3.29	3.27	3.27	3.24	3.11	3.06	3.06
	15.0	17.1	17.1	16.8	17.0	16.0	15.8	17.4	17.8	17.5	17.3
	3.06	2.90	2.90	2.78	2.48	1.90					
	16.4	16.6	16.2	17.6	16.8	16.7					

103 Æ (15)

Obv.: Bust of the king l., diademed; hair in bunches; headdress with spiked appendages and flaps; long beard; necklace and V-necked tunic.

Rev.: Bust of Tyche r., draped; turreted headdress.

Symbol: In the reverse field l. Λ. This can be distinguished on nine coins; on the rest this portion of the field is off flan or has been obscured.

Date: In the reverse field r., up (6) ΘΚΥ, 118/19 A.D.; (1) ΛΥ, 119/20 A.D.; (8) the date incomplete, obscured, or off flan.

There is a border of dots on obverse and reverse. The edges are approximately straight.

Cf. Wroth, 207, No. 21. See discussion, p. 123.

gr.	1.72	1.58	1.45	1.40	1.38	1.23	1.20	1.20	1.14	1.11	1.09
mm.	12.4	12.9	12.4	12.0	12.5	11.5	13.2	12.1	11.7	12.3	12.7
	1.03	0.95	0.89	0.62							
	11.4	12.1	11.6	11.2							

104 Æ (23)

Obv.: Bust of the king facing front, diademed; hair in bunches at the sides and the top; short beard.

Rev.: Bust of Tyche r., draped; turreted headdress.

Symbol: In the reverse field l. Λ. This can be discerned on eight coins; on the rest this portion of the field is off flan or has been obscured.

Date: In the reverse field r., up (4) ΘΚΥ, 118/19 A.D.; (1) ΛΥ, 119/20 A.D.; (18) the date off flan or obscured.

There is a border of dots on obverse and reverse. The edges are somewhat beveled.

Wroth, 207, Nos. 18–19; XXXI, 15. See Pl. V and discussion, p. 123.

gr.	1.35	1.29	1.22	1.20	1.20	1.14	1.13	1.07	1.07	0.99	0.95	0.91
mm.	11.2	10.8	11.2	11.5	10.7	10.2	11.7	11.1	10.9	11.2	11.4	10.8
	0.87	0.86	0.82	0.82	0.77	0.75	0.75	0.74	0.74	0.55	0.45*	
	9.80	11.8	11.8	10.3	10.6	11.4	9.40	10.7	9.90	9.90	10.0	

* Broken

105 Æ (16)

Obv.: Bust of the king l., diademed; hair in bunches; headdress with spiked appendages but no flaps; long beard; necklace and V-necked tunic.

Rev.: Bust of Tyche r., draped; turreted headdress.

Symbol: In the reverse field r., a caduceus. This can be distinguished on three coins; on two others there are traces that may represent this symbol. On the rest none appears, and it is not possible to determine whether one was intended to be shown on all the coins.

Date: In the reverse field r., up (5) ΒΛΤ, 121/22 A.D.; (4) [ ]ΛΤ; (7) the date entirely obscured or off flan.

There is a border of dots on obverse and reverse. The edges are approximately straight.

Wroth, 207, No. 20; XXXII, 1.

gr.	: 1.65	1.40	1.33	1.32	1.24	1.21	1.21	1.19	1.17	1.16	1.13
mm.	: 11.7	11.4	13.2	12.7	11.8	11.8	11.7	11.2	11.2	11.4	11.0
	1.01	1.00	0.92	0.91	0.77						
	11.8	11.5	11.0	13.3	10.5						

106 Æ (28)

Obv.: Bust of the king l., diademed; hair in bunches; long beard.

Rev.: Bust of Tyche r., draped; turreted headdress.

Symbol: None appears to occur.

Date: In the reverse field r. (3) ΔΛΤ, 123/24 A.D.; (1) ϚΛΤ, 125/26 A.D.; (7) ΖΛΤ, 126/27 A.D.; (2) ΗΛΤ, 127/28 A.D.; (15) the date incomplete or off flan.

There is a border of dots on obverse and reverse. The edges are roughly beveled.

Pl. V. See discussion, p. 123.

gr.	: 1.92	1.81	1.49	1.44	1.42	1.42	1.40	1.40	1.38	1.35	1.27
mm.	: 13.6	12.3	12.0	12.2	13.2	12.4	12.8	12.0	12.3	12.5	12.8
	1.25	1.24	1.24	1.23	1.20	1.20	1.15	1.15	1.13	1.12	1.09
	11.4	12.8	11.8	12.5	12.4	12.0	12.4	10.7	11.2	12.2	12.3
	1.09	1.03	0.97	0.95	0.95	0.80					
	11.4	11.7	11.8	11.4	11.0	11.6					

107 Æ (8)

Obv.: Bust of the king l., diademed; hair in a bunch behind; helmet with flaps; medium beard.

Rev.: Bust of Tyche r., draped; turreted headdress. Tyche holds a palm.

Symbol: None occurs.

Date: In the reverse field l., down (6) ΘΛΤ, 128/29 A.D.; (2) the date off flan.

There is a border of dots on obverse and reverse. The edges are straight.

Wroth, 207, No. 22; XXXII, 3.

gr.	: 3.72	3.61	3.33	3.17	3.12	2.99	2.88	2.83
mm.	: 16.8	15.6	15.7	15.9	15.2	16.2	17.0	15.0

108 Æ (2)

Obv.: Bust of the king l., diademed; hair in a bunch behind; helmet with flaps; medium beard.

Rev.: Tyche standing r. holding in the r. hand a long palm tied with fillets and in the l., a scepter; turreted headdress.

Symbol: None occurs.

Date: In the reverse field l., down ΘΛΥ, 128/29 A.D.

There is a border of dots on obverse and reverse. The edges are straight.

Wroth, 208, Nos. 23–24; XXXII, 4.

gr. : 6.19 5.81
mm. : 18.8 19.3

VOLAGASES II

(105/06 ?–147/48 A.D.)

109 AR (3)

Obv.: Bust of the king l., diademed; helmet with hooked appendages but no flaps; short beard. No border can be distinguished.

Rev.: The king seated l. on a throne with a high back, receiving a diadem from Tyche standing r. Tyche holds a scepter in the l. hand.

Legend: Above, 1st, off flan
2nd ΒΑΣΙΛΕΩΝ
l., 1st ΕΠΙΦΑΝΟΥΣ
2nd [ΦΙ]ΛΕΛΛΗΝ[ΟΣ]
r., 1st [Α]ΡΣΑΚΟ[Υ]
2nd ΟΛΑΓΑΣΟΥ
ex., 1st ΔΙΚΑΙΟΥ

Symbol: In the obverse field r. A.

Date: In the field center (1) ΓΛΥ, 122/23 A.D.; (2) [ ]ΛΥ; in the ex., 2nd, on the coin dated 122/23, ΠΕΡΙΤΕΙΟΥ, the 11th month.

Wroth, 210–212, Nos. 8–26; XXXII, 8–9. See discussion, p. 123.

gr. : 12.23 10.12 8.51
mm. : 27.50 24.30 25.7

109a AR (1)

Obv.: As on No. 109.

Rev.: As on No. 109.

Legend: As on No. 109, but blundered in part.

Symbol: In the obverse field r. Δ.

Date: In the field center ΘΜΥ, 138/39 A.D.; in the ex., 2nd ΔΙΟΥ, the 8th month.

Wroth, 212, Nos. 27–28. See discussion, p. 124.

gr. : 6.63
mm. : 28.6

110 AR (1)

Obv.: Bust of the king l., diademed; helmet with curved flaps and hooked appendages; long beard squared at the bottom. Border of dots.

Rev.: The king seated l. on a throne with a high back, receiving a diadem from Tyche standing r. Tyche holds a scepter in the l. hand.

Legend: Above, off flan
l., 1st [Ε]ΤΕΡΓΕ[ΤΟΥ]
2nd, off flan
r., off flan
ex., 1st, obscure

Symbol: In the obverse field r. B.

Date: In the field center ΓΛΥ, 122/23 A.D.; in the ex., 2nd ΠΑΝΗΜΟΥ, the 4th month.

Pl. V. See discussion, p. 124.

gr. : 5.26
mm. : 26.5

111 Æ (29)

Obv.: Bust of the king l., diademed; hair in three formal rows; long beard; necklace and V-necked tunic.

Rev.: Bust of Tyche r., draped; turreted headdress.

Symbol: None can be distinguished.

Date: In the reverse field r., up (1) ϚΙΥ, 105/06 A.D.; (7) ΗΙΥ, 107/08 A.D.; (2) ΘΙΥ, 108/09 A.D.; (19) the date partly or entirely obscured or off flan.

There is a border of dots on obverse and reverse. The edges are straight.

Wroth, 204, Nos. 1–2; XXXI, 6–7. See discussion, p. 125.

gr. :	1.51	1.24	1.14	1.09	1.07	1.06	1.05	1.04	0.98	0.93	0.91
mm. :	11.3	10.8	11.9	10.5	9.60	11.4	10.8	9.80	11.0	9.80	11.2
	0.91	0.89	0.89	0.89	0.87	0.85	0.82	0.82	0.80	0.80	0.80
	11.0	11.9	10.2	9.80	10.3	11.5	10.7	10.2	11.0	10.2	9.70
	0.76	0.76	0.74	0.72	0.64	0.60*	0.60				
	10.5	9.90	10.2	10.4	10.6	10.5	10.2				

* Broken

112 Æ (7)

Obv.: Bust of the king l., diademed; helmet with flaps and hooked appendages; medium beard.

Rev.: Tyche seated l. on a short column, the r. elbow resting on the knee and the hand raised to the face; turreted headdress.

Symbol: In the obverse field r., A on three coins, two of which bear the date 112/13, and B on one coin dated 113/14. On the rest this portion of the field is off flan.

Date: In the reverse field r., down (2) ΓKϒ, 112/13 A.D.; (2) ΔKϒ, 113/14 A.D.; (3) the date incomplete or off flan.

There is a border of dots on obverse and reverse. The edges are straight.

Wroth, 215, Nos. 46–47; XXXIII, 1–2. Cf. Petrowicz, 141, No. 40a. See discussion, p. 126.

gr.	6.81	6.65	6.35	6.33	6.25	6.04	4.61
mm.	18.6	18.4	17.4	19.0	18.2	17.7	18.9

113 Æ (45)

Obv.: Bust of the king l., diademed; helmet with hooked appendages and short flaps; medium beard.

Rev.: Bust of Tyche r., draped; turreted headdress.

Symbol: None occurs.

Date: In the reverse field r., up (23) Λϒ, 119/20 A.D.; (8) AΛϒ, 120/21 A.D.; (4) AΛϒ or ΔΛϒ; (10) the date partly or entirely obscured or off flan.

There is a border of dots on obverse and reverse. The edges are straight.

Wroth, 216, Nos. 49–55; XXXIII, 3–4. Cf. Petrowicz, 141–142, Nos. 41–46. See discussion, p. 127.

gr.	8.06	5.28	4.67	4.61	4.47	4.38	4.33	4.26	4.23	4.21	4.18	4.13
mm.	20.9	17.8	16.7	16.4	16.4	17.6	16.4	16.2	15.9	17.3	16.9	17.0
	4.04	4.00	3.97	3.96	3.95	3.89	3.88	3.88	3.87	3.84	3.82	3.74
	16.2	16.9	17.0	17.8	17.1	16.6	17.1	15.7	15.1	16.7	17.1	13.6
	3.72	3.62	3.61	3.61	3.60	3.40	3.37	3.32	3.18	3.18	3.10	3.08
	17.2	15.9	16.5	16.2	16.6	16.0	16.0	16.1	16.7	15.4	16.0	16.9
	3.06	2.93	2.91	2.85	2.82	2.74	2.65	2.60	2.18			
	16.8	10.5	16.0	16.3	15.8	16.7	16.2	17.2	15.6			

114 Æ (15)

Obv.: Bust of the king l., diademed; helmet with curved flaps and no spiked appendages; rather long beard; necklace and tunic do not appear on the flan.

Rev.: Tyche seated l. on a short column; turreted headdress. The r. hand holds a short palm in front; the l. rests on the lap.

Symbol: In the reverse field l., A on six coins, two of which are dated 129/30, and B on one coin with the same date. On the rest this portion of the field is off flan.

Date: In the reverse field l., down (7) Mϒ, 129/30 A.D.; (1) ΓMϒ, 132/33 A.D.; (7) the date off flan.

There is a border of dots on obverse and reverse. The edges are straight.

Wroth, 216, No. 56; XXXIII, 5. See Pl. V and discussion, p. 127

gr. :	1.60	1.51	1.28	1.26	1.18	1.17	1.15	1.12	1.07	1.07	1.06
mm. :	11.1	11.7	10.3	9.80	10.0	11.6	10.7	10.1	10.5	9.90	12.3
	1.04	1.00	0.99	0.96							
	11.1	10.3	10.8	10.6							

115 Æ (3)

Obv.: As on No. 114.

Rev.: Bust of Tyche r., draped; turreted headdress; necklace (?). In front is an object partly off flan, probably a wreath.

Symbol: In the reverse field r. A.

Date: In the obverse field l., down ΔΜΥ, 133/34 A.D.

There is a border of dots on obverse and reverse. The edges are straight.

Cf. Wroth, 234, No. 80; Petrowicz, 142, Nos. 47–49. See discussion, p. 127.

gr. :	4.13	4.10	3.89
mm. :	12.3	15.7	15.8

VOLAGASES III

(148–192 A.D.)

116 AR (11)

Obv.: Bust of the king l., diademed; helmet with long curved flaps; long beard squared at the bottom. Border of dots.

Rev.: The king seated l. on a throne with a high back, receiving a diadem from Tyche standing r. Tyche holds a scepter in the l. hand.

Legend: Above, 1st [B]ΑΣΙΛΕ[ΩΣ]
2nd ΒΑΣΙΛΕΩ[Ν]
l., 1st ΕΠΙΦΑΝΟΥ[Σ]
2nd ΦΙΛΕΛΛΗΝ[ΟΣ]
r., 1st [Α]ΡΣΑΚ[ΟΥ]
2nd ΟΛΑΓΑΣΟΥ
ex., 2nd [ΔΙΚΑΙΟΥ]

Symbol: In the obverse field r. (10) B; (1), obscured.

Date: In the field center, the year, and in the ex., 1st, the month;
- (3) ΔΞΥ, 153/54 A.D., of these (2) ΑΠΕΛΛ[ΙΟΥ], 9th month;
- (1) ΖΞΥ, 156/57 A.D., month obscure;
- (2) ΘΞΥ, 158/59 A.D., ΔΙΟΥ, 8th month;
- (1) ΑΟΥ, 160/61 A.D., [Α]ΠΕΛΛΑΙΟΥ, 9th month;
- (2) ΒΟΥ, 161/62 A.D., ΔΙΟΥ, 8th month;
- (1) ΘΠΥ, 178/79 A.D., [ΑΠΕ]ΛΛΑΙΟΥ, 9th month;
- (1) year obscure, ΔΙΟΥ, 8th month.

Wroth, 224–228, Nos. 1–34; XXXIV, 1–3. See discussion, p. 128.

gr. :	13.60	12.96	12.92	11.07	10.54	10.29	10.25	9.04	8.06	7.70	7.65
mm. :	28.20	27.50	28.70	27.70	28.30	26.70	29.70	27.4	25.4	26.4	27.0

116a Æ (213; a cache, see p. 128)

Obv.: As on No. 116. Rev.: As on No. 116.

Legend: As on No. 116 (but see discussion, p. 128, under No. 116a).

Symbol: In the obverse field r., A on coins dating from 148/49 to 150/51 and B on those dating from 151/52 to 165/66.

Date: In the field center, the year, and in the ex., either 1st or 2nd, the month;

(17) ΘΝΥ, 148/49 A.D., of these (4) ΑΡΤΕΜΙΣΙΟΥ, 2nd month, (3) ΔΑΙ-ΣΙΟΥ, 3rd month, (9) ΠΑΝΗΜΟΥ, 4th month, (1) ΔΙΟΥ, 8th month;
(20) ΞΥ, 149/50 A.D., of these (19) ΔΙΟΥ, 8th month, (1) month off flan;
(25) ΑΞΥ, 150/51 A.D., ΔΙΟΥ, 8th month;
(3) ΒΞΥ, 151/52 A.D., ΑΠΕΛΛΑΙΟΥ, 9th month;
(2) ΓΞΥ, 152/53 A.D., ΑΠΕΛΛΑΙΟΥ, 9th month;
(59) ΔΞΥ, 153/54 A.D., of these (1) ΔΑΙΣΙΟΥ, 3rd month, (51) ΑΠΕΛΛΑΙΟΥ, 9th month, (7) month obscure;
(22) ΕΞΥ, 154/55 A.D., ΔΙΟΥ, 8th month;
(5) ϚΞΥ, 155/56 A.D., of these (4) ΔΙΟΥ, 8th month, (1) month obscure;
(1) ΖΞΥ, 156/57 A.D., ΔΙΟΥ, 8th month;
(2) ΗΞΥ, 157/58 A.D., ΔΙΟΥ, 8th month;
(3) ΘΞΥ, 158/59 A.D., ΔΙΟΥ, 8th month;
(2) ΑΟΥ, 160/61 A.D., ΑΠΕΛΛΑΙΟΥ, 9th month;
(1) ΒΟΥ, 161/62 A.D., ΔΙΟΥ, 8th month;
(2) ΔΟΥ, 163/64 A.D., ΔΙΟΥ, 8th month;
(1) ΕΟΥ, 164/65 A.D., ΑΠΕΛΛΑΙΟΥ, 9th month;
(42) ϚΟΥ, 165/66 A.D., ΑΠΕΛΛΑΙΟΥ, 9th month;
(6) year obscure, of these (1) ΔΙΟΥ, 8th month, (4) ΑΠΕΛΛΑΙΟΥ, 9th month, (1) month off flan.

Wroth, 224–227, Nos. 1–25; XXXIV, 1–3. See also Petrowicz, 158, No. 1, for a coin dated in 148/49. See discussion, p. 128.

gr. : 148/49:	2nd mo.	13.62	13.26	13.18	12.96	3rd mo.	13.46	12.75
mm. :		29.40	27.90	29.70	28.50		29.60	28.80
12.70	4th mo.	13.65	13.63	13.59	13.50	13.20	13.12	12.99
29.70		26.90	29.50	28.90	29.60	28.10	29.90	26.90
12.95	12.87	8th mo.	13.26	149/50: 8th mo.		13.81	13.62	13.60
31.90	29.30		30.80			28.30	27.00	27.80
13.58	13.50	13.42	13.38	13.37	13.31	13.30	13.29	13.16
29.10	28.20	27.80	27.40	28.30	28.80	29.20	27.80	27.30
13.15	13.15	13.06	12.86	11.05	9.23	8.26	Month obscure	
29.40	27.80	28.90	28.30	29.50	28.7	28.5		
6.77	150/51:	8th mo.	13.72	13.55	13.54	13.54	13.48	13.43
29.3			29.40	28.60	28.80	28.40	27.90	27.80
13.42	13.41	13.41	13.36	13.32	13.20	13.13	13.13	13.11
29.20	28.50	27.80	29.50	31.00	30.50	29.30	28.20	29.20

gr. :	13.03	13.03	13.01	12.84	12.82	12.74	12.46	12.09	11.87
mm. :	28.10	27.60	28.90	30.50	29.90	29.20	28.80	30.90	28.90
	9.46	151/52: 9th mo.		13.80	13.64	6.47	152/53: 9th mo.		13.43
	28.0			26.80	30.10	29.0			30.10
	12.55	153/54: 3rd mo.			13.45	9th mo.		13.89	13.80
	28.20				26.90			27.40	28.30
	13.79	13.76	13.75	13.74	13.71	13.68	13.68	13.67	13.63
	26.80	29.00	28.30	28.60	26.90	27.10	26.80	27.30	27.80
	13.62	13.62	13.61	13.58	13.54	13.53	13.51	13.51	13.50
	26.40	26.00	27.00	26.40	27.20	27.30	28.90	28.30	27.80
	13.46	13.45	13.44	13.41	13.40	13.38	13.34	13.29	13.24
	28.50	25.90	26.90	30.80	27.10	27.40	28.90	28.70	30.00
	13.21	13.18	13.13	13.11	13.09	13.04	13.04	13.01	12.92
	27.90	27.00	28.80	28.20	30.20	28.70	25.60	27.90	28.30
	12.78	12.74	12.72	12.71	12.56	12.54	12.24	12.02	10.33
	28.40	28.30	28.20	28.90	29.90	25.90	27.20	28.70	26.80
	9.92	9.18	7.97	6.79	Month obscure		13.89	13.70	13.62
	26.8	27.7	27.5	29.2			27.00	28.20	26.40
	13.52	13.51	13.34	12.94	154/55: 8th mo.			13.72	13.68
	29.60	26.90	29.30	28.80				26.90	26.90
	13.60	13.55	13.52	13.49	13.46	13.43	13.35	13.35	13.31
	28.10	28.40	27.40	25.90	27.50	28.00	29.70	28.30	27.10
	13.12	13.12	12.97	12.96	12.82	12.53	12.39	11.25	11.18
	28.60	28.50	29.10	28.00	31.30	29.70	28.00	27.60	27.80
	10.72	10.43	155/56: 8th mo.			13.45	13.44	13.33	13.04
	28.00	26.90				28.30	26.80	28.20	26.40
	Month obscure		13.44	156/57: 8th mo.		13.42	157/58: 8th mo.		13.55
			27.40			29.70			26.90
	11.77	158/59: 8th mo.		13.53	13.46	12.87	160/61: 9th mo.		13.81
	26.90			26.40	28.30	29.20			26.00
	10.55	161/62: 8th mo.			12.95	163/64: 8th mo.		13.66	13.57
	28.40				29.80			27.50	27.40
	164/65: 9th mo.			13.35	165/66: 9th mo.		14.21	14.16	14.10
				28.30			27.80	26.00	27.50
	14.09	14.03	14.01	14.00	14.00	13.99	13.97	13.94	13.93
	26.90	28.90	28.90	28.30	26.50	28.20	27.80	27.30	29.40
	13.93	13.91	13.89	13.88	13.87	13.87	13.84	13.82	13.80
	27.90	28.20	28.90	27.60	29.30	26.10	28.20	29.10	27.20
	13.78	13.75	13.69	13.67	13.67	13.61	13.48	13.33	13.26
	28.30	26.90	28.00	28.00	26.40	27.30	29.00	28.80	28.40

gr. : 12.74	12.57	12.44	11.90	11.42	11.33	10.93	10.74	9.95
mm. : 30.20	28.50	26.10	27.80	30.20	28.80	27.10	27.00	28.2
7.25	6.42	6.40	Year obscure:		13.92	13.50	13.46	11.27
28.9	28.2	30.7			29.30	27.80	26.80	28.20
11.00	9.07							
29.00	27.10							

116b Æ (5; a cache, see p. 128)

Obv.: As on No. 116. Rev.: As on No. 116.

Legend: As on No. 116.

Symbol: In the obverse field r., A on the coin dated 150/51, B on the coins dated from 153/54 to 156/57.

Date: In the field center, the year, and in the ex., 1st, the month;

(1) AΞΥ, 150/51 A.D., ΔΙΟΥ, 8th month;
(1) ΔΞΥ, 153/54 A.D., ΑΠΕΛΛΑΙΟΥ, 9th month;
(2) ΕΞΥ, 154/55 A.D., month obscure or off flan;
(1) ΖΞΥ, 156/57 A.D., ΔΙΟΥ, 8th month.

Wroth, 224–226, Nos. 1–16; XXXIV, 1–2. See discussion, p. 128.

gr. : 11.45	10.73	10.14	9.51	7.77
mm. : 27.50	26.40	27.40	26.4	27.0

116c Æ (13; a cache, see p. 129)

Obv.: As on No. 116. Rev.: As on No. 116.

Legend: As on No. 116.

Symbol: In the obverse field r. B.

Date: In the field center, the year, and in the ex., 1st, the month;

(2) ΔΞΥ, 153/54 A.D., ΑΠΕΛΛΑΙΟΥ, 9th month;
(3) ΕΞΥ, 154/55 A.D., ΔΙΟΥ, 8th month;
(1) ΗΞΥ, 157/58 A.D., ΔΙΟΥ, 8th month;
(1) ΔΟΥ, 163/64 A.D., ΔΙΟΥ, 8th month;
(6) ϚΟΥ, 165/66 A.D., ΑΠΕΛΛΑΙΟΥ, 9th month.

Wroth, 224–227, Nos. 1–25; XXXIV, 1–3. See discussion, p. 129.

gr. : 13.47	11.16	10.92	10.91	10.75	10.74	10.64	10.63	10.53	10.20
mm. : 30.80	26.50	25.90	26.10	26.40	29.10	26.40	28.70	26.90	28.10
10.04	9.92	9.73							
27.90	29.4	28.9							

117 Æ (23)

Obv.: Bust of the king facing front; helmet with flaps; long beard.

Rev.: Tyche seated l. on a short column, the r. hand raised to the face; turreted headdress; in front a palm.

Symbol: None occurs.

Date: In the obverse field r., up (5) ΘΝΤ, 148/49 A.D.; (2) ΑΞΤ, 150/51 A.D.; (1) ΔΞΤ, 153/54 A.D.; (2) ϚΞΤ, 155/56 A.D.; (13) date obscured or off flan.

There is a border of dots on obverse and reverse. The edges are somewhat flattened.

Wroth, 232, Nos. 68–72; XXXIV, 8–9. See discussion, p. 129.

gr. :	4.08	3.87	3.73	3.67	3.59	3.57	3.29	3.13	3.11	2.97	2.89	2.87
mm. :	16.9	16.7	17.5	16.7	16.0	16.5	14.6	15.0	15.0	15.5	15.5	17.0
	2.78	2.73	2.70	2.63	2.54	2.45	2.40	2.34	2.15	2.07	1.07*	
	16.4	19.3	17.0	18.2	15.1	14.8	15.2	14.4	14.6	15.2	14.2	

* Broken

118 Æ (65; a cache, see p. 129)

Obv.: Bust of the king l., diademed; helmet with long curved flaps; long beard.

Rev.: Bust of Tyche r., draped; turreted headdress.

Symbol: In the reverse field r. A.

Date: In the obverse field l., down (12) ΕΟΤ, 164/65 A.D.; (34) ϚΟΤ, 165/66 A.D.; (19) date off flan.

There is a border of dots on obverse and reverse. The edges are rounded. The coins are practically in mint condition.

Wroth, 233, Nos. 73–76; XXXIV, 10. See discussion, p. 129.

gr. :	164/65:		4.35	4.05	3.88	3.76	3.74	3.72	3.58	3.56	3.38
mm. :			16.1	15.9	15.5	15.4	17.3	17.0	15.2	14.0	15.5
	3.23	3.19	3.08	165/66:		4.27	3.90	3.85	3.81	3.77	3.76
	15.7	14.8	14.3			15.0	13.8	15.9	13.5	15.7	15.0
	3.74	3.73	3.68	3.68	3.66	3.64	3.57	3.56	3.55	3.54	3.53
	14.7	14.8	15.0	14.5	14.6	14.0	14.2	17.5	14.3	14.9	16.0
	3.47	3.46	3.46	3.44	3.42	3.41	3.37	3.36	3.31	3.28	3.25
	15.1	15.9	15.6	14.0	14.2	15.8	14.9	14.4	14.9	16.0	14.0
	3.22	3.11	3.09	3.04	2.94	2.48	No date:		4.20	4.14	4.08
	15.3	15.2	14.3	14.8	13.5	15.0			14.6	16.2	17.5
	4.07	3.86	3.79	3.72	3.66	3.63	3.63	3.62	3.57	3.52	3.47
	15.2	15.6	14.0	15.5	16.7	15.0	14.7	13.9	13.8	13.8	14.2
	3.31	3.27	3.11	2.67	2.66						
	14.8	14.6	14.4	14.6	14.3						

118a Æ (110; a cache, see p. 129)

Obv.: As on No. 118.

Rev.: As on No. 118.

Symbol: In the reverse field r. A.

Date: In the obverse field l., down (25) EOΥ, 164/65 A.D.; (44) ϛOΥ, 165/66 A.D.; (41) date off flan or obscure.

There is a border of dots on obverse and reverse. The edges are rounded.

Wroth, 233, Nos. 73–76; XXXIV, 10. See discussion, p. 129.

gr. :	164/65:		4.58	4.42	4.33	4.18	4.13	4.10	4.02	4.01	3.90
mm. :			15.0	14.7	15.6	15.9	15.5	14.9	17.4	16.7	15.5
	3.74	3.73	3.71	3.65	3.64	3.53	3.45	3.33	3.29	3.21	3.14
	15.0	15.0	15.5	14.6	15.8	14.9	16.9	15.7	15.0	14.9	15.7
	3.08	3.05	3.03	2.97	2.89	165/66:	4.27	4.13	3.73	3.58	3.55
	13.7	15.5	15.2	14.3	15.0		15.1	16.4	15.6	14.2	14.1
	3.53	3.45	3.45	3.44	3.39	3.38	3.37	3.33	3.32	3.29	3.28
	14.6	15.3	14.2	14.9	14.6	14.0	14.6	15.3	14.4	14.9	13.8
	3.27	3.27	3.27	3.26	3.25	3.23	3.21	3.21	3.19	3.19	3.14
	14.9	14.1	13.9	14.9	14.4	14.5	14.8	13.6	14.3	14.1	14.6
	3.14	3.13	3.12	3.12	3.12	3.11	3.09	3.02	3.02	2.96	2.95
	14.5	14.8	14.6	13.9	13.8	14.6	14.7	16.0	14.5	14.0	14.8
	2.84	2.79	2.76	2.55	2.54	2.47	No date:		5.00	4.09	3.93
	14.4	14.5	14.5	16.0	14.8	13.3			18.3	15.2	16.3
	3.93	3.90	3.89	3.61	3.60	3.56	3.55	3.43	3.43	3.41	3.41
	15.6	15.0	17.5	15.6	15.5	16.9	15.1	15.0	14.2	14.6	14.2
	3.40	3.37	3.36	3.35	3.34	3.34	3.27	3.27	3.27	3.26	3.24
	14.9	14.5	14.5	14.2	15.2	13.6	14.2	14.1	13.6	14.1	13.9
	3.19	3.17	3.13	3.13	3.11	3.05	3.00	2.97	2.92	2.87	2.79
	14.7	14.5	17.1	14.5	14.3	14.6	14.2	14.9	14.1	13.4	16.7
	2.78	2.66	2.63	2.38	2.01						
	14.3	14.6	15.8	13.7	14.3						

118b Æ (50)

Obv.: As on No. 118. Rev.: As on No. 118.

Symbol: In the reverse field r. A; off flan on a number of coins.

Date: In the obverse field l., down (4) ϛOΥ, 165/66 A.D.; (2) ΠΥ, 169/70 A.D.; (1) AΠΥ, 170/71 A.D.; (1) EΠΥ, 174/75 A.D.; (2) ϛΠΥ, 175/76 A.D.; (5) [ ]ΠΥ; (35) the date off flan or obscured.

There is a border of dots on obverse and reverse. The edges are rounded.

Wroth, 233, Nos. 73–76; XXXIV, 10. Cf. Petrowicz, 166, Nos. 55–57. See discussion, p. 129.

gr. :	4.34	3.76	3.52	3.39	3.33	3.23	3.18	3.18	3.05	3.04	3.03
mm. :	16.6	17.0	14.3	14.2	14.7	15.8	14.6	13.4	16.8	15.4	15.0

gr. :	3.02	3.00	2.98	2.97	2.91	2.86	2.84	2.79	2.78	2.76	2.69
mm. :	13.8	13.0	14.0	13.9	13.9	13.6	13.7	13.9	13.7	14.8	15.0
	2.68	2.67	2.64	2.57	2.55	2.55	2.52	2.47	2.42	2.28	2.25
	12.6	16.4	14.3	14.3	13.9	12.4	12.2	13.5	15.0	13.2	12.9
	2.23	2.19	2.17	2.02	1.94	1.34	1.33	1.15	1.06	1.06	0.98
	13.6	15.8	13.2	14.2	12.0	10.3	11.3	11.7	10.3	9.70	12.1
	0.86	0.85	0.84	0.72*	0.64	0.59					
	10.8	9.30	10.8	11.2	10.7	10.5					

* Broken

119 Æ (4)

Obv.: The king mounted on a horse advancing l. The l. hand of the king rests on his sword; the r. hand is advanced over the head of the horse, grasping or receiving an object off flan. The king wears a helmet with curved flaps, a tunic, and loose trousers.

Rev.: Tyche standing r., holding a palm; turreted headdress.

Symbol: None can be distinguished.

Date: In the reverse field l., down (3) ΔΠΥ, 173/74 A.D.; (1) date off flan.

No border can be distinguished. The edges are slightly rounded.

Pl. V. See discussion, p. 129.

gr. :	2.92	2.57	2.50	2.40
mm. :	13.8	12.3	13.5	12.4

120 Æ (36)

Obv.: Bust of the king l., diademed; helmet with long curved flaps; long beard.

Rev.: Tyche seated l. on a short column, the r. hand raised to the face; turreted headdress; in front a palm.

Symbol: None occurs.

Date: In the obverse field l., down (1) ΕΠΥ, 174/75 A.D.; (2) ϚΠΥ, 175/76 A.D.; (6) ΖΠΥ, 176/77 A.D.; (5) ΗΠΥ, 177/78 A.D.; (10) [ ]ΠΥ; (12) date entirely obscured or off flan.

There is a border of dots on obverse and reverse. The edges are slightly rounded.

Wroth, 233, Nos. 77–79; XXXIV, 11. Cf. Petrowicz, 166, Nos. 58–59a. See discussion, p. 129.

gr. :	4.04	3.65	3.53	3.27	3.15	3.12	3.10	3.09	3.07	3.04	2.88	2.74
mm. :	14.8	14.0	14.4	14.2	15.2	13.9	12.4	15.6	14.6	14.3	13.9	14.6
	2.73	2.71	2.65	2.63	2.61	2.59	2.48	2.48	2.44	2.44	2.35	2.33
	14.4	14.6	13.6	14.3	12.8	14.5	14.6	13.7	14.6	13.8	14.7	14.8
	2.29	2.27	2.25	2.23	1.99	1.94	1.92	1.91	1.83	1.78	1.00	0.82
	15.0	16.5	15.5	13.9	13.5	13.7	13.8	12.6	14.0	14.0	12.8	13.3

121 Æ (7)

Obv.: Bust of the king l., diademed; helmet with long curved flaps; long beard.

Rev.: Bust of Tyche r., draped, with arm holding a wreath; turreted headdress.

Symbol: In the reverse field r. A.

Date: In the obverse field l., down (3) ΑϘΥ, 180/81 A.D.; (1) [ ]ϘΥ; (3) date obscure or off flan.

There is a border of dots on obverse and reverse. The edges are slightly rounded.

Wroth, 234, No. 80; XXXIV, 12. See discussion, p. 130.

gr. :	3.85	3.65	3.50	3.46	3.42	3.26	2.89
mm. :	15.8	16.2	16.8	15.7	15.9	15.5	15.6

VOLAGASES IV

(191–208/09 A.D.)

122 AR (116; a cache, see p. 130.)

Obv.: Bust of the king l., diademed; hair in bunches; long, pointed beard. Border of dots.

Rev.: The king seated l. on a throne with a high back, receiving a diadem from Tyche standing r.

Legend: This is largely off flan on all coins. The surviving traces, with their frequent blunders, are discussed on pages 234–235.

Symbol: None occurs.

Date: In the field center, the year, and in the ex., 1st, the month

(40) ΔΦ, 193/94 A.D.; of these (1) [A]PT[EMIΣIOY], 2nd month, (1) ΠΑ-NH[MOY], 4th month, (1) [ΓO]PΠ[IAIOY], 6th month, (1) [AΠ]E-ΛΛ[IOY], 9th month, (1) ΠΕΡΙΤ[IOY], 11th month, (2) [Δ]ΥΣΤ[POY], 12th month;

(18) ΕΦ, 194/95 A.D.; of these (1) ΞΑ[ΝΔΙΚΟΥ], 1st month, (1) ΠΑΝΗ-Μ[ΟΥ], 4th month;

(14) ϚΦ, 195/96 A.D.; of these (1) ΞΑΝΔΙΚ[ΟΥ], 1st month, (1) [A]PTE-M[IΣIOY], 2nd month;

(22) ΖΦ, 196/97 A.D.; of these (1) ΑΥΔΝ[ΑΙΟΥ], 10th month;

(15) ΗΦ, 197/98 A.D.;

(6) ΘΦ, 198/99 A.D.;
(1) [ ]Φ.
The greater number of the month dates are off flan.

Wroth, 238, Nos. 4–10; XXXV, 8. See discussion, p. 130.

gr. :	193/94:	12.71	12.33	12.27	12.24	12.21	12.11	12.10	12.01
mm. :		24.70	26.20	25.90	25.50	25.50	24.60	25.50	25.90
	12.01	11.93	11.86	11.86	11.84	11.53	11.52	11.47	11.43
	25.60	25.90	25.60	25.20	25.60	24.70	26.50	26.40	26.30
	11.42	11.41	11.40	11.31	11.31	11.29	11.28	11.27	11.21
	25.30	25.20	24.60	28.00	26.30	26.70	26.90	25.50	24.60
	11.18	11.16	11.00	10.99	10.84	10.78	10.77	10.72	10.71
	25.80	26.40	27.10	26.50	24.80	26.40	26.30	24.90	26.00
	10.63	10.37	10.18	9.77	9.52	194/95:	12.21	12.21	12.10
	26.80	28.80	27.90	25.4	27.8		26.90	25.50	26.40
	12.08	12.00	11.71	11.70	11.62	11.54	11.54	11.44	11.37
	26.40	25.80	26.50	24.10	26.00	25.20	24.60	26.70	26.50
	11.09	10.92	10.84	10.83	10.82	10.77	195/96:	12.50	12.06
	24.90	28.40	25.60	26.10	24.70	25.00		25.50	27.20
	11.94	11.52	11.42	11.40	11.38	11.32	11.31	11.27	11.17
	25.50	24.20	26.60	26.80	25.80	26.70	27.00	26.70	27.00
	10.96	10.87	10.73	196/97:	12.70	12.23	12.17	12.15	12.09
	26.20	27.50	26.00		25.50	25.60	25.40	25.00	26.90
	12.03	12.00	11.94	11.90	11.83	11.80	11.59	11.38	11.37
	26.40	26.00	25.60	26.00	26.20	25.40	25.90	26.00	26.00
	11.32	11.26	11.17	11.14	10.66	10.64	10.47	10.00	197/98:
	26.30	27.20	25.50	28.40	26.30	26.90	25.20	29.40	
	12.45	12.36	12.27	12.20	12.08	12.05	12.02	12.01	12.00
	26.70	24.80	25.40	24.40	26.20	25.10	26.00	24.80	26.10
	11.85	11.59	11.58	11.51	11.35	11.35	198/99:	12.79	12.53
	26.80	25.70	25.50	24.90	25.50	25.40		24.60	24.30
	12.38	12.25	11.99	11.82	10.84				
	25.80	24.70	24.50	28.20	27.40				

122a Æ (6)

Obv.: As on No. 122. Rev.: As on No. 122.

Legend: Largely off flan. See discussion, p. 130, under No. 122.

Symbol: None occurs.

Date: In the field center (1) ΔΦ, 193/94 A.D.; (1) ϚΦ, 195/96 A.D.; (1) ΗΦ, 197/98 A.D.; (1) ΒΙΦ, 201/02 A.D.; (1) ΓΙΦ, 202/03 A.D.; (1) date obscure. On all the coins the month date is off flan.

Wroth, 238–239, Nos. 4–16; XXXV, 8.

gr.	: 11.51	11.14	10.30	9.58	8.53	7.00
mm.	: 25.00	24.60	25.20	24.9	24.8	23.4

123 Æ (4)

Obv.: Bust of the king facing front, diademed; hair in bunches; long, pointed beard; presumably tunic.

Rev.: Bust of Tyche r.; turreted headdress.

Symbol: In the reverse field r. A.

Date: None can be distinguished. This may be due to the small size of the flans in comparison with the dies.

No border can be distinguished. The edges are flattened.

Pl. V. See discussion, p. 130.

gr.	: 2.85	2.24	1.90	1.45
mm.	: 15.6	15.2	15.7	14.1

VOLAGASES V

(208/09–222/23 A.D.)

124 Æ (27; a cache, see p. 131)

Obv.: Bust of the king l., diademed; helmet with flaps; long beard. Border of dots.

Rev.: The king seated l. on a throne with a high back, receiving a diadem from Tyche standing r. Tyche holds a scepter in the l. hand.

Legend: Almost entirely off flan.

Symbol: In the obverse field r. B.

Date: In the field center (4) ΚΦ, 209/10 A.D.; (8) ΑΚΦ, 210/11 A.D.; (1) ΒΚΦ, 211/12 A.D.; (1) ΓΚΦ, 212/13 A.D.; (8) [ ]ΚΦ; (5) date entirely obscured. On all coins the month date is off flan.

Wroth, 241–243, Nos. 1–18; XXXV, 14–15. See discussion, p. 131.

gr.	: 11.4	11.2	8.72	8.10	8.00	8.00	8.00	8.00	7.30	7.20	7.20
mm.	: 24.9	24.4	27.0	26.0	26.1	25.8	25.5	24.7	26.2	26.3	26.3
	7.20	7.00	7.00	6.90	6.90	6.50	6.30	5.90	5.79	5.70	5.30
	26.0	26.1	25.6	26.0	25.6	26.3	25.0	26.5	24.0	25.2	24.5
	5.14	5.10	4.70	3.60	2.72						
	27.1	27.2	25.9	25.2	25.0						

124a Æ (12)

Obv.: As on No. 124.

Rev.: As on No. 124.

Legend: Almost entirely off flan. On a number of coins traces of the first line on the left may be discerned, ΔΕΠΙΦ[.

Symbol: In the obverse field r. B.

Date: In the field center (2) KΦ, 209/10 A.D.; (2) AKΦ, 210/11 A.D.; (2) BKΦ, 211/12 A.D.; (1) ΔKΦ, 213/14 A.D.; (2) EKΦ, 214/15 A.D.; (2) [ ]KΦ; (1) date entirely obscured. On all coins the month date is off flan.

Wroth, 241–243, Nos. 1–18; XXXV, 14–15.

gr.	: 12.86	12.77	12.44	9.80	9.32	8.99	8.80	8.67	8.58	8.05
mm.	: 26.20	25.50	26.40	25.7	23.7	24.5	24.6	25.2	25.0	24.8
	5.42	5.17								
	25.8	24.8								

125 Æ (5)

Obv.: Bust of the king l., diademed; helmet with flaps; long beard.

Rev.: Tyche standing r., holding a palm; turreted headdress.

Symbol: None can be distinguished.

Date: In the reverse field l., down (1) EK[Φ], 214/15 A.D.; (2) ϛKΦ, 215/16 A.D.; (2) the date off flan.

A border can be distinguished only on the obverse of one coin; this is probably due to the small size of the flans in comparison with the dies. The edges are slightly flattened.

Pl. V. See discussion, p. 131.

gr.	: 1.93	1.81	1.66	1.35	1.32
mm.	: 12.4	12.2	11.1	10.8	12.2

2. THE AUTONOMOUS COINAGE

The bronze coins with civic types found at Seleucia are all of the Parthian period. Their relation to the Parthian coinage as a whole has been discussed on pages 153–158. On the coins of some groups dates cannot be distinguished, and their chronological sequence has been discussed in the "Notes on the Coins," to which references are made in the catalog.

ZEUS AËTOPHOROS

126 Æ (28)

Obv.: Bust of Tyche r. draped; turreted headdress; hair done in a knot from which fall curls.

Rev.: Zeus seated l. on a throne without a back, half-draped; details of the hairdressing obscured. The r. hand, advanced, holds a bird r.; the l. rests on a long scepter behind.

Legend: r. ΣΕΛΕΥΚΕΩΝ, l. ΤΩΝΠΡΟΣΤΩΙ, ex. ΤΙΓΡΕΙ. On no coin is the legend complete.

Monogram: None can be distinguished.

Date: On one coin in the second line of the exergue appear traces of characters that must represent a date. On all other coins of the group this portion of the field is either off flan or badly obscured.

The adjustment of the dies is normal. There is a border of dots on the obverse. The edges are flattened.

Pl. V. See discussion, p. 131.

gr. :	5.98	5.28	4.68	4.62	4.54	4.46	3.99	3.88	3.81	3.71	3.48
mm. :	22.2	22.2	21.1	22.4	22.5	19.8	21.7	20.3	19.1	17.9	20.7
	3.45	3.39	3.37	3.33	3.26	3.04	2.88	2.74	2.58	2.54	2.05
	17.8	18.9	18.7	20.5	17.1	18.2	18.7	19.9	16.8	18.8	15.4
	1.97	1.76	1.56	1.46	1.08	0.85					
	16.3	17.7	15.9	15.7	15.1	13.9					

TRIPOD

127 Æ (76)

Obv.: Bust of Tyche r., turreted headdress; hair done in a knot from which fall curls.

Rev.: Tripod-lebes.

Legend: r. ΣΕΛΕΥΚΕΩΝ, l., 1st ΤΩΝΠΡΟΣΤΩΙ, 2nd ΤΙΓΡΕΙ. On no coin is the legend complete.

Monogram: In the reverse field l. on two coins, traces of monograms. On the rest this portion of the field has been obscured or is off flan.

Date: In the exergue on a number of coins appear traces of characters which may represent dates. On no coin is the exergue sufficiently clear to demonstrate that a date was not intended to be shown.

The adjustment of the dies is normal. No border can be distinguished. The edges are beveled. In form the coins approximate Seleucid issues.

Hill, 140, Nos. 1–2; XXIII, 3–4. See Pl. V (rev. only) and discussion, p. 133.

gr. :	4.63	4.03	3.99	3.73	3.72	3.68	3.66	3.63	3.62	3.61	3.59
mm. :	16.2	16.0	16.7	15.9	17.8	16.6	17.3	16.1	17.5	16.8	15.9
	3.55	3.49	3.45	3.38	3.38	3.33	3.29	3.28	3.26	3.25	3.24
	17.1	15.9	17.1	16.4	16.2	16.4	15.9	16.5	16.5	16.8	16.0
	3.21	3.18	3.08	3.07	3.02	2.96	2.92	2.92	2.75	2.63	2.63
	16.8	17.3	17.2	15.2	16.9	15.5	16.8	16.7	15.8	17.3	15.9
	2.58	2.57	2.57	2.52	2.45	2.44	2.32	2.27	2.26	2.26	2.23
	16.4	15.9	15.5	15.6	15.9	15.0	14.3	15.4	15.7	14.8	15.3

gr. :	2.21	2.20	2.19	2.10	2.09	2.05	1.99	1.93	1.93	1.90	1.86
mm. :	15.1	15.3	15.0	15.5	16.0	14.9	16.3	15.5	14.9	15.2	15.4
	1.86	1.85	1.83	1.81	1.81	1.75	1.73	1.72	1.71	1.70	1.63
	15.2	13.0	15.5	15.5	15.0	15.0	14.6	15.2	14.5	14.6	15.9
	1.62	1.60	1.55	1.54	1.50	1.44*	1.35	1.28	1.22	1.09*	
	15.4	15.8	15.5	14.5	16.0	15.4	15.3	14.5	15.1	15.1	

* Broken

TYCHE NIKEPHOROS (SEATED)

128 Æ (205)

Obv.: Bust of Tyche r.; turreted headdress; hair done in a knot from which fall curls.

Rev.: Tyche seated l. on a throne without a back, on her head a kalathos. The r. hand, advanced, holds a Nike r., who extends a wreath with fillets. In the l. arm is a cornucopiae.

Legend: r. ΣΕΛΕΥΚΕΩΝ, l. ΤΩΝΠΡΟΣΤΩΙ, ex. ΤΙΓΡΕΙ. On no coin is the legend complete.

Monograms: In the reverse field l. on five coins, No. 44. On two of these the same monogram appears in the obverse field l. Two of the five are dated in 102/01 and 99/98. In the same position on another coin appears No. 45. In the obverse field l. on still another coin N can be discerned. A number of other coins show traces of monograms on one or the other field at the l. On the rest this portion of the field is off flan or has been obscured. It is probable that all the coins were intended to show a monogram on the reverse, but this was not invariably repeated on the obverse.

Date: In the ex., 2nd, (2) ΘΣ, 103/02 B.C.; (1) ΙΣ, 102/01 B.C.; (1) ΓΙΣ, 99/98 B.C.; (5) ϚΙΣ, 96/95 B.C.; (1) ΖΙΣ, 95/94 B.C.; (3) ΔΚΣ, 88/87 B.C.; (1) ΖΚΣ, 85/84 B.C.; (2) ΗΚΣ, 84/83 B.C. A number of coins show traces of the date; on the rest this portion of the field is off flan or has been obscured.

The adjustment of the dies is normal with one exception, ↑ →. There is a border of dots on the obverse. Some of the coins have beveled edges and in form resemble Seleucid issues; others have the edges flattened.

Hill, 141, No. 4; XXIII, 6. See Pl. V (rev. only) and discussion, p. 133.

gr. :	5.22	5.19	5.17	5.09	5.07	4.96	4.96	4.95	4.92	4.91	4.83
mm. :	17.5	20.0	18.8	19.7	18.6	18.7	18.2	18.1	18.2	17.8	18.6
	4.80	4.79	4.68	4.64	4.64	4.57	4.51	4.51	4.50	4.49	4.39
	18.3	19.4	19.6	18.2	18.0	18.0	18.2	18.0	19.0	18.7	17.8
	4.38	4.36	4.35	4.32	4.32	4.31	4.30	4.29	4.25	4.25	4.22
	19.7	19.8	17.8	19.0	18.9	17.8	18.1	18.4	18.6	17.5	17.4

gr. :	4.21	4.19	4.16	4.15	4.10	4.05	4.04	4.03	3.98	3.98	3.91
mm. :	18.3	16.8	17.5	18.3	18.2	19.2	17.9	18.0	18.3	17.8	18.8
	3.89	3.87	3.85	3.82	3.78	3.77	3.77	3.75	3.74	3.72	3.70
	18.7	18.9	17.9	18.4	18.9	17.5	17.3	18.9	18.0	17.4	17.7
	3.69	3.68	3.66	3.63	3.60	3.56	3.55	3.54	3.51	3.50	3.47
	20.0	18.9	19.4	17.9	17.3	16.9	17.9	17.8	18.3	17.6	19.8
	3.45	3.43	3.39	3.38	3.35	3.34	3.33	3.31	3.30	3.29	3.27
	17.2	17.3	17.1	18.9	19.5	18.9	18.1	17.4	18.5	18.5	19.1
	3.25	3.22	3.21	3.18	3.17	3.15	3.14	3.12	3.09	3.07	3.05
	16.8	17.9	18.9	16.5	18.5	17.8	18.4	17.6	17.5	18.4	16.9
	3.01	3.00	2.99	2.98	2.97	2.97	2.95	2.94	2.93	2.93	2.92
	19.2	17.3	18.8	17.8	19.3	17.4	17.3	18.3	17.7	17.6	17.8
	2.90	2.90	2.89	2.82	2.81	2.80	2.77	2.74	2.72	2.68	2.66
	18.5	17.6	16.9	19.3	16.7	16.5	15.3	16.9	17.8	17.9	18.0
	2.65	2.63	2.62	2.61	2.55	2.54	2.49	2.48	2.47	2.47	2.45
	17.8	16.4	16.5	15.9	16.7	17.6	18.3	16.9	17.5	17.2	17.8
	2.44	2.43	2.42	2.41	2.40	2.40	2.39	2.36	2.35	2.31	2.28
	16.6	17.7	17.2	16.3	17.9	16.8	17.2	15.9	17.9	16.1	17.4
	2.28	2.25	2.23	2.22	2.22	2.20	2.20	2.19	2.19	2.18	2.18
	16.6	16.1	18.0	16.3	15.7	16.8	15.8	18.2	15.9	15.9	15.8
	2.17	2.16	2.15	2.12	2.11	2.11	2.10	2.10	2.09	2.05	2.05
	16.5	15.9	17.0	18.1	17.8	14.7	17.5	14.6	17.0	16.1	16.0
	2.02	2.02	2.00	1.98	1.97*	1.97*	1.95	1.95	1.95	1.93	1.87
	16.6	16.1	17.7	15.2	18.2	17.3	17.5	16.9	15.2	15.5	15.9
	1.86	1.83	1.83	1.82	1.81	1.81	1.81	1.81	1.73	1.73	1.70
	15.2	16.1	14.9	16.0	16.9	16.5	16.4	16.2	16.6	16.3	15.7
	1.69	1.68	1.63	1.61	1.60	1.49	1.47	1.46	1.37	1.36*	1.36
	15.9	15.6	16.2	14.4	17.0	16.6	16.1	16.1	17.0	15.7	15.4
	1.34	1.34	1.31	1.30	1.25	1.21	1.21	1.19	1.17	1.14	1.06
	16.4	14.8	15.2	14.7	14.0	15.4	15.3	14.4	15.0	17.3	14.4
	1.02	0.99	0.92	0.90	0.88	0.81	0.74				
	13.8	15.1	15.0	13.9	15.4	14.5	16.2				

* Broken

CORNUCOPIAE

129 Æ (16)

Obv.: Bust of Tyche r.; turreted headdress; hair done in a knot from which fall curls; the presence or absence of drapery cannot be determined.

Rev.: A cornucopiae, upright.

Legend: r., 1st ΣΕΛΕΥΚΕΩΝ, 2nd ΤΩΝΠΡΟΣ, l. ΤΩΙΤΙΓΡΕΙ. On no coin is the legend complete.

Monogram: None can be distinguished.

Date: In the reverse field l., down (3) ΜΣ, 72/71 B.C.; (2) probably ΜΣ but possibly [ ]ΜΣ; (11) the date largely or entirely off flan or obscured.

The adjustment of the dies is normal. There is a border of dots on the obverse. The edges are flattened.

Hill, 140, No. 3; XXIII, 5. See Pl. V (rev. only) and discussion, p. 134.

gr. :	2.67	2.01	1.99	1.92	1.77	1.63	1.61	1.52	1.44	1.42	1.71
mm. :	14.9	14.3	16.2	14.2	13.9	12.6	13.9	12.2	13.7	13.9	13.2
	1.06	1.06	1.03	1.01	0.41*						
	12.1	12.0	11.9	13.0	11.4						

* Broken

TYCHE AND RIVER GOD

130 Æ (72)

Obv.: Head of Tyche r.; turreted headdress; hair done in a knot from which fall curls.

Rev.: Tyche, wearing a turreted headdress, seated r. on a short column and holding a palm in the r. hand. At her feet, the river god swimming r.

Legend: Circular, starting at the upper r. ΣΕΛΕΥΚΙΑΣΤΗΣΠΡΟΣΤΩΤΙΓΡΙ. On no coin is the legend complete. On some of the coins the final sigma of the city name is omitted.

Monogram: In the obverse field l., No. 46. This can be distinguished on thirteen coins. On the rest this portion of the field is obscured or off flan.

Date: In the field r. (15) ΟΣ, 42/41 B.C.; (11) ΑΟΣ, 41/40 B.C. On the rest this portion of the field has been obscured.

The adjustment of the dies is normal. There is a border of dots on the obverse. The edges are flattened.

Hill, 141, No. 6; XXIII, 8. See Pl. V and discussion, p. 134.

gr. :	3.07	3.02	2.95	2.95	2.95	2.83	2.78	2.77	2.73	2.60	2.60
mm.	17.9	18.8	18.2	17.1	16.9	16.9	16.5	18.0	17.9	18.2	18.2
	2.56	2.45	2.43	2.42	2.42	2.35	2.29	2.26	2.24	2.23	2.21
	14.9	16.9	17.9	17.7	15.3	17.1	17.3	16.5	17.6	17.7	16.9
	2.10	2.09	2.08	2.08	2.06	2.06	2.05	2.05	2.04	2.02	2.00
	18.6	14.8	16.8	15.1	16.5	14.9	17.7	16.5	17.9	17.3	17.8
	1.98	1.96	1.95	1.93	1.92	1.89	1.88	1.86	1.86	1.81	1.80
	19.3	16.0	14.5	16.2	15.0	16.4	15.4	16.6	15.8	15.5	15.8

gr.	: 1.76	1.74	1.73	1.72	1.70	1.67	1.67	1.65	1.62	1.61	1.58
mm.	: 15.5	14.3	15.8	14.5	15.9	16.8	15.8	16.1	14.5	16.6	15.1
	1.55	1.54	1.53	1.52	1.52	1.45	1.45	1.39	1.34	1.34	1.25
	17.0	15.0	17.7	17.1	16.2	16.5	15.4	15.3	15.5	14.9	15.5
	1.24	1.16	1.12	1.01	0.85	0.63					
	15.8	15.7	17.0	14.5	15.2	15.2					

130a Æ (7)

Obv.: As on No. 130.

Rev.: As on No. 130, save that the column is definitely longer.

Legend: None can be distinguished at the top or the r.; this, however, may be due to the poor condition of the coins. No legend occurs along the bottom. On two coins traces of legend can be discerned at the l.; on one, reading up]ΤΩΩΛΑ.

Monogram: None can be distinguished.

Date: In the field r., traces only.

The adjustment of the dies is normal except on one coin which has ↑ →. There is a border of dots on the reverse; though none can be distinguished on the obverse this may be due to the condition of the coins. The edges are flattened.

Pl. V. See discussion, p. 135.

gr.	: 2.16	2.01	1.55	1.34	1.13	1.10	1.04
mm.	: 16.0	15.8	14.5	15.8	14.9	14.9	13.7

TYCHE NIKEPHOROS (STANDING)

131 Æ (46)

Obv.: Head of Tyche r.; turreted headdress; hair done in a knot, no curls.

Rev.: Tyche standing l. The form of the headdress cannot be distinguished. The r. hand, advanced, holds a Nike r.; in the l. arm rests a cornucopiae.

Legend: r. ΣΕΛΕΥΚΕΩ[Ν], l. [ΤΩ]Ν ΠΡΟΣ ΤΩ[Ι], ex. ΤΙΓΡΕΙ.

Monogram: In the obverse field l. apparently No. 46. This can be distinguished on one coin only. Both faces of all the coins of this group are in an obscure condition, and the apparent absence of monograms lacks significance.

Date: In the field l. (7) ΔΟΣ, 38/37 B.C.; (8) [ ]ΟΣ; in the ex., 2nd (3) ΠΣ, 32/31 B.C.; (2) traces only. On the rest of the coins no date can be distinguished.

The adjustments of the dies are ↑ ↑, ↑ ↗, ↑ →. There is a border of dots on the obverse. The edges are flattened.

Imhoof-Blumer, 452, No. 67. See Pl. V and discussion, p. 135.

gr. :	3.53	3.35	3.25	3.23	2.90	2.65	2.60	2.57	2.50	2.49	2.49	2.44
mm. :	15.9	18.3	13.9	19.1	18.5	17.2	18.4	17.2	16.3	16.7	16.4	16.3
	2.39	2.37	2.33	2.30	2.29	2.27	2.20	2.20	2.08	2.00	1.99	1.99
	18.9	17.1	17.2	17.1	17.0	17.1	20.5	15.0	16.6	15.5	16.6	16.5
	1.92	1.85	1.85	1.81	1.80	1.75	1.74	1.70	1.68	1.66	1.56	1.46
	14.9	18.9	16.7	16.7	16.5	17.7	14.9	16.8	15.7	17.9	15.9	15.8
	1.41	1.34	1.27	1.26	1.26	1.23	1.23	1.20	1.13*	0.79*		
	15.8	15.9	14.1	13.1	15.0	17.1	13.9	14.9	15.0	15.6		

* Broken

TWO CITY-GODDESSES

132 Æ (129)

Obv.: Bust of Tyche r.; turreted headdress; hair done in a knot from which curls fall along the neck.

Rev.: Two figures standing facing each other with their r. hands held over a tripod between them. Each figure is fully draped and has the head covered by a kalathos; in the l. arm of each rests a cornucopiae. The sex is not definitely indicated but presumably is female. It is not certain whether the r. hands are clasped or whether each holds an object.

Legend: (rarely completely visible on a single coin) r. ΣΕΛΕΥΚΕΩΝ, l. ΤΩΝΠΡΟΣΤΩΙ, ex. ΤΙΓΡΕΙ.

Monogram: None occurs.

Date: None can be distinguished. The second line of the exergue in all instances is off flan; it is possible that dates were intended to be shown here.

The adjustment of the dies is approximately normal. There is a border of dots on the obverse. Some of the coins have beveled edges and in form resemble typical Seleucid issues. On others the edges are entirely flattened in the manner most characteristic of civic issues. On the rest the edges show variations of these extremes.

Imhoof-Blumer, 451, No. 60; Hill, cxv, No. 1. See Pl. VI and discussion, p. 136.

gr. :	3.95	3.95	3.93	3.89	3.87	3.72	3.68	3.63	3.59	3.45	3.38
mm. :	17.8	17.2	16.4	17.3	17.5	11.7	16.6	16.0	17.2	18.0	17.1
	3.33	3.29	3.06	3.02	2.98	2.85	2.82	2.82	2.72	2.69	2.52
	17.5	16.2	16.1	17.5	17.5	16.5	16.1	15.8	18.6	16.1	15.4
	2.51	2.48	2.48	2.41	2.39	2.35	2.33	2.29	2.25	2.23	2.20
	16.9	16.6	15.7	16.1	15.7	15.5	15.3	14.8	15.3	15.9	16.3

gr. :	2.15	2.15	2.15	2.11	2.10	2.10	2.07	2.06	1.96	1.93	1.93
mm. :	18.5	15.6	14.4	14.5	16.4	15.4	13.7	16.0	18.2	16.6	15.1
	1.92	1.92	1.91	1.88	1.86	1.86	1.85	1.85	1.84	1.84	1.83
	15.5	15.2	16.5	15.3	14.9	14.7	16.2	15.5	15.8	15.1	14.3
	1.81	1.80	1.79	1.78	1.78	1.75	1.75	1.72	1.69	1.69	1.67
	14.6	17.7	15.0	15.3	15.0	15.8	15.1	16.4	14.7	16.3	15.7
	1.66	1.65	1.65	1.63	1.63	1.62	1.62	1.62	1.61	1.60	1.60
	15.4	16.3	15.9	15.3	14.3	16.5	14.6	14.2	15.5	15.1	14.6
	1.59	1.55	1.55	1.54	1.54	1.53	1.53	1.53	1.50	1.50	1.49
	15.5	15.6	14.4	15.6	15.6	15.8	15.0	14.9	14.6	14.5	15.1
	1.47	1.47	1.45	1.44	1.44	1.43	1.42	1.41	1.41	1.39	1.39
	15.5	13.2	15.1	14.9	14.3	16.2	14.7	15.3	14.1	15.2	14.6
	1.38	1.38	1.37	1.36	1.36	1.35	1.34	1.32	1.32	1.29	1.29
	15.1	14.3	14.8	15.3	14.9	14.2	14.7	16.1	13.9	15.7	14.6
	1.25	1.25	1.24	1.23	1.19	1.17	1.16	1.15	1.14	1.13	1.11
	16.4	15.6	14.9	15.8	14.8	15.6	12.7	15.5	13.9	14.9	14.9
	1.11	1.10	1.07	1.06	1.05	0.93	0.79	0.77			
	14.5	15.0	13.9	14.6	14.0	12.6	12.6	13.9			

MALE DEITY WITH KALATHOS AND LYRE

133 Æ (14)

Obv.: Bust of Tyche r.; turreted headdress; the hair done in a knot from which fall curls. The presence or absence of drapery cannot be determined.

Rev.: A nude male figure seated l. on the edge of a cippus-like seat. The head is covered by a kalathos and the hair is done in a knot. Behind the figure a large cithara rests on the back of the seat. The r. hand, advanced, holds a palm, reversed on two coins, upright on the rest.

Legend: Circular, starting at the upper l. ΣΕ ΛΕ ΥΚΕΩ[ΝΠΡΟ]Σ ΤΩΙ[ΤΙΓΡΕΙ]. On all the coins the legend is badly obscured.

Monograms: In the reverse field l. and the obverse field l., No. 47. This can be distinguished in both fields on seven coins, on the reverse alone on four others. Without doubt it was intended to be shown on both faces of all the coins.

In the reverse field r. and on the obverse between two of the turrets of the headdress, either Π or Π̄. This can be distinguished on both faces on eight coins and on the one face or the other on the rest.

Date: None can be distinguished. It is possible that this is due to the condition of the coins.

The adjustment of the dies is normal. There is a border of dots on obverse and reverse. The edges are flattened.

Hill, 141, No. 5; XXIII, 7. See Pl. VI and discussion, p. 137.

gr. :	4.23	4.16	3.98	3.65	3.64	3.60	3.60	3.57	3.37	3.33	3.33
mm. :	18.6	18.5	18.9	18.2	19.1	20.1	19.1	19.5	19.0	18.6	18.2
	3.07	3.04	2.51								
	18.7	18.1	17.7								

DRAPED FIGURE ON A THRONE

134 Æ (22)

Obv.: Head of Tyche r.; turreted headdress; hair done in a knot from which fall two formal curls.

Rev.: A draped figure seated l. on a throne with a low back. The head appears to be bare and beardless; other details have been obscured. There is nothing definite to indicate the sex, but the character of the drapery suggests that the figure is male. The l. hand rests on the lap. The r. rests on a short staff or scepter immediately in front of the knees.

Legend: Quadrangular, above ΕΤΟΥΣ, r. ΚΤΣΕΛ[Ε], ex. (inverted) ΥΚΙΑΣΤ, l., up ΗΣΠΡΟΣ. There is no indication in the legend of a reference to the name of the river, the Tigris. It is possible that the river name with the article occupied an outer line at the top, off flan on all the coins.

Monograms: In the reverse field l., No. 47, and r., No. 48.

Date: As a part of the legend, on the r., down (1) ΚΤ, 9/10 A.D.; (2) [·]Τ. On the rest this portion of the field is obscured or off flan.

The adjustment of the dies is normal. There is a border of dots on the obverse. The edges are straight.

Pl. VI. See discussion, p. 137.

gr. :	6.21	6.07	5.82	5.74	5.63	5.63	5.34	5.16	4.99	4.95	4.59
mm. :	19.0	21.0	19.0	19.6	19.6	18.4	18.9	20.2	19.0	18.8	21.5
	4.54	4.45	4.38	4.31	4.20	3.82	3.64	3.35	3.32	3.15	2.67
	20.5	17.9	19.4	20.8	20.4	18.8	18.5	19.4	18.9	18.9	17.0

ANCHOR

135 Æ (6)

Obv.: Head of Tyche r.; turreted headdress; hair done in a knot from which fall two formal curls.

Rev.: An anchor, inverted.

Legend: Semicircular starting at the l., up ΣΕ[ΛΕΥΚ]ΙΑΣ. Although the legend is at least partly obscure on all of the coins, it clearly comprised only the one word.

Monogram: Between the flukes of the anchor, at the r., obscure traces that suggest monograms.

Date: Between the flukes of the anchor, at the l., traces of what may be dates.

The adjustment of the dies is normal. There is a border of dots on obverse and reverse. The edges are somewhat rounded.

Pl. VI (rev. only). See discussion, p. 138.

gr. :	1.98	1.95	1.80	1.76	1.66	1.57
mm. :	15.5	14.1	15.7	14.3	14.8	15.7

FEMALE BUST WITH KALATHOS AND VEIL

136 Æ (28)

Obv.: Bust of Tyche r., draped; turreted headdress; hair done in a knot from which falls a curl.

Rev.: A female bust r., wearing kalathos and veil.

Legend: None occurs.

Monograms: In the field l., No. 49 on three coins dated in 15/16, months Hyperberetaios, Apellaios, and Audynaios; No. 50 on four coins dated in 15/16, months Peritios, Dystros, and Xandikos, and on ten coins dated in 16/17. On the rest the monogram is off flan or has been obscured.

Date: In semicircular form starting at the l.

(7) ϚΚΤ, 15/16 A.D.: (1) ΥΠΕΡΒΕΡΕΤΑΙΟΥ, the 6th month, (1) ΑΠ-[Ε]Λ[Α]ΙΟΥ, the 8th month, (1) Α[ΥΔΥ]ΝΑΙΟΥ, the 9th month, (1) ΠΕΙΡΙΤΙΟΥ, the 10th month, (2) ΔΥΣΤ[ΡΟΥ], the 11th month, (1) ΞΑ[ΝΔΙΚΟΥ], the 12th month;

(14) ΖΚΤ, 16/17 A.D.: (1) ΑΡΤΕΜ[ΙΣΙΟΥ], the 1st month, (2) ΠΑΝΗ-[ΜΟΥ], the 3rd month, (5) ΠΕΙΡΙΤΙΟΥ, the 10th month, (6) month obscure:

(7) the year date obscured or off flan.

The adjustment of the dies varies according to the monogram: with the first the adjustment is ↑ ↓ ; with the second it is normal. There is a border of dots on obverse and reverse. The edges are either straight or beveled, without reference to the chronological sequence of the coins.

Hill, 145, No. 41; XXIII, 16. See Pl. VI (rev. only) and discussion, p. 138.

gr. :	5.56	5.16	4.00	4.00	3.96	3.86	3.82	3.68	3.68	3.33	3.32
mm. :	21.5	20.5	18.6	17.8	19.9	17.4	18.3	17.7	17.3	18.2	16.9
	3.31	3.27	3.15	3.13	3.04	2.99	2.93	2.86	2.56*	2.50	2.21
	17.4	17.9	17.6	18.9	17.5	18.0	18.6	17.9	18.6	17.4	15.8

* Broken

gr.	: 2.17	1.83	1.76	1.67	1.35	1.06
mm.	: 18.2	16.5	16.7	14.8	15.0	12.7

MONOGRAM AS TYPE

137 Æ (27)

Obv.: Bust of Tyche r., draped; turreted headdress; hair done in a knot.

Rev.: A monogram as type.

Monogram: In the center of the field, No. 49 on seven coins, six dated in 15/16 and one in 16/17; No. 51 on twenty coins, ten dated in 16/17 and ten on which the date has been obscured.

Legend: From the upper r., down ΒΟΥΛΗΣ.

Date: At the l. below, up (6) ϚΚΤ, 15/16 A.D.; (11) ΖΚΤ, 16/17 A.D.; (10) date obscure.

The adjustment of the dies is normal on most of the coins; a few, without relation to date or monogram, show ↑ ↗ and ↑ ↓ . There is a border of dots on obverse and reverse. The edges show a wide variation with some straight and others beveled or flattened.

Hill, cxvi–cxvii, No. 6. See Pl. VI (rev. only) and discussion, p. 139.

gr.	: 3.94	3.56	3.40	2.80	2.63	2.11	2.02	1.97	1.93	1.84	1.65
mm.	: 18.6	18.4	18.9	16.6	16.8	15.3	15.3	16.2	15.8	14.5	15.0
	1.55	1.45	1.44	1.44	1.42	1.35	1.33	1.28	1.20	1.19	1.17
	16.0	15.8	15.1	14.6	15.8	15.9	14.8	15.7	13.0	14.5	15.0
	1.04	0.95	0.95	0.93	0.79						
	15.2	15.7	14.9	13.9	16.1						

THE KING AS ZEUS NIKEPHOROS

138 Æ (26)

Obv.: Bust of Tyche r., draped; turreted headdress; hair done in a knot from which fall fillets.

Rev.: The king seated l. on a throne without a back. The head is bare, the body clad in loose trousers and tunic with V-shaped neck. The r. hand, advanced, holds a Nike r. who extends a wreath toward the king. The l. hand rests on a long scepter behind.

Legend: None occurs.

Monogram: None appears to occur.

Date: None can be distinguished.

The adjustment of the dies is normal. There is a border of dots on obverse and reverse. The edges are beveled. The fabric is that of Parthian bronze of the reign of Artabanus II.

Hill, 143, No. 16; XXIII, 11. See Pl. VI and discussion, p. 139.

gr. :	1.83	1.75	1.69	1.68	1.68	1.62	1.61	1.59	1.57	1.54	1.53
mm. :	12.5	12.7	12.8	12.6	12.2	12.5	14.2	12.8	12.6	12.7	13.1
	1.50	1.43	1.41	1.36	1.34	1.33	1.31	1.28	1.11	1.09	1.08
	12.9	12.6	12.3	12.6	12.3	13.2	12.4	12.9	12.2	13.0	12.0
	1.02	0.95	0.87	0.82							
	13.1	12.7	12.0	11.6							

THE KING RECEIVING A DIADEM FROM TYCHE

139 Æ (6)

Obv.: A draped female figure seated l. The form of the headdress cannot be determined. The r. hand, advanced, holds a wreath with streamers. Presumably the figure represents Tyche.

Rev.: The king seated l. receiving a diadem from Tyche standing r. The king appears to be wearing the characteristic trousers and tunic. All other details have been obscured.

Legend: None occurs.

Monogram: None can be distinguished.

Date: In the reverse field r., down (1) ΘK[T], 18/19 A.D. On the rest this portion of the field is off flan.

The adjustment of the dies is normal. There is a border of dots on obverse and reverse. The edges are roughly flattened. The fabric is that of Parthian bronze coins.

Hill, cxvi, No. 4; XXIII, 12–13. See Pl. VI (rev. only) and discussion, p. 140.

gr. :	1.61	1.38	1.34	1.25	0.92	0.34*
mm. :	11.7	10.3	14.4	12.1	12.8	10.7

* Broken

THE KING SEATED ON A THRONE

140 Æ (3)

Obv.: Tyche seated l. on a cippus-like seat; turreted headdress. The r. hand rests on a short staff or scepter immediately in front of the knees. The l. arm is dropped at the side.

Rev.: The king seated l. on a throne, the details of which cannot be determined. The form of the headdress cannot be distinguished. The costume is that usually worn. The l. arm is dropped at the side. The r. arm is outstretched in front, the hand off flan.

Legend: None occurs.

Monogram: None occurs.

Date: In the obverse field l., up (2) ΔΛΤ, 23/24 A.D. On the third coin this portion of the field has been obscured.

The adjustment of the dies is normal. There is a border of dots on obverse and reverse. The edges are roughly flattened.

Pl. VI. See discussion, p. 141.

gr.	: 1.05	0.88	0.78
mm.	: 13.5	13.0	12.2

HUMPED BULL

141 Æ (153)

Obv.: Bust of Tyche r.; turreted headdress; hair done in a knot from which fall two formal curls.

Rev.: A humped bull standing r., the head on a level with the body but turned front, the tail raised.

Legend: Above ΣΕΛΕΥ, r. ΚΙΑΣ, ex. (inverted) ΤΗΣΠΡΟΣ, l. ΤΙΓΡΕΙ. The legend at the left reads up on some coins and down on others. On no coin can the entire legend be distinguished. On the majority it is largely or entirely off flan or obscured.

Monogram/Initials: In the reverse field r. (5), No. 52; (18) groups of two letters written vertically, very obscure, possibly ΗΥ or ΝΥ. On the rest this portion of the field is entirely obscure or is off flan. The initials are more readily obscured than is the monogram, and it is probable that the great majority of the coins bore one or more groups of letters.

Date: Probably none was intended to be shown.

The adjustment of the dies on most of the coins is normal; a few show ↑ ↗ and ↑ ↓. There is a border of dots on the obverse. The edges are flattened. The metal is of poor quality and the coins are all badly worn and chipped. The execution of the types is below the average for the civic issues.

Pl. VI. See discussion, p. 141.

gr.	: 2.78	2.67	2.54	2.34	2.33	2.30	2.27	2.26	2.19	2.18	2.16
mm.	: 16.8	16.7	16.9	16.8	18.6	17.4	16.9	16.7	16.5	18.7	16.4
	2.14	2.11	2.09	2.07	2.06	2.02	2.02	2.02	2.01	2.00*	1.99
	18.5	16.0	15.8	16.5	18.1	17.0	16.2	15.7	15.0	15.3	17.7
	1.96	1.93	1.92	1.90	1.86	1.85	1.84	1.84	1.83	1.81*	1.78
	15.9	17.5	17.3	15.9	15.8	16.3	18.0	15.1	15.6	17.0	17.6
	1.77	1.76	1.75	1.75	1.74	1.73	1.73	1.70	1.67	1.65	1.64
	17.1	16.0	17.0	16.4	14.6	16.4	15.1	16.4	18.2	16.7	15.6
	1.63*	1.62	1.62	1.60	1.60	1.58	1.57	1.57	1.55	1.55*	1.55
	15.9	18.4	14.3	15.3	14.9	15.7	15.5	15.0	17.0	15.9	15.2

gr.	1.54	1.54*	1.53	1.53	1.52*	1.51*	1.48	1.48	1.48	1.47	1.47
mm.	16.9	16.7	16.5	15.8	15.9	14.7	17.4	15.4	14.9	16.9	16.8
	1.47	1.45	1.44*	1.44	1.44	1.43	1.42	1.42	1.41	1.41*	1.40
	15.2	16.5	19.2	16.6	15.2	16.1	16.2	15.7	15.6	15.0	14.7
	1.39	1.39	1.38	1.37	1.37	1.37	1.35	1.35	1.33	1.33	1.32
	15.4	15.2	16.1	18.2	16.3	15.2	16.2	15.7	15.5	15.3	16.0
	1.30	1.28	1.27*	1.27	1.26	1.24	1.24*	1.23	1.21	1.21	1.19
	13.2	14.4	16.4	16.1	15.6	19.4	16.0	14.4	14.9	14.3	14.8
	1.17*	1.17*	1.17	1.14	1.13	1.13	1.13*	1.13	1.12	1.11	1.11
	16.9	15.9	15.3	16.3	15.5	15.4	15.1	14.9	15.2	16.1	14.3
	1.08	1.04	1.01	0.99	0.94*	0.94	0.92	0.89	0.88*	0.87	0.87*
	14.9	15.0	15.5	14.1	14.4	14.2	15.0	13.9	15.4	16.4	13.9
	0.86*	0.85*	0.79	0.78	0.78	0.77	0.76	0.73*	0.72	0.72	0.68
	13.3	14.7	14.9	13.1	12.6	15.6	14.8	12.7	12.2	9.90	13.7
	0.68	0.61*	0.60*	0.60	0.59	0.57	0.56	0.54	0.49*	0.43	0.42*
	10.4	11.3	14.3	11.1	12.1	11.6	11.8	10.8	12.3	11.7	10.5
	0.41	0.41	0.40	0.39	0.38	0.38*	0.35	0.35	0.32	0.28	
	11.7	10.7	10.4	9.40	11.2	10.2	11.6	9.90	9.40	8.50	

* Broken

NIKE WITH PALM

142 Æ (53)

Obv.: Bust of Tyche r., draped; turreted headdress; hair done in a knot from which hangs a fillet.

Rev.: Nike advancing l., holding a palm upright in the r. hand.

Legend: None occurs.

Monogram: None occurs. On one coin, date obscure, in the obverse field l. the symbol A can be observed. This may recur on some other coins which are obscure; it is clear that a symbol was not intended to be shown on the great majority in this group.

Date: In the reverse field l., down (18) ANT, 40/41 A.D.; (11) BNT, 41/42 A.D.; (3) ΓNT, 42/43 A.D.; (21) date partly or entirely obscured or off flan.

The adjustment of the dies is normal with one exception, which has ↑ ↓. There is a border of dots on obverse and reverse. The edges are straight. The quality of the metal and of the execution is noticeably superior to that of the two groups immediately preceding.

Hill, 145–146, Nos. 43–48; XXIII, 18–21. See Pl. VI and discussion, p. 142.

gr.	3.70	3.62	3.59	3.57	3.50	3.49	3.45	3.42	3.39	3.33	3.31
mm.	16.2	15.8	14.9	15.2	14.7	16.0	14.8	15.3	15.5	14.9	16.1
	3.31	3.31	3.30	3.24	3.23	3.23	3.15	3.11	2.99	2.98	2.96
	14.4	14.1	14.8	14.6	15.3	15.2	16.4	15.5	15.0	13.3	14.1

gr.	: 2.91*	2.88	2.88	2.86	2.84	2.75	2.72	2.72	2.71	2.70	2.65
mm.	: 16.2	14.7	14.5	14.3	15.8	15.2	15.9	15.0	14.9	16.5	16.3
	2.65	2.64	2.61	2.53	2.50	2.48	2.44	2.39	2.36	2.33	2.24
	15.1	15.1	16.8	15.8	14.4	13.6	15.3	16.3	15.4	15.9	14.1
	2.15	2.09	1.95	1.90*	1.89	1.69	1.55	1.52	1.49		
	13.4	16.2	13.6	15.0	14.9	14.2	16.5	15.5	15.5		

* Broken

THE DEIFIED KING

143 Æ (26; in a cache, see p. 143)

Obv.: Tyche seated l. on a short column. The headdress cannot be distinguished. A cornucopiae is held in the l. arm. The r. arm appears to be advanced, but the hand is off flan.

Rev.: A male figure seated l. The form of the seat cannot be determined. The figure is clad, apparently in a long robe. The head is bare; details of the hairdressing cannot be distinguished. The figure wears a beard, rather long and executed in a style common to Parthian coins. The l. arm is raised behind, as though grasping a long scepter; the hand is off flan. The r. arm is advanced; the hand grasps either a small wreath or a flat vessel.

Legend: None occurs.

Monogram: None occurs.

Date: In the reverse field l., down (5) ΔNT, 43/44 A.D. On the rest this portion of the field has been obscured or is off flan.

The adjustment of the dies is normal. There is a border of dots on obverse and reverse. The edges are roughly flattened. The fabric is that of Parthian bronze issues.

Pl. VI. See discussion, p. 143.

gr.	: 1.19	1.09	1.08	1.05	0.95	0.87	0.84	0.84	0.83	0.83	0.79
mm.	: 12.7	11.8	12.9	13.4	12.9	11.5	13.0	12.7	12.4	11.5	12.8
	0.76	0.75	0.75	0.74	0.73	0.70	0.70	0.70	0.69	0.65	0.65
	12.4	13.2	12.6	12.0	12.8	12.1	11.9	10.7	11.5	13.2	11.5
	0.61	0.59	0.59	0.52							
	12.2	13.3	11.9	12.5							

EAGLE

144 Æ (9)

Obv.: Head of Tyche r.; turreted headdress; all other details obscured.

Rev.: An eagle standing ¾ r., wings outstretched; probably a wreath held in the beak.

Legend: None can be distinguished; probably none was intended to be shown.

Monogram: None can be distinguished.

Date: None can be distinguished.

The adjustments of the dies are ↑ ↑, ↑ ↗, ↑ →. There is a border of dots on obverse and reverse. The edges are flattened. The fabric is more related to that of Parthian bronze than of civic issues.

Pl. VI. See discussion, p. 143.

gr.	: 1.47	1.20	1.14	1.08	1.01	0.87	0.67*	0.65	0.57*
mm.	: 15.0	14.6	15.5	14.6	14.6	14.6	14.8	13.3	14.0

* Broken

ARTEMIS

145 Æ (37)

Obv.: Bust of Tyche r.; turreted headdress. A curl lies along the neck.

Rev.: A female figure standing facing front with head turned l. The head appears to be bare. The figure is clad in a short tunic; a folded chlamys hangs from the elbows. The l. arm is raised, the hand grasping a spear held upright. The r. hand rests on the head of a deer-like animal which stands ¾ l. The representation is of Artemis.

Legend: None occurs.

Monograms: In the reverse field r. (16), No. 53; (6), No. 47. On the rest this portion of the field has been obscured or is off flan. On a few coins the monogram is repeated in the obverse field l. One coin, however, which has the first monogram on the reverse, on the obverse shows No. 54.

Date: In the field l., top (2) OT, 59/60 A.D.; (1) BOT, 61/62 A.D.; (4) [ ]OT. On the rest this portion of the field is off flan or has been obscured.

The adjustment of the dies is normal with a few exceptions which show ↑ ↗. There is a border of dots on obverse and reverse. The edges are abruptly beveled. The metal is of reddish tinge.

Pl. VI. See discussion, p. 144.

gr. :	4.17	3.43	3.37	3.36	3.24	2.73	2.63	2.53	2.53	2.48	2.39
mm. :	18.2	17.4	17.2	16.4	17.3	17.8	14.9	17.1	16.5	16.6	17.2
	2.36	2.20*	2.19	2.17	2.17	2.03	2.00	1.97	1.95	1.94	1.84
	15.2	18.8	14.8	17.1	16.7	16.9	17.8	17.5	15.9	15.2	14.3
	1.75	1.66*	1.51	1.40	1.30	1.27	1.21	1.11	1.04	0.97	0.97
	15.9	12.0	14.3	15.7	16.9	15.0	16.2	13.9	12.7	13.9	13.7
	0.94	0.93	0.81	0.77							
	14.6	12.5	13.6	14.6							

* Broken

HUMPED BULL

146 Æ (47)

Obv.: Bust of Tyche r.; turreted headdress. Either a curl or a fillet hangs along the back of the neck.

Rev.: A humped bull standing r., the head held on a level with the body, the tail raised.

Legend: None occurs.

Initials: In the reverse field r., written horizontally (15) ΔΥ; on the rest this portion of the field has been obscured or is off flan.

Symbol: On the obverse field l., on one coin, a cornucopiae. It may have been intended to show this symbol on other coins which have this portion of the field off flan or obscured. On a number, however, it is clear that the symbol does not occur.

Date: In the reverse field at the top (27) ΠΤ, 69/70 A.D. On the rest this portion of the field is off flan or has been obscured.

The adjustment of the dies is normal. There is a border of continuous fillet on obverse and reverse. The edges are beveled.

Pl. VI. See discussion, p. 145.

gr. :	2.62	2.16	2.14	2.04	1.81	1.77	1.67	1.60	1.59	1.57	1.52
mm. :	14.6	13.0	13.2	14.1	13.7	11.7	14.0	13.2	13.5	13.0	13.1
	1.51	1.48	1.47	1.44	1.44	1.42*	1.41	1.36	1.36	1.31	1.29
	13.9	12.7	13.8	15.7	13.4	13.5	11.7	13.2	12.9	14.1	12.8
	1.27	1.27	1.25	1.18	1.18	1.15	1.14	1.14	1.10*	1.10	1.10
	14.6	13.7	12.5	14.4	12.8	13.6	13.2	12.9	13.9	12.6	12.6
	1.09	1.01	0.98	0.96	0.94	0.89	0.88	0.87*	0.85*	0.83*	0.74
	14.9	12.6	13.5	13.7	12.8	12.9	13.4	13.8	13.7	12.8	11.7
	0.74	0.72	0.31								
	11.9	10.7	11.8								

* Broken

TYCHE SEATED ON A COLUMN

147 Æ (12)

Obv.: Head of Tyche r.; turreted headdress; hair done in a knot from which fall two formal curls.

Rev.: Tyche seated l. on a short column; turreted headdress. The r. hand is raised to the face; the l. arm is dropped at the side.

Legend: Above [ΣΕΛΕΥΚΙΑΣ], r. ΤΗΣΠΡ[ΟΣ], l. ΤΙΓΡΕ. The legend is entirely off flan on the majority of the coins.

Monogram: In the reverse field l., No. 42. This can be distinguished on seven coins. On the rest this portion of the field has been obscured or is off flan.

Date: In the reverse field l., up (5) ΠΤ, 69/70 A.D. On the rest this portion of the field is off flan.

The adjustment of the dies is normal. There is a border of dots on the obverse. The edges are rounded.

See discussion, p. 145.

gr. :	1.36	1.33	1.27	1.25	1.21	1.12	0.95	0.78	0.78	0.78*	0.67	0.37*
mm. :	12.9	15.0	13.0	12.4	12.8	13.9	12.8	13.5	13.3	12.8	13.2	11.4

* Broken

NIKE WITH WREATH

148 Æ (3)

Obv.: Head of Tyche r.; turreted headdress; hair done in a knot.

Rev.: Nike standing l. The r. hand, advanced, holds a wreath from which fall two short streamers. The l. arm is dropped at the side.

Legend: None occurs.

Monogram: None can be distinguished. This may be due to the fact that the flans are too small for the dies.

Date: None can be distinguished.

The adjustment of the dies is normal. No border can be distinguished. The edges are somewhat flattened.

Pl. VI. See discussion, p. 146.

gr. :	1.22	1.20	1.04
mm. :	11.4	11.4	10.7

CHAPTER V

NOTES ON THE COINS

In this chapter have been brought together under the serial headings employed in the catalog all discussions having to do with the individual type groups. The purpose has been to make the catalog more readily available for rapid reference to the various types. As in the catalog the Royal Coinage is treated first, then the Autonomous Coinage.

1. THE ROYAL COINAGE

PERIOD OF MITHRADATES I

66. The coins with similar types published by Wroth comprise three varieties, two of which bear dates, 139/38 and 138/37 B.C. Owing to the obscured condition of its details the specimen from Seleucia cannot be assigned to a particular variety. The examples which lack a date were probably struck shortly before those on which the date appears (see below, p. 147).

ARTABANUS I

67. The coin from Seleucia is apparently similar to that in the Berlin Museum; Wroth, however, gives the second monogram on that specimen as alpha enclosed by pi. Both coins lack a date. Another, published by Wroth (20, No. 1), is dated in the year 124/23 B.C. The undated examples probably represent an issue which preceded that on which the date occurs (see below, p. 147).

MITHRADATES II

68. The coins in Wroth show a monogram behind the figure of Arsaces, a feature which cannot be distinguished on the examples from Seleucia. The characters in the exergue, TΥ, appear on one of the coins cited and also on a tetradrachm of Phraates II (Wroth, 23, No. 1, attributed to Himerus).

ORODES II

69. The coin cited in the catalog is similar in respect to types and monogram, but bears the month date Peritios. The months

on this and all succeeding coins have been calculated on the basis of the Babylonian calendar. The problem of the calendar employed by the Seleucia mint has been discussed on pages 147–153. The issue represented by No. 69 was struck probably shortly prior to type group No. 70. In the legend the letter phi has the form reproduced on page 244, No. 15.

70. On this issue we find for the first time on the coins from Seleucia the use of the rectangular sigma. The forms of the upsilon and the phi have also been changed. See page 244, Nos. 13, 14, and 15. Although the two types of Orodes found at Seleucia fail to show year dates, a variety of type No. 70 published by Wroth (73, No. 37) bears the date 39/38 B.C. The issue of which No. 70 is an example may be presumed to have been struck just prior to the dated variety. Since the legend on group No. 69 employs the older form of the sigma, this issue was probably struck before No. 70.

PHRAATES IV

71. On the coin cited a pellet is shown in the reverse field. Possibly this has been obscured on the coin from Seleucia. The form of the upsilon and the phi of the legend are reproduced on page 244, Nos. 14 and 15.

72. The coin cited is similar in respect to the types, but bears a different year date, 25/24 B.C. Wroth does show a specimen with the year and month dates of group No. 72, but the types are those of No. 71 (103, No. 18). The issue of variant types of tetradrachms within the same month, a feature of the coinage of Phraates IV, is discussed on pages 174–175. It should be noted that the epsilon in the legend of type No. 72 lacks the middle horizontal bar. Its form and those of the sigma, upsilon, and phi are reproduced on page 244, Nos. 5, 13, 14, and 15.

73. The coin in Wroth bears the month date Apellaios. Note the peculiar spelling of Panemos on one of the coins from Seleucia. The forms of the alpha, sigma, upsilon, and phi of the legend are reproduced on page 244, Nos. 1, 13, 14, and 15.

74. The coins cited bear the first monogram which occurs on the specimens from Seleucia. Under the throne, however, Wroth has noted a simple Λ in place of our lambda and rho in monogram. In the legend of this group and that of No. 75 the older form of the sigma temporarily reappears. The forms of the up-

silon and the phi of the legend and of the alpha of the date are reproduced on page 244, Nos. 14, 15, and 1. The issues represented by groups Nos. 74 and 75 alone among those struck under Phraates IV appear to be undated. In style they are closely similar to the dated issues and probably succeeded them.

75. In addition to the adjunct characters which appear on the examples from Seleucia, the coins in Wroth show the same monogram which occurs on group No. 74. This has undoubtedly been obscured on our single specimen of group No. 75. The forms of the upsilon and phi of the legend are reproduced on page 244, Nos. 14 and 15.

PHRAATACES (PHRAATES V)

76. The coins cited are dated in the month Artemisios of the year in which the specimens from Seleucia were struck. They appear to lack the pellets in the reverse field. Two of the coins of group No. 76, weighing 9.83 and 6.01 grams, have what seems to be a bronze core under a plating of silver. In the legends of this group the sigmas again have the rectangular form. In addition the epsilons lack the middle horizontal bar and the crossbar of the alpha is represented by a dot. These forms and those of the upsilon and the phi are reproduced on page 244, Nos. 13, 5, 2, 14, and 15. So far as I have been able to read the legends, the debased forms are common to the succeeding issues of Phraataces which have been found at Seleucia. They became aggravated on the coinage of Artabanus II, who followed Phraataces, but disappeared thereafter. The significance of this temporary debasement of the legends is discussed on pages 216–217.

77. The coin cited is similar except in the date which is equivalent to 1 B.C./1 A.D.

79. The reverse type of the coin in Wroth is partly off flan. It is probable that the types are similar to those of the coin from Seleucia, but the presence or absence of a monogram cannot be determined. The style of the engraving and the form of the monogram of our specimen are characteristic of the Parthian bronze coinage struck in the mints of Iran. Presumably the coin had been brought to Seleucia by some chance. See page 157 for further discussion.

ARTABANUS II

80. On this group, as on the other issues of silver of this reign, the Greek letters of the legends retain the debased forms which have been noted for the reign of Phraataces. The cross-bar of the alphas disappears entirely, and this character cannot be distinguished from lambda. Similarly the epsilons and the sigmas have the same form. These characters along with the letters omicron, upsilon, and phi are reproduced on page 244, Nos. 3, 5, 13, 11, 14, and 15.

81. Petrowicz (106, No. 4) shows a tetradrachm, wrongly assigned by him to Vonones I, which has types similar to those of the coin from Seleucia and of the examples cited from Wroth, but which bears on the second line of the exergue the legend [E]TOΥΣ Γ[KT]. The date is equivalent to 12/13 A.D. Petrowicz has noted traces of this legend in a corresponding position on another tetradrachm of Artabanus (108, No. 3). On an autonomous issue of Seleucia struck three years earlier ETOΥΣ is again found associated with the date. On the coin from Seleucia with which we are now concerned the second line of the exergue has been obscured. It is very possible that the coins in the British Museum have suffered in a similar manner, and I have tentatively assigned all the examples of this group to the year 12/13 A.D. It should be noted that these coins, alone among the tetradrachms of Artabanus II, have been considered to have lacked the year date. The examples cited from Wroth and from Petrowicz are dated in Loos and Gorpiaios, the fourth and fifth months.

82. One of the coins in this group, of 7.78 grams, has a bronze core under a silver plating. On all of the specimens the first line of the legend has as the final character a nu, reversed, in place of a sigma. The final letter of the second line cannot be distinguished, but it is probably a sigma instead of the normal nu. The engraver appears to have inverted the order of the two lines. On one coin of the group the word in the exergue reads ΔIKAIOΥ in place of EΥEPΓETOΥ. The types have been struck over an earlier issue of Artabanus. In the legend the alpha, epsilon, omicron, sigma, upsilon, and phi have the forms reproduced on page 244, Nos. 3, 5, 11, 13, 14, and 15.

The title Phil-hellenos, which had only rarely been omitted

from the legends of the tetradrachms since the reign of Mithradates I, does not occur on groups Nos. 82 and 83. The significance of the omission is not certain.

83. The coins cited bear various monograms, one of which includes A. Possibly the alpha which can be discerned on the coins from Seleucia constitutes one element of a similar monogram, the other characters of which have been obscured. The alpha, epsilon, omicron, sigma, upsilon, and phi in the legend have the forms reproduced on page 244, Nos. 3, 5, 11, 13, 14, and 15.

84. This group represents the earliest issue of Parthian royal bronze currency struck for use in the Seleucia mint area. The transition from the autonomous coinage of Seleucia to the royal coinage is discussed on page 156.

85. The reverse type of this bronze piece is essentially that of an earlier tetradrachm (Wroth, 102, Nos. 13–17). The choice was probably inspired, however, by the appearance of this motif on autonomous coins struck about 17/18 A.D. (see p. 104, No. 138).

86. The form of the character mu of the date, which closely resembles the letter pi, is of not infrequent occurrence on Parthian coins (see p. 244, No. 8; cf. Wroth, lxxviii). Although the dates on all the examples are somewhat obscure, the attribution of the group to Artabanus II receives support from other factors. The manner of representation of the hair on the head and the beard is definitely that of the full-faced portrait of Artabanus on his tetradrachms. Vardanes II, Osroes, and Volagases IV are pictured in the frontal position on certain of their issues (Wroth, XXIX, 16; XXXI, 15; XXXV, 7), but the treatment of the hair differs significantly. The nine coins which constitute the group under consideration were found in Level III of the Great House, two together in one room and seven together in another. Occupation of this level came to an end about 43 A.D., three or four years after the death of Artabanus. Vardanes II was in successful revolt for only a short period around 55 A.D.; Osroes and Volagases IV came to the throne in turn during the next century. The provenance of the coins, therefore, requires their assignment to Artabanus II and supports the reading of the dates. The latest date on coins of Artabanus hitherto published is 27/28 A.D. (Wroth, 148, No. 20).

VARDANES I

87. One coin of this group (10.21 gr.) appears to have a bronze core under silver plating; another (7.91 gr.) is apparently of a base metal. The coin of the year 42/43 has been overstruck, but it is not possible to identify the earlier types. On this and all succeeding issues of tetradrachms through the reign of Volagases III the Greek letters of the legend are again correctly formed, although, in some instances, in a different style. See page 244, Nos. 4, 11, 13, 14, 15, and 17.

88. This issue is of unusual interest. The obverse type with the bust of the king turned right follows a practice which on Parthian coinage had been abandoned since the period of Artabanus I, about a century and a half earlier. The reverse type appears to be related to that of an autonomous issue of an earlier date which was struck by the Boule, the organization of the aristocratic party at Seleucia (see p. 103, No. 136). This title occurs on the succeeding issue of Vardanes, on coins of this same year, 43/44 A.D. The quality of the engraving of the group is markedly superior to that of any other Parthian bronze and is equaled only by certain of the early issues of silver. The group constitutes the first known issue of the royal bronze currency at Seleucia after the close of the period of anarchy and revolt which marked the latter part of the reign of Artabanus II. The issue appears to have been light, and was followed in the course of the same year by another of more nearly normal fabric and design.

The fragmentary legend on the reverse of the group is puzzling. The two surviving characters constituted the final letters of the word of which they formed a part. The most reasonable explanation appears to be that the coins were dated by the month as well as by the year. This would be the more natural if, as is likely, they commemorated a particular event.

89. Wroth fails to show any examples of this group for the year 45/46 A.D. Although the British Museum specimens do not show the symbol letter on the reverse at the left, Petrowicz has noted this feature on one of the coins in his collection (115, No. 13).

The figure of the reverse type appears to symbolize the Boule, the council of the aristocratic party at Seleucia. The significance of this motif on the first normal issue of the royal bronze currency in Seleucia after the revolt is discussed on pages 224 to 226 below. On a few specimens of the group under consideration, on which unfortunately the dates have been obscured, the technique of the engraving appears to be related to that of an autonomous issue of the reign of Artabanus (see p. 105, No. 139). Aside from these the group represents a quality of engraving superior to that found on either the royal or the civic bronze of that reign. The execution is decidedly superior to that of the coins struck in the revolt period, No. 141, but there is a close similarity in respect to both style and fabric between the coins of this group and those of the autonomous issue, type No. 142, which marked the victory of the aristocratic party over the rebels and the return of the city to its allegiance to the Parthian dynasty. It is probable that the few coins representing an inferior technique were the earliest struck, from a die that was soon discarded along with the engraver responsible for it. The reverse reproduced on Plate IV illustrates the technique.

It should be noted that there is no relation between the variation in the size of the coins and the changes in date; if two denominations are represented, as is likely, both were issued in each of the three years.

GOTARZES II

90. The coin has been overstruck on the types of Vardanes. On the obverse the outline of the bust of Vardanes can be distinguished and on the reverse the palm branch represented in the hand of Tyche on the tetradrachms of that reign. The legend and the dates recorded in the catalog belong to the second striking. The month Xandikos does not appear on the coins for this year published by Wroth. The date of the types of Vardanes on our coin cannot be distinguished. In the legend the alpha, omicron, sigma, upsilon, phi, and omega have the forms reproduced on page 244, Nos. 1, 11, 13, 14, 15, and 17.

Beginning with the year 46/47 A.D. in the reign of Gotarzes the dates on all coins discussed in this volume have been calculated on the basis of the Babylonian calendar as before, but a change of one month has been assumed in the correspondence of the Greek months with the Babylonian. Xandikos rather than Artemisios has been correlated with Nisannu, the initial month of the year. The reasons for this modification have been discussed on pages 151–153.

91. The coins cited appear to be similar, although the presence of a symbol has not been noted. The style of the engraving is that characteristic of the later Parthian mints in Iran, and it must be presumed that the single example found at Seleucia had not been intended to circulate in the local mint area. The distinctions between the bronze struck at Seleucia and in the other Parthian mints are discussed on page 158.

92. The group constitutes the sole established instance in the Parthian royal coinage of the occurrence of month dates on bronze issues. What may be a fragmentary month date on an issue of Vardanes I has already been noted (p. 117, No. 88). The month as well as the year has been indicated also on an autonomous issue from Seleucia (p. 103, No. 136) and on a commemorative issue of an unidentified city (pp. 155–156). The group under consideration is important because of the light which it throws on the form of the calendar employed by the mint at Seleucia. The evidence is presented on pages 152–153. In the date the numeral xi has the form reproduced on page 244, No. 10.

Petrowicz has published (115, No. 14) what appears to be an example of type group No. 92. The coin is not illustrated, but the obverse is said to be similar to that of an issue of Vardanes, and the specimen has been assigned to that reign. Aside from the coin published by Petrowicz no issue of Vardanes is known which has as the reverse type a head or bust of Tyche. Petrowicz gives the monogram as alpha and rho linked, and a query is placed after the reading of the date ΓNT. I suggest that the date should be read ΣNT, with the zeta reversed as on some of the examples of this group from Seleucia, and that on the monogram the vertical stroke of the tau has been obscured. The month date presumably is off flan or has been obscured. De Morgan also has published a coin of the type under consideration (298, No. 223), which he erroneously assigns to Vardanes. The portrait is clearly that of Gotarzes and the coin is dated in 46/47 A.D., after the death of Vardanes.

VOLAGASES I

94. Wroth has published examples of this group which are dated variously in 78/79 and 79/80 A.D. He assigns the group

to Volagases II on the grounds of the close similarity of the types to those of this reign. He is compelled to assume that the second Volagases came to the throne about 78 A.D., reigned until about 80, and then disappeared until 122, from which date he reigned until 147. The decision of Wroth appears to have been based on the fact that although literary evidence cited by him suggests the continued tenure of the throne by Volagases I as late as 75 A.D., dated coins known to him "carry the reign only as far as A.D. 67/68" (*op. cit.*, l). In making this statement he has entirely ignored a series of tetradrachms published by Lindsay which reproduce exactly the types of Volagases and which are said to be dated in 69/70, 73/74, 74/75, 75/76, and 77/78 (185, Nos. 76–80). A hitherto unpublished series of bronze coins found at Seleucia (p. 75, No. 96) bears dates which cover the period from 69/70 through 77/78 and very probably through 78/79. This group can be assigned only to Volagases I and, with the series noted by Lindsay, it serves to bridge entirely the gap between the earlier coinage of Volagases I and the group of tetradrachms dated in 78/79 and 79/80, which Wroth would assign to Volagases II.

The group of tetradrachms which are in question have a reverse generally similar to that of the coinage of Volagases II and of the earliest coinage of Volagases I (Wroth, XXXII, 8–10; XXVIII, 12–14). It differs from the second coinage of Volagases I (*ibid.*, XXIX, 5) in the substitution on the latter of a palm for a diadem in the hand of Tyche. On the obverse of the first two coinages of Volagases I the king is represented with the head bare; on that of the group in question and of the coinage of Volagases II, the head is covered by a helmet. Actually the relationship of the group to the earlier coinage of Volagases I as well as to the coinage of Volagases II is superficial and of secondary importance. A close examination demonstrates that the reverse type of the group is a literal reproduction of the type chosen by Pacorus II for his first coinage (Wroth, XXX, 1–2). At this period Pacorus was in revolt against Volagases (see pp. 229–230); he seized the mint and struck tetradrachms about April, 78 A.D. About June Volagases reoccupied the mint and struck the first of the group of tetradrachms with which we are concerned. He came into possession of the mint again about June, 79 A.D., and about January,

80 A.D., at which times the rest of the group were issued. During the greater part of this period Pacorus maintained control and Volagases contented himself with the reverse type employed by his rival. The distinguishing feature of the design is the crosspiece forming the back of the throne which had been absent from the earlier coinages of Volagases I and which was not reproduced on the coinage of Volagases II. It was employed again by Pacorus on his third coinage. On the obverse of the group in question there appears to have been no attempt to reproduce the features of Volagases. The portrait, indeed, is more nearly that of the bearded Pacorus (Wroth, XXXI, 1) than of either Volagases I or Volagases II. The coins were obviously struck under the stress of conflict, and it is only the presence of the royal name on the legend which identifies the group. In assigning the group to Volagases I the latter is not provided with a greater variety of portraiture than his three coinages afforded Pacorus II. There is nothing strange in the adóption of the types of Volagases I by Volagases II some forty years later. Pacorus had been a rebel under whose reign the paramount power had been seriously weakened; when Volagases II finally reëstablished the unity of the empire it must have served to increase public confidence that he should have chosen the types of the last legitimate monarch. In the legend of this group alpha, beta, omicron, sigma, upsilon, phi, and omega have the forms reproduced on page 244, Nos. 1, 4, 11, 13, 14, 15, and 17.

95. On one of the coins in this type group the date has been obscured, but the form of the monogram and the fabric of the coin require its inclusion. On another example both the date and the monogram are illegible, and identification has been based on style and fabric alone. The first coin weighs 0.94 gram; the second, 1.08 grams. The assignment of the group to Volagases I is required by the date, which is entirely too early for Pacorus II. The portrait on the obverse might be attributed to either of these two kings, and the group affords an illustration of the unreliability of portraiture at this late period as a principal means for the identification of coins.

96. It is unfortunate that the reading of the latest date on the coins of this group must be classed as tentative. The pi and the tau are distinct, but only the upper portion of the theta can

be discerned. Although I am convinced that the fragmentary character is neither alpha, nor beta, nor delta — the other possibilities — the fact that the date constitutes the latest in the series and is unsupported by other evidence requires its limitation to a tentative reading. Wroth has published a coin with types apparently similar to those of the group under consideration (158, No. 40, note 1). He describes the date as having the appearance of ΑΠΤ, but he tentatively reads it as ΔΝΤ. The first reading is undoubtedly correct. It should be noted again in respect to this group of coins that variations in the weight have no relationship to the year of issue.

97. A general similarity will be noted between the types of this coin and those of a group published by Wroth, which he assigns to the reign of Volagases II (214, Nos. 40–45). In details of execution, however, they differ, and because of the absence of a date from the coins in Wroth they must be attributed to a mint other than that at Seleucia. Our specimen must be assigned to the reign of Volagases I not only because of the character of the date but by reason of the closer relationship of the obverse to the types of this reign than to those of Pacorus II. It is very possible that the group of coins cited likewise belong to the earlier reign.

PACORUS II

98. The coin has been overstruck, the types of Pacorus appearing over others, which probably are those of the first coinage of Volagases I. The name of the latter cannot be distinguished. In the legend the alpha, beta, omicron, sigma, upsilon, phi, and omega have the forms reproduced on page 244, Nos. 1, 4, 11, 13, 14, 15, and 17.

99. The obverse type shows a characteristic portrait of Pacorus. The reverse, however, is unusual in respect to both motif and execution. Both of these factors reveal a fresh and direct western influence generally lacking in the Parthian coinage after the reign of Phraates II. Owing to the condition of the coin one cannot be certain of the significance of the reverse motif. It is scarcely possible that a portrait of the king was intended. Probably the representation is of deity — Dionysos rather than Zeus or Hercules.

100. In addition to the dates which occur on the examples found at Seleucia, Petrowicz has published coins of this type

group dated in 80/81 and 85/86 A.D. (147, Nos. 15, 18); Longpérier, one of 87/88 (p. 131); and Lindsay, one of 93/94 (208, No. 100). The variation in the weight of these coins has no relation to the date of issue.

101. The coin cited appears to be entirely similar to those from Seleucia; the palm on the reverse presumably is off flan. As Wroth has noted, Longpérier in the first publication of this coin read the date as ΓΚΥ, but Gardner, whom Wroth follows, preferred ϚΥ. By comparison of the reproduction of this coin in Wroth with the specimens from Seleucia I am entirely satisfied that the correct reading is ϚΚ[Υ]. In spite of the late date the attribution of the group to Pacorus II is required by the character of the obverse.

OSROES

102. The coins of this group represent two denominations, the one comprising only two examples (7.77 and 6.81 gr.). The types of group No. 106 are similar, but the denomination is smaller. On the coins of 114/15 A.D. the epsilon of the date has the form reproduced on page 244, No. 6. In addition to the dates found on the coins of these groups from Seleucia Wroth gives 110/11 A.D. (205, No. 8) and Petrowicz 109/10, 112/13, 121/22, and 122/23 (150–152, Nos. 3, 5, 15, 16).

103. The coin cited is similar to the group from Seleucia in respect to the types and the symbol. It is reasonable, therefore, to change Wroth's restoration of the date from ΘΛΥ to ΘΚΥ.

104. The coins in Wroth bear only the one date, 118/19 A.D., and the symbol has been read as A rather than as Λ.

106. See discussion under No. 102, above. On group No. 106 no symbol can be distinguished, and apparently none was intended to be shown. On the coins of this group dated in 123/24, 125/26, and 127/28 A.D. the dates read up; for the year 126/27 on two examples the date reads up, on five, down.

VOLAGASES II

109. Tetradrachms of Volagases II are known for the greater number of the years between 122 and 147 A.D. The two examples from Seleucia on which dates cannot be read may belong anywhere within this period. In this volume the so-called early coinage of Volagases II has been attributed to Volagases I

(see p. 119, under No. 94). In the legend alpha, beta, omicron, sigma, upsilon, phi, and omega have the forms reproduced on page 244, Nos. 1, 4, 11, 13, 14, 15, and 17.

109a. This specimen is of a base, spongy metal. In view of this fact and of the blundered legend it is possible that we have here an example of ancient counterfeiting. In addition to the forms noted under No. 109 the theta of the legend has the form reproduced on page 244, No. 7.

110. The example from Seleucia is dated five months prior to the earliest tetradrachm of Volagases II hitherto published (see the table on p. 194). The details of the obverse closely approximate those characteristic of the coinage of Volagases III; this is particularly true of the long squared beard and the helmet with rather long curved flaps. Because of the conventionalization of the portraiture on late Parthian coins, it is not possible to determine whether the features are those of the second or the third Volagases. The reverse type is that common to both reigns. Although the greater part of the legend has been obscured, the epithet ΕΥΕΡΓΕΤΟΥ which has survived demonstrates that this portion of the design has been drawn from the coinage of Volagases I. This particular title had been dropped from the legend on the latest issues of that reign and on those of Pacorus II in order to provide space for the royal name. This had been a requisite during a period when rival kings claimed the paramount power. Although Volagases II during the latter portion of his reign and Volagases III throughout his reign were untroubled by rivals, on all examples of their tetradrachms except that with which we are now concerned the royal name continued to form a part of the legend. The month date appears on the tetradrachms of Volagases II on the second line of the exergue except in the case of the latest issues, on which, as on all the issues of Volagases III, this date has been placed as the first line of the exergue. In this respect the specimen with which we are concerned is related to the coinage of the second Volagases.

The coin is abnormally light and may well be of a base metal. The question arises whether it may be counterfeit. On this supposition the coin could be assigned to the reign of Volagases III, with the early date an error on the part of the illegal engraver. It is unreasonable, however, to suggest that a counterfeiter would err so patently in respect not only to the year of issue, but to the character of the legend. I have assumed, therefore, that if the coin is counterfeit it was copied from a legal issue of Volagases II which bore corresponding types, legend, and date. There have been found at Seleucia bronze coins of the later years of the reign of Volagases II (type groups Nos. 114 and 115) which have obverse types very similar to those of Volagases III. I suggest that curved rather than straight flaps for helmets, and beards worn long, became the style sometime after 120 A.D. On one of his late issues Osroes is pictured with the new style of helmet (Wroth, XXXII, 4). I suggest further that our coin reproduces the design chosen for the first issue of tetradrachms by Volagases II. On this he is portrayed in the actual style of the day. The fact that his administration reinaugurated the minting of tetradrachms after a lapse of twenty-five years (see discussion on pp. 233–234) affords evidence that conditions within the empire were rapidly being restored to normal. The choice of the traditional form of the legend, omitting the royal name, expressed confidence in this trend. The abrupt abandonment of this design on the tetradrachms can reasonably be explained by the supposition that the public displayed a lack of confidence in the new types and that it became necessary to reëmploy those of Volagases I, the last legitimate king from whom Volagases II derived his right to rule (see discussion under No. 94, p. 119, and on pp. 228–229). The use of the current style of headdress on later bronze issues indicates simply that by this date Volagases II had entirely established his political strength in the area within which these coins were intended to circulate. With the accession of Volagases III, the legitimate successor of Volagases II, the administration was in a position to complete the shift from an archaistic to a natural representation of the royal portrait on the coinage.

111. Wroth tentatively assigned this type group to the reign of Osroes. He quotes Gardner's suggestion that it may belong to another, unidentified, rival king of the period (204, note 1; Gardner, 54). Since the extensive coinage of Osroes is entirely homogeneous and shows an obverse which differs in every significant characteristic from that of the group with which we are concerned, I feel that the suggestion of Wroth is not admissible. On the other hand, I see no necessity for introducing an unknown king, nor any objections to the attribution of the group to Vola-

gases II. From the year 112/13 A.D. the issues of this king recur with adequate regularity. No difficulty is presented by the fact that on the obverse of the coins under consideration the king is shown bareheaded, with the hair in formal rows, whereas on the succeeding coinage of Volagases he is represented helmeted. A similar change in the obverse took place in the coinages of Volagases I and Pacorus II. This variation involved no break with traditional style such as is caused by the introduction of the peculiar hairdressing represented on the coinage of Osroes — a break which points to a change in cultural domination. In view of these conditions, therefore, I have tentatively assigned the group to Volagases II and have accepted the earliest date, 105/06 A.D., as the first year of this reign.

112. This type group and the two following, Nos. 113 and 114, have been attributed by Wroth to Volagases II, but with a query. He notes two objections to the attribution: first, that the form of the helmet and of the beard differs from that characteristic of the known issues of this king and, second, that the dates on this bronze fail to coincide with those on the tetradrachms (215, note 1). An explanation of the early form of helmet pictured on the tetradrachms of Volagases II has been presented above under No. 110. The helmet on the bronze under consideration shows a form intermediate between that on the tetradrachms and that on the later bronze of Volagases (type groups Nos. 114 and 115). Wroth describes the beard of the portrait on the coins as long and pointed. Actually it is of medium length and squared at the bottom. That is, the beard, like the helmet, is represented with greater naturalness on the bronze than was feasible for the tetradrachms. The bronze unquestioningly assigned to Volagases II by Wroth (XXXII, 13–14) is not a product of the Seleucia mint and quite naturally, therefore, differs in style from the local issues. If the coins with which we are concerned are not assigned to Volagases II, his long reign at Seleucia after 122 A.D. is entirely unrepresented by bronze issues, whereas his tetradrachms are numerous during this period. Of the five type groups of bronze attributed to Volagases II in this volume, the last four, Nos. 112–115, cannot reasonably be separated. The reverse motif of No. 114 repeats that of No. 112; of No. 115, that of No. 113. The changes in the style of the obverses reflect simply the progressive stabilization of the political situation (see

above under No. 110), and in this respect the bronze constitutes one link in the continuity of the legitimate coin types between the reigns of Volagases I and Volagases III. There is nothing in the details of either the obverses or the reverses of the four type groups to warrant their separation and attribution to two different kings, one of whom, in the entire absence of historical evidence, would have to be created for this particular purpose. The example of group No. 112 cited from Petrowicz is dated in the year 115/16 A.D.

113. The attribution of this group to Volagases II has been discussed under No. 112 above. Examples of the group which have been published by the authors cited in the catalog bear the following additional dates: 122/23, 123/24, 124/25, and 126/27 A.D. The variation in the weight of the coins appears to have no relation to the year of issue.

114. This group and No. 115 below are dated in the reign of Volagases II, but the obverse types of both approximate that characteristic of the coinage of Volagases III. This is particularly true in respect to the curved flaps of the helmet and the form of the beard. As has been suggested under the discussion of group No. 110 above, the coins with which we are now concerned probably portray Volagases II as he actually appeared, in the current style of his day, whereas on the tetradrachms his likeness had been approximated to that of Volagases I. Volagases III, in turn, as the legitimate successor of Volagases II, continued the latest type adopted by the latter. The coin cited in the catalog under No. 114 appears to be entirely similar, although the palm in the hand of Tyche cannot be distinguished. The form of the beard and that of the helmet can be distinctly discerned on the reproduction of this coin in Wroth (XXXIII, 5). The specimen is dated in 128/29 A.D.

115. The obverse type of this group appears to be entirely similar to that of No. 114. The coins cited in the catalog are without doubt examples of group No. 115. Although Petrowicz has failed to state that the flaps of the helmet are curved, he compares his coins with a type of Volagases III published by Wroth which possesses these features. The dates on the examples in Petrowicz, 133/34 and 138/39 A.D., require their attribution to Volagases II.

VOLAGASES III

116. One coin in this group, weighing 8.06 grams and dated in 178/79 A.D., has a bronze core under silver plating. The variation in weight within the group has no relation to the sequence of dates. In the legend alpha, beta, omicron, sigma, upsilon, phi, and omega have the forms reproduced on page 244, Nos. 1, 4, 11, 13, 14, 15, and 17.

116a. The coins of this group were found together below the floor of room 92, Level I of the Great House. The latest coin in the group establishes approximately the date at which the cache was constituted — the ninth month of the year 165/66 A.D. The relationship of the cache to current events at Seleucia is discussed on page 234.

In the case of this as of other large caches described in this volume the weights and the measurements have been listed according to the dates on the coins. This reveals the degree of variation among coins presumably of a single issue. It should be noted that on the series of tetradrachms of Volagases III the symbols A and B are mutually exclusive in time. It is very possible that these characters represent mint offices or titles which might be rendered as "First Controller" and "Second Controller," and that the officials concerned alternately rather than concurrently assumed responsibility for issues or series of issues.

The coins of this group reveal a certain carelessness in both the engraving and the striking. There are several instances of double and even triple striking with the same dies. On four coins dated in 149/50 the month date occupies the second line of the exergue rather than the first, the normal position. On some specimens initial or final letters have been dropped from an upper to a lower line of the legend.

116b. The coins of this group were found together below the floor of room 190, Level I of the Great House. In the same room two caches of bronze coins were uncovered, groups Nos. 118 and 118a, each of which has for its latest date the year 165/66 A.D. It is not possible to determine definitely whether the burial of the five tetradrachms was connected with that of the bronze. The latest date on the silver, 156/57 A.D., suggests no political event which might have caused the secretion of valuables at that time. Our knowledge of the domestic history of

Parthia is so limited, however, that little significance can be accorded a negative condition. In view of the number of caches which appear to be connected with events in the year 165/66 A.D., it is not unreasonable to assume that the five coins under discussion were buried along with one of the two lots of bronze.

116c. These coins were found together below the floor of room 226, Level I of the Great House. As in the case of the cache constituted by group No. 116a, the latest coin of the group is dated in the ninth month of 165/66 A.D.

117. Among the coins cited are two, published by Petrowicz, which bear dates not found on the examples from Seleucia, 149/50 and 154/55 A.D.

118. The coins of this group were found together below the floor of room 190, Level I of the Great House. The latest coins of the group are of the year 165/66 A.D. Although buried in the same room with group No. 118a, and at the same general time, this cache is distinct from the other. There is a possibility, however, that the silver coins listed under No. 116b above formed a part of this lot.

118a. The coins of this group constitute a cache found below the floor of room 190, Level I of the Great House. The latest date in the group is 165/66 A.D. Forming a part of the cache were a large number of bronze coins with similar types, carelessly struck, but of a fractional denomination. These specimens averaged a little over one gram in weight and about eight millimeters in diameter. Owing to the slight value which attaches to them such coins have not been listed in the catalog.

118b. One of the coins in Petrowicz bears the date 172/73 A.D., not found on the examples of this group from Seleucia.

119. The representation of the king in full figure and mounted as the obverse type of these coins is most unusual. I suggest that the two types constitute details from a common motif — the king on horseback receiving a palm from the standing Tyche. This appears as the reverse type on tetradrachms of Artabanus II (see p. 69, No. 83).

120. The obverse type of these coins is that of group No. 118, the reverse type that of group No. 117. One of the examples cited from Petrowicz bears the date 173/74 A.D., which does not occur on the coins of the group found at Seleucia. The vari-

ation in the weight of the coins has no relation to the sequence of dates.

121. On the coin cited the date has been obscured, but, so far as one may judge from the reproduction, it appears to be similar to that which can be distinguished on the coins from Seleucia. The types of the group are closely related to those of group No. 115 of the reign of Volagases II (see p. 127).

VOLAGASES IV

122. These coins constitute a cache found below the floor of room 192, part of a late occupation of Level I of the Great House. The latest coins in the group are dated in the year 198/99 A.D., with the month dates obscured or off flan. The relationship of the cache to events in Seleucia at this time is discussed on page 235.

As is true of nearly all extant tetradrachms of this reign, on the examples from Seleucia the legends are in large measure off flan. The outer lines at the top and the right are entirely missing on all our specimens. This was due to the general use of flans too small for the dies and points to a change in mint practice and policy under the new administration. Such words of the legend as survive are in many instances hopelessly blundered. The inner line at the right besides the normal form ΟΛΟΓΑΣΟΥ shows the following: ΛΠΛΙ, ΟΛΙ, ΛΟΛΓΑ, ΤΟΣ, ΛΟΑΓ, ΟΛΙΗ, ΛΑΣΙΛ, etc. In the corresponding position at the left for ΕΠΙΦΑΝΟΥΣ appear ΔΙΑΝΟ, ΠΙΑΝΟ, ΕΤΙΦ, ΠΙΦΦ, ΜΗΝΟΣ, ΜΗΝΟΥ, ΔΙΚΑΙ, ΔΙΚΗΟ, ΙΚΟΗ, ΕΥΕΡΓΕ, ΑΟΛΟΓ, etc. Without doubt the engravers responsible for the tetradrachms of Volagases IV copied the legends from earlier coins and were themselves largely or entirely ignorant of Greek. The significance of this fact is discussed on page 235. It is interesting to note that the character phi as a numeral of the date retains its early form, whereas in the legend proper it appears as a simple cross. Similarly the character nu has been reversed in the legend, but not in the date. These and other letters with special forms are reproduced on page 244, Nos. 15, 9, 1, 4, 11, 13, 14, and 17.

123. The representation of the royal bust on the obverse of these coins in the frontal position relates them to the early issues of tetradrachms of this reign, and they were probably struck within the same period (Wroth, 237, Nos. 1–3).

VOLAGASES V

124. These coins formed part of a larger lot of tetradrachms found adhered together in débris of Level I, block A (just north of the Great House). The majority of the specimens could not be disengaged and cleaned. The silver is of an unusually low quality. The coins undoubtedly constituted a cache or hoard. Since those cleaned formed only a small proportion of the total, no estimate can be made of the date limits represented by the lot.

125. The two examples of this group dated in 215/16 A.D. are the latest Parthian coins which have as yet been recovered at Seleucia. Both were found on the surface of the mounds.

2. THE AUTONOMOUS COINAGE

ZEUS AËTOPHOROS

126. Although the dates on these coins are not legible their chronological associations can be determined by other means. The right to issue an autonomous coinage was accorded Seleucia by the Arsacid dynasty (see pp. 218–219); no groups in this coinage, therefore, were struck prior to 141 B.C., when Mithradates I occupied Babylonia for the first time. The privilege of coinage was withdrawn about 24 A.D.; subsequently autonomous types, easily identified, were issued only during periods of revolt when the central authority became ineffective (see pp. 141–142, 143–145, and 216–229). Of the twenty-three autonomous type groups which have been identified as belonging to Seleucia, there are nine on which dates cannot be distinguished. On the basis of monograms, motifs, style, or fabric six of the nine can be assigned to the period beginning with the close of the first century B.C. On the basis of the character of the legend, the form of the edge of the flans, and the denominations the remaining three groups — Nos. 126, 127, and 132 — can well be attributed only to the early Parthian period at Seleucia. For the interval between 141 and the end of the first century B.C. we possess autonomous coins dated in 103/02, 102/01, 99/98, 96/95, 95/94, 88/87, 85/84, 84/83, 72/71, 42/41, 41/40, 38/37, and 32/31 B.C. (see the table, pp. 183–185). It will be remarked at once that between 141 and 103 B.C., 71 and 42 B.C., and 31 B.C. to the close of the century there were long periods for which we have no dated coins. It is

reasonable to assume that the issue of the newly won autonomous coinage would have been especially heavy during the early decades of the Parthian occupation. Two occasions stand out at which in particular it is likely that issues would have been struck — the presence in Seleucia of Mithradates I either upon its initial occupation or after the defeat of Demetrius II, and of Phraates II after the defeat of Antiochus VII.

It is to the first of these two occasions that I suggest the attribution of the group with which we are now concerned. The reverse type of the group reproduces that of a series of drachms of Mithradates I (Wroth, 13, No. 51; 14, No. 57; 15, No. 61). What is apparently the latest issue of these drachms is dated in 138/37 B.C. The assignment of this silver to the mint of Seleucia may be questioned in favor of its attribution to the mint of Ecbatana, for aside from this series, and one assigned by Wroth to Himerus (Prokesch-Osten, 21, No. 4; cf. Wroth, 23, No. 2 and note 2), I believe that no drachms were struck at Seleucia (see the more general discussion on pp. 153–172). I assign the drachms of Mithradates to Seleucia because they share common monograms with a series of tetradrachms (Wroth, 12, No. 48; 14, No. 55; 15, No. 58), and there is no evidence to suggest that any Parthian tetradrachms were struck except in the Seleucia mint (see pp. 153–172). Zeus Aëtophoros occurs as a coin type under Parthian rule only on the series of drachms and on the bronze which is under discussion. The portrayal on a later tetradrachm of the living king Phraates III in the pose of Zeus Aëtophoros represents a different concept (Wroth, 48, No. 25). In the absence of any hostile evidence it appears necessary to assign the two series not alone to a common mint, Seleucia, but to approximately the same date. Added evidence regarding group No. 126 is afforded by the size of the coins. Their average weight and diameter are greater than those of any other group of autonomous coins. The autonomous coinage in turn includes heavier denominations on the whole than occur in the Parthian royal bronze coinage — with a significant exception. A series of bronze of Mithradates I, probably of the mint at Ecbatana, shows weights and diameters closely equivalent to those of group No. 126 (Wroth, 8, Nos. 14 and 15; 9, Nos. 21 and 22). The position in respect to these factors which each of these groups occupies within its class suggests that they are contemporary. On these several grounds, therefore, I have assigned the group under discussion to the reign of Mithradates I, and, within that reign, to the years around 140–137 B.C. The extant examples of the group are not numerous, and it is probable that they were issued within a relatively short period. It should be noted that most of the coins are badly worn. They represent a single denomination, the variation in the weight and the diameter being due in large measure to the wear.

TRIPOD

127. That this group is among the earliest within the autonomous coinage is demonstrated by the form of the letters and the use of the ethnikon in the legend and by the fabric of the coins, which approaches that of Seleucid issues. An attribution of the group to the reign of Phraates II can be based on the relation between the reverse type, the tripod, and that of an issue of tetradrachms of this king which shows Apollo seated on the omphalos (Wroth, p. 16). The evidence obviously is suggestive rather than conclusive, but the attribution satisfactorily meets the need for an issue at this period as well as for an interval during the first few Parthian reigns into which the group may be fitted. The number of the examples of the group which have been recovered suggest that its issue may have been continued over a number of years.

TYCHE NIKEPHOROS (SEATED)

128. Dates can be read on sixteen examples of this unusually large group. On many others traces of dates can be distinguished, and there can be no doubt that they were intended to be read on all the coins of the group. The surviving dates cover the period from 103/02 to 84/83 B.C., but in view of the number of specimens which have been found, there is no reason to doubt that the group was struck over a more extensive period. The reverse type reproduces in a general way that of a series of tetradrachms struck during the reigns of Phraates II and Artabanus I (Wroth, 23, No. 1; 20, Nos. 1–2). Mithradates II, who succeeded Artabanus in 123 or 122 B.C., appears to have spent some time in Babylonia shortly after his accession (see pp. 202–203). I suggest, therefore, that the issue of group No. 128 was inaugurated at, or shortly after, that date. Monogram

No. 44 of this group appears to be that which occurs on tetradrachms of Gotarzes I (assigned by Wroth to an Artabanus II; 38, Nos. 3–4). On the examples of No. 128 which have hitherto been published no dates have been remarked. It should be noted, also, that the group appears to represent a single denomination; the wide variations in weight and diameter are in large measure due to unequal wear. In the reference cited in the catalog Mr. Hill refers to a possible thymiaterion behind the seated Tyche. No such object forms a part of the design on the specimens from Seleucia. Confusion may have been caused by the fact that the rear leg of the throne on some coins gives the impression that it is distinct from the body of the seat.

CORNUCOPIAE

129. On the coin cited no date has been distinguished, but the presence of an obscure monogram on the obverse has been noted. On all the examples from Seleucia the left edge of the obverse, where a monogram would normally appear, has been obscured or is off flan. The dates which are legible on the coins of this group fall in the reign of Sinatruces (*c.* 77–70 B.C.). Since but a few specimens have survived, it is very possible that the issue of this type was confined to the single year 72/71 B.C.

TYCHE AND RIVER GOD

130. On twenty-six coins of a total of seventy-two dates can be distinguished. Since the dates which have survived represent only two successive years, it is probable that the entire group was struck during this period, 42/41–41/40 B.C., in the reign of Orodes II.

Type group No. 130 initiates a number of changes in the autonomous coinage. One remarks a definite decrease in the quality of execution of both obverse and reverse. The legend is circular rather than rectangular. The date for the first time appears in the field rather than in the exergue. In the legend alpha, omicron, and sigma have the forms reproduced on page 244, Nos. 1, 11, and 13. The final letters of the river name and its accompanying particle have been dropped. On some coins a similar degradation marks the name of the city. Of greater significance still is the fact that the city is referred to by the place name rather than by the ethnikon. The changes in the form of the letters and in the position of the date can be noticed on the tetradrachms of this same period. These features and the new shape of the legend indicate simply a development in style. A blundered legend has been noted by Wroth on an issue of tetradrachms of Orodes II dated in 39/38 B.C. (73, No. 37). The significance of the temporary debasement in the quality of the design and of the change in the form of the city name which mark this group of coins is discussed on pages 221–222.

It should be noted that, whereas on the legend proper the sigma is rectangular, on the date it retains the older form. In the date of two numerals the omicron is rectangular, but in that of three numerals it is represented by a large dot. In his description of the coin of this group in the British Museum Mr. Hill makes no mention of any peculiarities in the rendering of the legend. In spite of the great variation in weight among the coins of the group, they appear to represent a single denomination.

130a. These seven coins stand out among those comprising group No. 130 by reason of the particular crudity of their design. There are no grounds for an assumption that they are counterfeit. I can offer no explanation of the fragmentary legend beyond a suggestion that the engravers responsible were ill acquainted with Greek. The alpha has the form referred to under No. 130. It is probable that the coins belong to the same period as does the larger group.

TYCHE NIKEPHOROS (STANDING)

131. The dates which can be read on the coins of this group fall in the reign of Phraates IV. Since specimens of the preceding group, No. 130, were struck as late as 41/40 B.C., it is probable that the new types were inaugurated in 38/37. It will be noted that the coins struck during this year show the date in the field at the left, whereas on the coins of 32/31 B.C. the date is in the exergue. Presumably the group comprised simply two issues struck in these two years.

The design for this group disregards the changes adopted for the engraving of group No. 130, and the quality of its execution is equivalent to that of the earlier autonomous issues. In the date but not in the legend omicron and sigma have the rectangular form. It should be noted that in the reference cited

Imhoof-Blumer reads the place name Σελευκία rather than as the ethnikon, which appears on all the specimens from Seleucia. If the reading published is correct, one may assume that it represents the earliest issue of this type group and that on the succeeding issues the place name was discarded in favor of the ethnikon.

TWO CITY-GODDESSES

132. The large number of examples of this group which have been preserved suggest that its issue extended over a period of years. In the discussion of group No. 126 three principal intervals were noted for which we possess no coins that bear legible dates. Type groups Nos. 126 and 127 were assigned to the earliest interval. On the basis of style, the form of the legend, the quality of execution, and corresponding criteria the group with which we are now concerned might be assigned to either the period 71–42 B.C. or the period from 31 B.C. to the end of the century. Certain other factors, however, favor the later interval. Prior to 71 B.C. the issue of autonomous types appears to have been heavy, and group No. 130, struck at the close of the earlier interval, represents again a heavy issue. On the other hand, after the final striking of this group in 41/40 no unusually heavy issues, aside from that under discussion, occur until about 36 A.D., with the inauguration of group No. 143. Further, it should be noted that the issue of tetradrachms at Seleucia was heavy during the years from 31 B.C. to the end of the century, whereas for the period 71–42 B.C. it was relatively light. In the absence of hostile evidence these factors appear to require the assignment of group No. 132 to the interval between 32/31 B.C. and the succeeding issue of the autonomous coinage, No. 133, which was struck in the opening years of the first century A.D.

The reverse type of the group under consideration is unusual. So far as I have knowledge it is found elsewhere only on an issue of Rhesaena in northern Mesopotamia of the Roman period (Hill, 130, Nos. 28–31; cf. also 131, No. 32). The reverse of a coin of Demetrius II shows a Tyche grasping the hand of a bearded deity (Babelon, XIX, 8). In his description of the type from Seleucia Imhoof-Blumer refers to a turreted headdress. This is an error since both the goddesses are represented with the kalathos. The possible significance of the motif has been discussed on pages 177–179.

MALE DEITY WITH KALATHOS AND LYRE

133. Although no dates can be distinguished on the coins of this group, they show a monogram which appears also on group No. 134, dated in 9/10 A.D. The two groups, that is, must have been struck within the same general period. Since after 9/10 the autonomous issues succeed one another with a fair degree of frequency, group No. 133 must be presumed to have been struck prior to No. 134, which falls in the reign of Vonones I. Since the examples of the group are few, they were probably struck within a few years. Without an attempt to fix a precise date it appears reasonable to assign group No. 133 to the reign of Phraataces, from about 2/1 B.C. to about 4/5 A.D. As do the preceding two, this group retains the ethnikon and the quality of execution of the earlier autonomous type groups.

In the references cited Imhoof-Blumer has largely misjudged the character of the reverse motif, and Hill has described an omphalos-shaped object behind the figure of the type which in reality is simply the base of the cithara. The nudity of the figure, the arrangement of the hair in a knot, and the presence of the cithara strongly support the identification of the type as a representation of Apollo. The presence of the kalathos and the palm fails to harmonize with this attribution, but may indicate that we have here some local concept of this deity.

DRAPED FIGURE ON A THRONE

134. The date, although legible on only one coin, is certain. It identifies the group as of the reign of Vonones I. The term *ἔτους*, which accompanies the date, is found nowhere else in the autonomous coinage, but occurs on tetradrachms of Artabanus II of about the same date (see p. 115, under No. 81). In the legend alpha and sigma have the forms reproduced on page 244, Nos. 1 and 13.

On this group we find again the place name substituted for the ethnikon, as on No. 130 above. The possible significance of the change at this time is discussed on pages 222–223. The significance of the reverse motif is difficult to determine. The figure presumably is symbolic of the city as represented by the particular party in power at this date. The quality of execution is generally inferior to that displayed by the preceding groups, with the exception of No. 130. In connection with this one remarks the carelessness in the placement of the legend. A corresponding lack of care characterized the striking of the coins. Although a wide variation in weight will be noted, they are all of a single denomination.

ANCHOR

135. Two factors in particular serve to distinguish this small group of autonomous coins from those which have preceded. The fabric of the coins is more closely related to that of the Parthian royal bronze which began to be struck at Seleucia in 24/25 A.D. than it is to the fabric of the earlier autonomous issues, and the legend bears simply the name of the city, with no reference to its position on the Tigris River. In the legend alpha and sigma have the forms reproduced on page 244, Nos. 1 and 13. Of the autonomous groups which can be given a date later than that assigned to the coins under consideration, the city name in any form occurs on two only, Nos. 141 and 147, which were issued by a revolted faction within the city (see pp. 141, 145, and 224–229). It is on the basis of these general factors that the group has been assigned a position in the series between groups Nos. 134 and 136. It is assumed, that is, that the coins were struck in some one of the years between 9/10 and 15/16 A.D. These years cover the close of the reign of Vonones I and the inauguration of that of Artabanus II. Since group No. 134 falls in the reign of the former and since it is unlikely that his short and troubled rule at Seleucia would have produced two distinct issues of bronze, group No. 135 has been tentatively assigned to the period between 11/12, the year in which Artabanus first secured control of the Seleucia mint, and 15/16 A.D.

FEMALE BUST WITH KALATHOS AND VEIL

136. With this group of autonomous coins of the reign of Artabanus II all reference to the city is dropped from the legend. The possible significance of the change is discussed on pages 223–224. The legend with the name of the city and of the river appears again only on two groups of the "revolt coinage" of Seleucia, Nos. 141 and 147. In the names of the month alpha and nu have the forms reproduced on page 244, Nos. 1 and 9. Group No. 136 is unique within the autonomous series

because of the presence of month as well as year dates. The conjunction on the same coins of the two forms of the date and of monograms affords important evidence concerning the calendar employed by the mint at Seleucia (see pp. 149–150). Although one of the coins in the group (1.06 gr.) is markedly smaller than the others, it is probable that they represent a single denomination. There is no relation between the variation in weight and the chronological sequence. The coin published by Hill is dated in Gorpiaios, 15/16 A.D.

MONOGRAM AS TYPE

137. The two monograms which appear on the various coins of this group as reverse types occurred on the coins of the preceding group with their normal value, that is, as representing mint controllers. It should be noted, however, that the center upright stroke of monogram 51 on the coins under discussion has been elaborated to form a palm branch. The significance of the use of the initials of mint controllers as coin types has been treated on page 224, note 46. The single word of the legend occurs nowhere else in the autonomous coinage, but in the nominative case is found on group No. 89 of the royal bronze struck at Seleucia (see p. 117). Its significance is discussed on pages 224–226. The sigma of the legend and the stigma of the date have the forms reproduced on page 244, Nos. 13 and 18. The reference in the catalog is to a coin dated in 15/16 A.D. The coins of the group represent a single denomination.

THE KING AS ZEUS NIKEPHOROS

138. In the absence of a date which can be read the chronological position of this group can be determined by other factors. With this group we are approaching the close of the period in which the right of Seleucia to strike its own bronze was recognized by the Parthian administration. On its reverse for the first time in the autonomous coinage appears a representation of the reigning Arsacid. It is perhaps significant that he is portrayed as deity (see pp. 219–221). The same reverse type is found on the second issue of the new royal bronze, No. 85, dated in 25/26 A.D. The fabric, also, of the coins under consideration is that of the new royal issues. It is evident that the group must be placed among the latest of the autonomous series. Two

groups, however, Nos. 139 and 140, must be assigned to the very end of the period. On their obverses the usual head or bust of Tyche has been replaced by seated figures of the city-goddess suggestive of reverse rather than obverse types. They exemplify the change from the autonomous to the royal coinage. Since group No. 139 bears the date 18/19, and since we already have issues struck in 16/17, group No. 138 has been assigned to the year 17/18 A.D. In the reference in the catalog Hill has assigned a coin of this type to the second century A.D. (cf. Hill, cxvi). This is entirely unnecessary since in respect to both style and fabric the coins are closely related to the earliest royal bronze struck at Seleucia in the first half of the first century A.D., examples of which were unknown to Mr. Hill. It should be noted that the reverse type of the group is in all essentials that of tetradrachms of Phraates IV struck at Seleucia in 27/26 B.C. (Wroth, 102, Nos. 13–17).

THE KING RECEIVING A DIADEM FROM TYCHE

139. The reverse motif of this group is that of tetradrachms of Phraataces dated in 2/1 B.C. (Wroth, 136, Nos. 1–4). The motif recurs on the silver with the accession of Gotarzes II in 44/45 A.D. The obverse of this, as of the succeeding group, has the appearance of a reverse type. Indeed Hill, in the passage cited in the catalog, has referred to the type which shows the seated Tyche as the reverse, and that which represents the king with Tyche as the obverse. Actually groups Nos. 139 and 140 were struck during the period which was marked by the transition from the autonomous to the royal bronze coinage at Seleucia. This transition was symbolic of a fundamental change in the relationship of the city to the dynasty, a change which, however, did not constitute an act of hostility on the part of the dynasty (see pp. 223–224) and for which, therefore, there could have been little precedent. That the nature of the sovereignty expressed by the coin types is obscure can reasonably be explained by the fact that the status of the city was itself in doubt at this time. On the coin published by Hill the date is apparently off flan. It should be noted that the quality of execution of this group is mediocre and is characterized by a peculiar style in the representation of the drapery. This can be observed on the reproductions both in this volume and in the catalog of the British Museum.

THE KING SEATED ON A THRONE

140. The peculiar character of the obverse of this group has been discussed under No. 139. There is a definite relationship between the motif of the obverse on the group under discussion and that of the reverse on group No. 134 (see p. 102). This is expressed principally by the character of the figure and by the form and the position of the staff or scepter held by the figure. The reverse type of group No. 140 probably represents a detail from the common reverse motif of the tetradrachms — the king seated and receiving a diadem or palm from Tyche. This group is the latest in the regular series of autonomous types. Issues with civic types which were struck at later dates represent either revolt coinages or coins struck by the loyalist party in the city at periods when the royal power had become ineffective. These circumstances are discussed on pages 224–226 and 228–229.

HUMPED BULL

141. In the absence of dates on these coins their chronological position must be established by other criteria. Their fabric is of poor quality and differs from those characteristic of the regular autonomous series and of the royal bronze. The execution of the design is likewise distinctly inferior to that of the preceding groups. The reverse type portrays a motif which though similar in form is entirely unrelated to that of early coins of Seleucus I (see p. 7, No. 11), but is characteristic of the Oriental glyptic art of the period with which we are now concerned. It represents, therefore, the influence of Oriental culture in Seleucia at this time. These factors which are all foreign to the regular autonomous coinage suggest strongly that group No. 141 was unconnected with that series. Four of the coins in the group formed part of a cache which contained a majority of specimens dated in 43/44 A.D. (group No. 143). In addition, a large number, in some instances comprising caches, were found in various rooms of Level III of the Great House, occupation of which came to an end about 43 A.D. A faction in the city held Seleucia in revolt during the years from about 36 to 40 A.D. (see pp. 224–226). All the factors are satisfied by the assignment of group No. 141 to this period, and this classification has been adopted for the purposes of this volume. It is assumed, that

is, that these coins were struck by the mint of Seleucia while that institution was held by a group within the city which was in revolt against the legitimate Arsacid succession. Since other types make their appearance in 40/41 the specific date limits of the group can best be fixed at 36–40 A.D. The fact that the examples number 153 presupposes that they were struck during each year of the period. Beyond this, however, the large total supports the assignment of the group to a rebel government. The evidence points to the existence of an ample coinage already in circulation upon the inauguration of group No. 141. The purpose of the heavy striking, therefore, must be presumed to have been largely political — the replacement of the old types with one more expressive of the cultural sympathies of the new government. One should note the recurrence of the legend on this revolt coinage after it had disappeared from the normal autonomous issues. In the legend alpha, epsilon, sigma, and upsilon have the forms reproduced on page 244, Nos. 1, 5, 13, and 14. Although it is difficult to fix a division point, it is probable that the coins of this group comprised two denominations.

NIKE WITH PALM

142. The quality of both the fabric and the execution represented by these coins is markedly superior to those features not only of the preceding group but of groups Nos. 139 and 140. In these respects they show a close relationship to the royal bronze of Vardanes I struck in 43/44, 44/45, and 45/46 A.D. (see p. 71, No. 89). On the latter we find associated the royal bust and a personification of the Boule, the council of the aristocratic party at Seleucia. These various factors appear to require the assumption that the group of autonomous coins with which we are now concerned was not issued under the same authority as the three preceding groups, and that the Nike motif was intended to commemorate the victory of the loyalist, aristocratic party which prepared the way for the resumption of the Arsacid rule in the city. The situation is discussed in further detail on pages 224–226. The exact date of the death of Artabanus II is not known, and the issue of group No. 142 may have been inaugurated either in the closing years of his reign or with the opening of the reign of Vardanes I. The alpha of the date has the form reproduced on page 244, No. 1. There is no relation

between the variation in the weights of the coins of this group and their chronological sequence.

THE DEIFIED KING

143. The obverse type with its seated figure in place of a head or bust is in a general way similar to those of Nos. 139 and 140 above. Just as the types of these two groups expressed the transition from the autonomous to the royal coinage prior to the revolt, group No. 143 represents the change from the autonomous issue which succeeded the revolt, No. 142, to the initial issue of the royal bronze after the central authority had been reëstablished. That is, there appears to have been again a certain hesitation on the part of those responsible for the choice of the coin types which would portray to the public the immediate relationship between Seleucia and the Arsacid dynasty. The reverse type is somewhat unusual. The general pose of the figure is that characteristic of Zeus. The garment appears to be a robe rather than tunic and trousers. The head, however, is typically Parthian. I suggest that we have here an assimilation of the reigning king to Zeus such as is represented by the reverse of No. 138 (see p. 104), and that this again illustrates the effort which was being made throughout this general period to arrive at a satisfactory basis for the relationship of Seleucia to the dynasty (see pp. 219–221). Group No. 143 must have been struck early in 43/44, since for the same year we have two groups of royal bronze, Nos. 88 and 89. Of the coins in this group twenty-three, along with four examples of No. 141, were found together in Street 36, below Level II of the Great House.

EAGLE

144. Although a date cannot be distinguished there is no indication that the coins of this group were not intended to show dates. Their chronological relationship to the series of coins with civic types must be determined by general factors. The motif of the reverse is characteristically Oriental of the first and second centuries A.D., and is foreign to the stock of motifs from which were drawn the reverse types of the regular autonomous issues. In this respect the group is related to the revolt coinage struck just prior to 40 A.D. (see p. 106, No. 141), on which the humped bull is shown. In fabric and in style, how-

ever, the group is later and suggests a relationship with the issues of royal bronze struck during the latter part of the first century. Type groups Nos. 145 and 146, which will be discussed just below, are characterized by Oriental motifs and by a style and fabric generally similar to that of group No. 144. The three groups, which revived the civic types given up in the reign of Artabanus II, must be classed as revolt coinage struck during the period of unrest which marked so much of the reign of Volagases I (see the more detailed discussion of this situation on pp. 228–229). Since the latest of the revolt issues is followed immediately by a loyalist issue, No. 148, group No. 144 must be placed at the outset of the revolt. Probably as a result of the disturbed conditions in Seleucia, no tetradrachms were struck between 58/59 and 61/62 A.D. The earliest examples of group No. 145, of the revolt coinage, were struck in 59/60. To this same year, therefore, I assign group No. 144. Since it is represented by only nine extant examples, it was probably limited to a single striking and was then superseded by group No. 145.

ARTEMIS

145. The presence of legible dates for the years 59/60 and 61/62 suggests that coins of this group were struck also in 60/61. Prior to 59/60 no bronze had been struck at Seleucia since 47/48 A.D. in the reign of Gotarzes II (see table on p. 190), and it must be presumed that a real need for new currency had arisen. In view of this condition the fact that only thirty-seven coins of group No. 145 have been preserved suggests that its issue was limited to a short period. The character of this group as a part of the revolt coinage struck during the reign of Volagases I has been discussed elsewhere (see pp. 228–229). On the basis of this character it is reasonable to assume that group No. 145 was struck only during the three years, 59/60–61/62, for which no tetradrachms are known. The reverse type is significant in view of the conditions under which the group appears to have been struck. Artemis represented originally, of course, an Anatolian religious concept adopted by the Greeks. Throughout Babylonia and Iran, however, this goddess had become assimilated to local forms of deity and in the first and second centuries A.D. represented a concept fundamentally much more Oriental than Greek, although clothed in Greek form. In fabric, style, and

quality of execution, group No. 145 is closely related to the succeeding group, No. 146. In spite of the wide variation in weight and size the group represents a single denomination.

HUMPED BULL

146. The fact that, out of a total of forty-seven in this group, the twenty-seven coins which show a legible date are all of the year 69/70 A.D. requires an assumption that the entire group was struck in this year. The reverse type is that of the revolt coinage issued between 36 and 40 A.D. (see p. 106, No. 141), but the style is entirely distinct in spite of a common crudity of execution. One cannot logically escape the conclusion that, although separated in time by a full generation, the two groups were struck by individuals who possessed a common cultural background. As has already been stated, group No. 146 is closely related to group No. 145 through a common quality of execution, style, and fabric. The significance of the relationship between the three groups is discussed on pages 228–229.

TYCHE SEATED ON A COLUMN

147. Although struck in the course of the same year this group differs from No. 146 in the presence of the legend and in the style, fabric, and quality of execution. The legend emphasizes the practical state of autonomy in which the city found itself at this period, but suggests no change in this respect subsequent to the issue of the two preceding groups; the three groups, through their use of the civic type for the obverse rather than the portrait of Volagases I, reveal in equal measure the failure of the royal administration to enforce its authority in Seleucia upon the occasion of their minting. The other distinctions are more significant and suggest that two different elements within the city were responsible for the issue of the two groups, Nos. 146 and 147. The suggestion is measurably strengthened by the fact that, in contrast to the preceding two groups, No. 147 has a reverse motif drawn from the stock which supplied the autonomous coinage prior to its abrogation under Artabanus II. It should be noted further that the monogram found on the group under discussion occurs also on the first issue of the royal bronze of Volagases I, struck later in the same year (see p. 75, No. 95). These two groups are similarly related in

respect to form and to the character of the bronze. The significance of these attributes of group No. 147 is discussed on page 228.

NIKE WITH WREATH

148. Although no date can be distinguished on the coins of this group, through certain factors it can be established that the issue was struck in 69/70 A.D. A detailed similarity exists between its reverse type and that of group No. 96 of the royal bronze which bears this date (see p. 75). In addition, the two groups are related through fabric and style. In these respects group No. 148 is also related to No. 147 above, likewise dated in 69/70. There can be no reasonable doubt, therefore, that the group under discussion was struck immediately after the other issue of civic types and shortly before the group of royal bronze. The concentration of issues in this one year is discussed on page 228. The relation of group No. 148 to the revolt coinage of this period is treated on the same page. It represents the latest issue of coins with autonomous types which has been found at Seleucia.

CHAPTER VI

THE PARTHIAN MINT AT SELEUCIA

1. THE CALENDAR EMPLOYED

NO DATED coins of the Seleucid period have been recovered at Seleucia, and it is to be presumed that the practice of placing dates on coins — at least those of bronze — was adopted by this mint from Syria or Phoenicia only after the occupation of Babylonia by the Parthians. Seleucia was the only mint of the Parthian Empire which followed this practice.[1] Dates first appear in the reign of Mithradates I, after 141 B.C., but irregularly; they occur on the majority of coins struck during the last half of the first century B.C. During this same period the tetradrachms begin to show month dates as well as year dates. Within the next half-century the use of dates became the invariable practice of the Seleucia mint.[2] Although the original idea was developed by the Phoenician mints, Seleucia appears to have been responsible for the technique of noting both the month and the year of issue. In the early period certain Parthian tetradrachms bear dates, and others, having similar types, lack the date. The value of the date on coins appears to have been primarily that of a serial number; it distinguished successive issues and strikings. In the beginning the first issue of a given type was struck without regard for the date, whereas, apparently, the second issue was given a date to distinguish it from the first. As issues became more numerous and frequent, it was a natural development to record the year on all issues and to employ the names of the months to distinguish the emissions within a single year.

The Seleucid Era differed from other eras in that the date from which were calculated the regnal years of the first king, Seleucus, was not replaced by the accession year of each succeeding king, but continued to serve as the fixed point for the era throughout the Seleucid period. The innovation, indeed, was so practical that as a popular institution the era far outlived the

[1] See pp. 157–158 and 167–168. [2] See pp. 189–200.

empire. As Bouché-Leclercq has pointed out, the Seleucid Era was instituted in Babylonia, and from there its use spread to Syria and the west.[3] The fixed point was the first New Year after the return of Seleucus to Babylonia as an independent ruler in fact if not in name. This took place in the early spring of 311 B.C. The Babylonian new year was inaugurated with the month Nisannu, corresponding generally with our April. The era, therefore, was originally based on Nisannu 1 (*c.* April 1), 311 B.C. After the Seleucid administration became centered in Syria, the fixed point appears to have been calculated from that Macedonian New Year which fell closest to the actual date of the accession of Seleucus, Dios 1 (*c.* October 1), 312 B.C. We have, therefore, a variation of about six months between the Babylonian and Macedonian calendars as applied to the Seleucid Era, and in transposing dates from that to the present era it becomes important to know which calendar was employed.

In the publication of Parthian coins it has generally been assumed that the dates on the coins are to be calculated on the basis of the Macedonian calendar. There is no question but that the Seleucid Era was employed by the Parthian mint of Seleucia. That they used the Macedonian calendar, however, is pure assumption. The exclusive use of the Babylonian calendar for the dating of tablets demonstrates the hold this system retained over the mass of the population of Babylonia. There is no evidence to suggest that the Seleucid administration east of the Euphrates imposed the western calendar for either popular or official use. The system of reckoning dates employed by the Babylonians of the Seleucid period was scientifically superior to that of the west. The Babylonian New Year represented an event much more important in the tradition and consciousness of the east than was true of the corresponding day among the Greeks. From every aspect the burden of proof appears to rest on those who assume that in the Seleucid period the Macedonian calendar was employed in Babylonia, either for official purposes or by the general public. I find no grounds for belief that the Arsacid dynasty would have preferred Babylonian usage in any respect to the Greek; there is nothing to indicate that the Parthian ruling class sensed a necessity for loyalty to eastern as opposed to western culture. Except where there is definite

[3] *Histoire de Séleucides*, II, 516–517.

evidence to the contrary, one must assume that the Parthians adopted the local administrative practices of each area which they conquered. In short, I suggest that the mint at Seleucia during the Parthian period employed the Babylonian calendar because the evidence available points to this system of reckoning as the standard at the moment of occupation of Babylonia by the Parthians.

Certain of the coins from Seleucia present concrete evidence that the Babylonian calendar was employed by the Seleucia mint in the dating of coins for the years 15/16 and 16/17 A.D. They comprise group No. 136 in the autonomous coinage.[4] The British Museum possesses an example with a month date not found on the specimens from Seleucia.[5] The value of the coins lies in the fact that they bear monograms — representing mint controllers — and month dates as well as the year dates. It should be noted that the position of the dies on all these coins varies in accordance with the particular monogram which they bear. It must be assumed that the monograms divide the group into two classes which are mutually exclusive in point of time. The coins of the group can be arranged successively according to the Babylonian and the Macedonian calendars, as follows:

1. *By the Babylonian calendar*

Year	Monogram	Dies	Month	
326 A.S. 15/16 A.D.	[monogram]	↑ ↓	Gorpiaios	5th month (Hill)
		↑ ↓	Hyperberetaios	6th "
		↑ ↓	Apellaios	8th "
		↑ ↓	Audynaios	9th "
	[monogram]	↑ ↑	Peritios	10th "
		↑ ↑	Dystros	11th "
		↑ ↑	Xandikos	12th "
327 A.S. 16/17 A.D.	[monogram]	↑ ↑	Artemisios	1st "
		↑ ↑	Panemos	3rd "
		↑ ↑	Peritios	10th "

[4] See p. 103, and note on p. 138.

[5] Hill, p. 145, No. 41.

2. *By the Macedonian calendar*

Year	Monogram	Axes	Month	Order	
326 A.S. 15/16 A.D.		↑ ↓	Apellaios	2nd month	
		↑ ↓	Audynaios	3rd "	
		↑ ↑	Peritios	4th "	
		↑ ↑	Dystros	5th "	
		↑ ↑	Xandikos	6th "	
		↑ ↓	Gorpiaios	11th "	(Hill)
		↑ ↓	Hyperberetaios	12th "	
327 A.S. 16/17 A.D.		↑ ↑	Peritios	4th "	
		↑ ↑	Artemisios	7th "	
		↑ ↑	Panemos	9th "	

The interchange of monograms required by the Macedonian calendar would mean that two individuals relieved each other in the office of mint controller every second or third month — an untenable conclusion. There can be little question that in the dating of this group of coins the mint employed the Babylonian calendar. It cannot be assumed that the Seleucia mint would employ one calendar in connection with the autonomous coinage and another for the royal coinage. The dates as substitutes for serial numbers were of primary value to the mint officials, and any calendar would have served their purpose; presumably they employed that with which they were most familiar. Nor can it be assumed that the use of the Babylonian calendar at the date with which we are concerned was the result of a change in national sentiment during the century and a half of Parthian rule. The group of coins which have served as evidence was struck under the order of the Boule, the council of Seleucia traditionally representative of the aristocratic and Hellenic elements in the city.[6] The city still enjoyed autonomy with a large measure of self-government.[7] I suggest, therefore, that in the absence of any indication pointing to Parthian interference with local practices or to the use of the Macedonian calendar in the east at any time, the coins must be accepted as reasonable evidence that the Babylonian calendar was employed by the mint at Seleucia throughout the Parthian period. One may well conclude, indeed, that the practice of the mint was followed by the city administration and the general public.

[6] See pp. 223–224. [7] See p. 224.

Dr. Jotham Johnson of the University of Pennsylvania has recently published an important study of the calendar employed at Dura-Europos.[8] This system of reckoning time he terms the "Seleucid Calendar" and describes it as differing from the Babylonian only in the selection of the fall rather than the spring equinox as the fixed point which determined the inauguration of the new year. The material collected by Johnson demonstrates the strength of the Babylonian practice in the area west of the Euphrates to a late period. It is important to note further that the sponsor of this importation from Babylonia must have been the administration of the Seleucid Empire.

Of particular interest is the evidence pointing to the insertion of an extra intercalary month in the cycle of Greek months, with the result that, whereas formerly Artemisios had corresponded with Nisannu — the initial month of the Babylonian year —, now this position was occupied by Xandikos. This change, according to Johnson, took place "at some moment between 229 B.C. and the *floruit* of Josephus." [9] The question naturally arises whether this shift can be remarked in the dating of the coins from Seleucia. According to it Xandikos became the initial month by the Babylonian calendar, Hyperberetaios by the Macedonian calendar. If this change is assumed for the group of coins which has just been examined, we get the following unsatisfactory results:

1. *By the Babylonian calendar*

Year	Monogram	Month	
326 A.S. 15/16 A.D.		↑ ↑ Xandikos	1st month
		↑ ↓ Gorpiaios	6th "
		↑ ↓ Hyperberetaios	7th "
		↑ ↓ Apellaios	9th "
		↑ ↓ Audynaios	10th "
		↑ ↑ Peritios	11th "
		↑ ↑ Dystros	12th "
327 A.S. 16/17 A.D.		↑ ↑ Artemisios	2nd "
		↑ ↑ Panemos	4th "
		↑ ↑ Peritios	11th "

[8] *Dura Studies*, I, 1–15.

[9] *Ibid.*, p. 15.

2. *By the Macedonian calendar*

Year	Monogram		Month	
		↑ ↓	Hyperberetaios	1st month
326 A.S. 15/16 A.D.	[monogram]	↑ ↓	Apellaios	3rd "
		↑ ↓	Audynaios	4th "
	[monogram]	↑ ↑	Peritios	5th "
		↑ ↑	Dystros	6th "
		↑ ↑	Xandikos	7th "
	[monogram]	↑ ↓	Gorpiaios	12th "
327 A.S. 16/17 A.D.	[monogram]	↑ ↑	Peritios	5th "
		↑ ↑	Artemisios	8th "
		↑ ↑	Panemos	10th "

The confused interchange in the monograms and in the fixation of the dies which results from this adjustment of the calendars requires an assumption that at Seleucia in 15/16 and 16/17 A.D. a shift had not taken place in the correlation of the Greek and the Babylonian months.

A different picture is presented by a group of bronze coins struck at Seleucia by Gotarzes II.[10] They are dated in the year 357 A.S., 46/47 A.D., and bear in addition the names of months. Since the Babylonian calendar was in force thirty years previously, the dates on these coins must likewise be reckoned by it. The two columns which follow represent the sequence of the months named in the group, in the first correlated conventionally, in the second shifted as suggested by Johnson.

1. *Conventional*		2. *Johnson's Intercalation*	
Artemisios	1st	Xandikos	1st
Daisios	2nd	Artemisios	2nd
Panemos	3rd	Daisios	3rd
Loos	4th	Panemos	4th
Gorpiaios	5th	Loos	5th
Hyperberetaios	6th	Gorpiaios	6th
Xandikos	12th	Hyperberetaios	7th

It should be noted that the same type of coin continued to be struck in the succeeding year, 47/48 A.D., but on these the month dates were omitted. The group constitutes the sole occurrence of month dates on Parthian royal bronze. Although the exact significance may not be determined, it is unlikely that

[10] See p. 73, No. 92, and note on p. 119.

coins of this unique character would have been issued at two disconnected intervals within a single year. It is possible that coins were struck in each of the twelve months of this year and that the absence of examples for five months is due to chance. However improbable it is that an unbroken sequence covering six of the twelve months should have been preserved and for five consecutive months no examples recovered, this factor of uncertainty cannot be disregarded. The coins do not constitute proof that between 16/17 and 46/47 A.D. the correspondence of the Greek months with the Babylonian had been shifted at Seleucia as indicated. Their evidence does support, however, an assumption of such a change.

Quite apart from the coins, in the absence of concrete evidence to the contrary concerning Seleucia, the very fact that the intercalation had been accepted at Dura appears to me to require the assumption. One must bear in mind the background. The shift in the correspondence of Greek and Semitic months cannot have been the product of political forces alone — the edict of an administration. We are concerned neither with the political nor with the economic interrelationship of Seleucia and Dura. Rather, the change constituted simply an example of a particular adjustment between two great cultures which, intermingled in each local area, jointly united all the peoples from the Mediterranean to the Iranian plateau. Granting that the shift took place at Dura, as the evidence adduced by Johnson appears to require, the fact of the change must be postulated for the entire region dominated by Graeco-Semitic culture. Because of these general factors, supported as they are by the coins from Seleucia, I have transposed the month dates on coins referred to in the present volume, beginning with 46/47 A.D., to accord with the correspondence of Xandikos with Nisannu as the initial month of the year. Actually the change may have taken place at any time between 16/17 and 46/47 A.D. Throughout the volume the dates on coins of the entire Parthian period, whether found at Seleucia or cited from other publications, have been calculated on the basis of the Babylonian calendar.

2. CLASSES OF COINS STRUCK

The allocation of ancient coins to particular mints and mint areas constitutes an essential element in the preparation of more general historical studies. The extant coins of the Parthian period already published form a body of material which, owing to its great size and the wide extent of the area from which it was obtained, must approximate a fair representation of the complete Parthian coinage, in respect to both chronological and geographical distribution. Attempts to assign this material to individual mints have in large measure failed because of the almost total absence of known factors upon which to base a study of the mints. The coins from Seleucia, coming as they do from a single well-stratified site which represents one of the principal cities of the empire, themselves establish certain facts and, in addition, aid in classifying the body of general material in respect to the characteristics which distinguish the issues of the various mints. In studying the published coins of Parthia I have employed the standard works cited in the Bibliography, but for the distribution of the coins to particular reigns I have generally followed the arrangement supported by Mr. Warwick Wroth, with a few modifications suggested by Mr. E. T. Newell and others.[11]

The coins of the Parthian period from Seleucia which have been included in this volume total 2,330. Of these 453 are tetradrachms, none are drachms, 826 are of the royal bronze, and 1,051 are bronze with civic obverse types. As a basis for the determination of the mint associations of the various classes of currency here represented, the following premises may be made: (1) The series of autonomous coins which bear the name of the city constitute proof that a mint existed at Seleucia during the Parthian period; (2) So far as the bronze coins are concerned, types of which at least three examples have been recovered in the excavations must be assumed to have been issued for circulation in the Seleucia area; (3) Since Seleucia possessed a mint, bronze coins which were intended to circulate in this area must be assumed to have been struck locally.

Eleven of the type groups of the autonomous coinage which have been listed in the catalog are not identified by the use of the city name as a part of the legend. That they were minted at Seleucia is evidenced not only by their satisfaction of the conditions laid down above but by the relationship of their types, legends, monograms, and style to other coins of the local

[11] See the Bibliography, pp. xiii–xiv.

mint. Of the known groups of coins with civic obverse types which appear to have been struck within the Parthian Empire, three are not represented in the series from Seleucia. Published references to these groups assume, at least tentatively, that they were minted at Seleucia.[12] The first has as reverse type Tyche Nikephoros seated left with a river god at her feet. This is a variation of group No. 130 found at Seleucia. No date appears, and the legend bears the single word πόλις. The second group lacks a type figure and shows on the reverse only the legend ΔΚΣ|ΔΙΟΥ|Α, the first day of the month Dios (the seventh month by the Babylonian calendar), 88/87 B.C. The third group, represented so far as I know only by a single specimen, has as reverse type either the figure of a dolphin or the head of an elephant. An obscure date is probably equivalent to 23/24 A.D. The style and the quality of execution of this coin correspond to those of other contemporary types from Seleucia, and it may well represent a light issue of the local mint.

The other two groups appear to be closely related in style and are probably of a single mint. This style, however, is definitely not characteristic of the coins from Seleucia for any period. Further, they appear to have represented heavy issues which, if struck locally, would almost certainly have contributed to the series found in the excavations. The peculiar elements present in the two groups — on the one the reference to a particular form of civic organization, on the other the replacement of the reverse type by a particular date — render doubtful their acceptance as representative of autonomous coinage struck in the exercise of a normal fiscal policy. I suggest that the two groups with which we are now concerned, although used as currency, constituted nonreplaceable commemorative medals rather than media of exchange. The date on the one marked not only the first day of the Macedonian year but the equivalent of the first of the month Tashritu, which was a Babylonian festival of some importance. On the other the presence of the term *polis* suggests that the issue celebrated the acquirement by some community of more formal civic rights. Viewed primarily as medals

[12] Hill, p. 142, Nos. 7–15; pp. 143–145, Nos. 19–40; p. 145, No. 42. I disregard, of course, the large number of civic coins of the Roman period struck by cities which had formerly been part of the Parthian Empire. Mr. E. T. Newell informs me that the first two of these groups appear to have been struck in Iran. See Preface, p. viii.

rather than as currency, they might be assigned to any one of a number of Babylonian cities which did not possess the right of autonomous coinage, but which may well have been granted the privilege of an especial commemorative issue. Whatever the value of these groups they do not constitute evidence that any Parthian city other than Seleucia maintained its own currency. In the complete absence of such evidence the further premise is established that the relation of the mint at Seleucia to the Parthian administration differed from that of the other mints in the empire.[13] The mint cannot logically be dissociated from the city as an active political force within the empire. One cannot state that the royal government maintained a mint in Seleucia; rather, Seleucia struck and issued coinage, whether royal or civic, for the Parthian government.

There is no evidence to indicate that the abrogation of the right to possess its own coinage was caused by or resulted in an estrangement between the dynasty and the traditional ruling class in Seleucia which, except for a short interval, had controlled the mint since Seleucid days. By all the evidence, indeed, the abrogation took place almost simultaneously with the consummation of an alliance between this group in the city and the dynasty.[14] There is no basis, therefore, for an assumption that the shift from a bronze currency with civic obverse type to one with the royal portrait as type constituted a break in mint policy or tradition. The shift took place about 24 A.D., in the reign of Artabanus II. Just prior to this date a marked change had occurred in the style of engraving employed for the obverse of the royal bronze currency which had circulated in those parts of the empire not served by the Seleucia mint. It involved a simplification of the design and the indication of the hair by straight lines which are almost vertical.[15] The royal bronze which began to be issued at Seleucia in place of the autonomous coinage presented, on the other hand, a style of obverse which was copied closely from the contemporary tetradrachms. The hair lay in formal rows and on both the head and the beard

[13] A more extended discussion of the status of Seleucia under the Parthians will be found on pages 216–229.

[14] See the more detailed discussion on pages 223–224, where is pointed out the significance of the interrelation of the latest autonomous and the earliest royal types.

[15] See pp. 161–162.

emphasized horizontal lines. Of the 826 bronze coins with royal obverse types included in our catalog, two single coins fail to follow the style of the tetradrachms, and they alone show the simplified design characteristic of the other Parthian mints.[16] These two specimens obviously are not of the Seleucia mint and were not intended to circulate in that area. The homogeneous character of the royal bronze struck at Seleucia is not limited to factors of style. With the exception of the two "foreign" coins noted, all bore dates. Only five of the type groups show a reverse motif other than some representation of the city-goddess.[17]

The 824 coins which are related by the factors cited above constitute thirty-one type groups. Three of these, Nos. 85, 97, and 99, are represented by single coins; another, No. 108, has two examples. There cannot be the slightest doubt that the twenty-seven larger groups circulated in Seleucia and were minted in Seleucia. This being so, the close relationship of the other four groups to the large majority requires an assumption that they, too, were products of the local mint.

It should next be noted that no type groups are known to exist which conform to the factors characteristic of the Seleucia royal bronze, but which are not included among the coins from the site. The bronze coinage of Parthia is abundantly represented in all the principal catalogs. This includes, naturally, a few individual examples of the thirty-one types from the Seleucia mint, duplicates of which have not as yet come to light from among the quantity of coins from the excavations. A few others have as reverse type some representation of Tyche, but executed in a style foreign to that of the series from Seleucia and accompanied by an obverse portraying either a king who reigned prior to 24 A.D. — when at Seleucia only civic types were struck — or one of the later kings — but in a style and quality of execution which set it apart from the portraits engraved at Seleucia. One issue of Phraates IV should be noted.[18] The reverse shows a bust of Tyche and a date equivalent to 32/31 B.C. At this

[16] Osroes struck bronze at Seleucia but no silver. He introduced momentarily a style foreign to the tradition of all the Parthian mints and himself appears to have been an interloper on the Arsacid throne. His reign is discussed further on pages 231–234.

[17] No. 85 (p. 69) reproduces a reverse from the tetradrachms; No. 89 (p. 71) shows a personification of the city council; No. 96 (p. 75), Nike with wreath, copied from an autonomous issue; No. 97 (p. 76), an eagle; No. 99 (p. 77), a deity head.

[18] Wroth, p. 128, Nos. 231–235.

period Seleucia still possessed the right to issue her own coinage, and for this very year we have a group with civic types, No. 131. Further, the style of the coins is entirely different from that characteristic of the Seleucia mint, and there can be no doubt that they were struck elsewhere in the empire. Among the great number of groups of the royal bronze from mints other than Seleucia which have been published, this one alone bears a date. The evidence presented by the general body of Parthian coins clearly requires the additional premise that the factors characteristic of the royal bronze from Seleucia do not occur together on the issues of any other Parthian mint.

We are now in a position to formulate certain statements with regard to the bronze currency of the Parthian Empire. It falls into two distinct classes: that of Seleucia and that of the other mints. Seleucia was the only Parthian city which possessed an autonomous coinage. All coins of the empire which bear a civic obverse type must be presumptively assigned to the Seleucia mint unless definite evidence to the contrary can be established. To mints other than that at Seleucia must be attributed all bronze coins which have as the obverse type the portrait of one of the kings who reigned prior to 24 A.D. All bronze coins later than this date must be assigned to Seleucia if their obverse portraits are styled after contemporary tetradrachms and if they were intended to show dates; to the other Parthian mints must belong all coins of this later period which display on either the obverse or the reverse a style and quality of execution that are foreign to the Seleucia issues and which were apparently not intended to show dates.[19]

It has been stated above that 453 Parthian tetradrachms have been found at Seleucia, but no drachms. These facts permit of only one conclusion, that the larger silver was in common use locally, the smaller, rarely or never. It follows, of course, that drachms were not minted at Seleucia except, perhaps, some rare and very light issues of which examples have not yet been uncovered. It is generally assumed, and rightly, that the Seleucia mint regularly struck tetradrachms. I believe, however, that it

[19] The bronze of the other Parthian mints followed closely the style characteristic of the drachms which is described on pages 159–165. Distinctions between the bronze coinage of Seleucia and of the other Parthian mints based on fabric cannot be discussed in the present volume.

is possible to proceed a step farther and to demonstrate that, with the exception, perhaps, of the earliest issues, Parthian tetradrachms were struck only at Seleucia. The conclusion is based on the essential dissimilarity of the two classes of silver, on the homogeneity of the tetradrachms and their relation to the bronze struck only at Seleucia, and on the relation of the drachms to the bronze of the other Parthian mints. An examination of the general body of published Parthian coins suggests certain fundamental points of distinction between tetradrachms and drachms. In particular I refer to (1) the position of the head on the obverses, (2) the arrangement of the hair of the head and beard on the obverses, (3) the motifs of the reverses, (4) the quality of execution of the types, (5) the quality and the content of the legends, (6) the presence or the absence of dates, (7) the character and the use of monograms, and (8) the relative abundance of the tetradrachms and drachms. The significance of most of these factors has been pointed out by earlier writers. Little effort has been made, however, to follow the evidence through to a logical conclusion.

The position of the head on the obverses

On the Seleucid and Bactrian coinages to which the Parthians succeeded the head is regularly turned right, although the frontal position was frequently chosen for bronze of the Seleucia mint.[20] The earliest Parthian coinage — drachms and bronze of Mithradates I (171–138/37 B.C.) with the beardless head on the obverse — broke away from this tradition and pictured the obverse head turned left.[21] Tetradrachms began to be struck only toward the close of the reign. On them, and on three series of drachms and bronze, probably contemporary,[22] the head faces right after the Seleucid tradition. This change was coincident with the expansion of Parthian territory to include Ecbatana and Seleucia. Immediately upon the death of Mithradates I the obverse of the drachms reverted to the style adopted for the earliest Parthian coins.[23] On the tetradrachms, on the other

[20] See pp. 47–48.

[21] One issue in this series (Wroth, p. 5, (vi)), probably the latest, has the obverse head turned right.

[22] Wroth, Pls. II, 1–5; II, 6–13; III, 8–9, 11, 13.

[23] As the sole exception should be noted an issue of drachms attributed by Wroth to Himerus (p. 23, No. 2), which may well have been struck at Seleucia.

hand, the head turned right continued to appear until the accession of Mithradates II (123/22–91/90 B.C.), under whom took place the first consolidation and organization of the empire. Thereafter the Parthian practice became general for all classes of the royal coinage, except for the occasional appearance of frontality on both tetradrachms and drachms.[24] The distinction between the two denominations of silver in respect to the positions of the obverse heads is supported by a corresponding distinction in the reverse type of the silver of Phraataces (2/1 B.C.–4/5 A.D.). On these issues the bust of the queen is shown on the reverse, on the tetradrachms turned right, on the drachms, left.[25]

The arrangement of the hair of the head and beard on the obverses

On the Parthian coinage minted in the earlier part of the reign of Mithradates I the head on the obverse is shown covered, and the face clean-shaven. Thereafter, throughout the Parthian coinage, the kings were represented as bearded and, generally, with the head bare. On the latest series of the issues of Mithradates I the hair of the head and beard was executed in a style distinctly naturalistic. Two techniques, however, can be distinguished. On the series which shows the obverse head turned left the hair is represented by rather fine, almost straight lines, which emphasize the vertical strokes. The other series of late coins of Mithradates, with the head turned right, emphasizes curly tufts of hair — a technique characteristic of contemporary Hellenistic engraving and sculpture. It recurs on a tetradrachm of Phraates II (138/37–128/27 B.C.).[26] This naturalistic tendency did not long survive; by the reign of Mithradates II (123/22–91/90 B.C.) one observes what appears to be a deliberate effort toward formalism, especially noticeable in the treatment of the beard.[27] In the reigns of Gotarzes I, "Arsaces," and Orodes I [28] (*c.* 91–*c.* 77 B.C.) further experimentation developed the technique of representing the hair by formal rows. A culmination was reached with the portrait of Orodes, which differs

[24] Frontality, so far as I know, never occurs on both classes of silver at the same time except in the reign of Volagases IV. What mint other than Seleucia employed this style cannot be determined at the present time.

[25] Wroth, Pl. XXIV, 1–3.

[26] *Ibid.*, Pls. III, 2–6; III, 7–13; IV, 1.

[27] *Ibid.*, Pl. VI, 5–11.

[28] *Ibid.*, Pls. VIII, 12; VIII, 11; VIII, 10, and IX, 1. Wroth assigned these coins to an Artabanus II. See discussion on pages 206–210.

markedly in style from that of Gotarzes. The unit in each row was the individual tuft of curly hair noted in respect to one of the series of Mithradates I, but the curl had now become entirely formalized. The rows emphasized horizontal rather than vertical lines, and came to be applied to the beard as well as to the hair of the head. The similarity of this technique to that employed on Assyrian and Achemenid sculpture is obvious. It appears, nevertheless, to have been an independent outgrowth of attempts to follow a naturalistic style of the Hellenistic west. The formalism was a recognition of the practical limitations in the way of a successful application of this style to coin engraving by the personnel available in Parthia.

The formalistic treatment of the hair reached a climax on the coins of Orodes II (57–38/37 B.C.) and Phraates IV (38/37–2/1 B.C.). Both denominations of silver were equally responsive to this development. On the tetradrachms, however, the individualism of portraiture was maintained to a large extent and, within a given reign, was uniform, whereas at least as early as the reign of Phraates IV the appearance of the drachms suggests that engravers of sufficient skill and feeling were not generally available. In the succeeding reigns, of Phraataces (2/1 B.C.–4/5 A.D.), Vonones I (9/10–12/13 A.D.), and Artabanus II (11/12–*c.* 40 A.D.), a distinct reaction took place and a wide break developed between the style of the tetradrachms and that of the drachms. On the former the horizontal lines of the rows continued to be emphasized, although on certain issues the formalism has been relaxed. The individuality of the portrait has perhaps been increased; certainly there was no lessening in the complexity of the design.[29] For the drachms the case is entirely distinct. The coins of this denomination of Vonones I have undergone a marked simplification in design.[30] Of immediate concern is the fact that on both the head and the beard the formal rows, with their emphasis on the horizontal, have been replaced by fine lines, nearly straight and with the emphasis definitely on vertical strokes. In contrast with contemporary tetradrachms, the formalism of expression has been retained to the detriment of the individuality. For the preceding reign, of Phraataces, a bronze coin exists that is characterized by the new

[29] Wroth, Pls. XXIII, 10; XXIV, 1, 6; XXV, 2–6.

[30] See below, pp. 164–165.

technique,[31] which, in all probability, was initiated in that reign. Actually the technique was not new but was a redevelopment, either conscious or unconscious, of that which had appeared briefly on a late series of Mithradates I,[32] as well as on scattered succeeding issues. By the accession of Vardanes I (*c.* 40/41–45 A.D.) there had taken place a stabilization in techniques of obverse style which survived to the end of the Parthian period. The tetradrachms retained the complicated design of formal horizontal rows, the drachms, the no less formal but greatly simplified design which emphasized the nearly straight and vertical lines of the hair.[33]

The motifs of the reverses

The reverse type of the earliest Parthian silver, drachms, portrayed a male figure in Parthian dress seated right on an omphalos, presumably the deified founder of the Arsacid dynasty. The omphalos in time was replaced by a throne. Though its prototype is obviously Seleucid, the motif is a definitely Parthian contribution to the stock of reverse types. With only four short-lived exceptions throughout the entire Parthian period, the drachms were marked by the uninspired repetition of this type.[34] In contrast to the uniform monotony of the drachms, the tetradrachms from the moment of their inauguration toward the close of the reign of Mithradates I developed a wide variety in motif, and finally became stereotyped only after the passage of more than two centuries. With a single exception to be noted below, the typically Parthian motif of the drachms was copied for the tetradrachms only during the period from the accession of Mithradates II, 123/22 B.C., to a point early in the reign of Orodes II, shortly after 57 B.C. During this interval the issue of tetradrachms was light and of relatively little importance. Prior

[31] Wroth, Pl. XXIII, 13.

[32] See above, p. 160.

[33] As an exception should be noted certain drachms of Volagases I which follow the lines of the tetradrachms. See Wroth, Pl. XXVIII, 15–16. I suggest that the obverse dies for this issue had been prepared at the mint for the tetradrachms, Seleucia, and forwarded to the mint where the drachms were struck, probably Ecbatana. See p. 165, note 41.

[34] The exceptions follow: issues of Mithradates I with reverse of Zeus Aëtophoros (Wroth, Pl. III, 8–9, 11, 13); of Himerus with reverse of Nike (*ibid.*, Pl. V, 10); of Phraataces with the portrait of the queen on the reverse (*ibid.*, Pl. XXIV, 2–3), and of Vonones I with Nike as reverse type (*ibid.*, Pl. XXIV, 7).

to this period the tetradrachms of Mithradates I, of Artabanus I, and of Phraates II had borrowed their reverse types directly from the Hellenistic coinages — Hercules, Apollo, and Tyche Nikephoros. Phraates III (*c.* 70–57 B.C.) for one of his issues discarded the seated bowman type and struck tetradrachms which portrayed him as Zeus Aëtophoros crowned by the city-goddess.[35] With the second coinage of Orodes II the issue of tetradrachms became, and thereafter remained, much more frequent and heavy than had heretofore been the case. This development was accompanied by the introduction of a new reverse in which the king, portrayed as a mortal, is shown with Tyche, the city-goddess. Occasionally, thereafter, the new type was replaced by one representing the king as Zeus. In special issues Phraataces employed again the bowman type and the portrait of his mother, Musa, and Vonones I celebrated his victory over Artabanus.[36] Of particular significance, however, is the fact that when the new type of the king with Tyche was repeated in a number of issues the individuality of each type was maintained by the introduction of distinctions in the details of the motif. This is in direct contrast with the early and complete acceptance of an unvarying design for the reverse of the drachms. The tetradrachms became stereotyped only in the reign of Pacorus II (78–115/16 A.D.) with the type of the king in the act of accepting a diadem from the standing Tyche. It should be noted finally that, with the exception of the rare use of the reverse copied from the drachms, all the varied motifs employed on the tetradrachms are either largely or entirely Hellenistic Greek rather than Oriental in concept, and that the portrayal of the city-goddess as a part of the motif on the great majority of the tetradrachms beginning with the reign of Mithradates I points to a special relationship between this class of silver and the city of Seleucia.[37]

The quality of execution of the types

Throughout the duration of the empire the quality of execution of the obverse and the reverse of Parthian tetradrachms remained approximately uniform in respect to one another. A

[35] Wroth, Pl. XI, 1.

[36] *Ibid.*, Pls. XV, 1–2; XVIII, 17; XXIII, 11; XXIV, 1, 6.

[37] See the discussion of the significance of this motif on pages 219–221.

decrease in quality can be remarked between the earlier and the later periods, but it was constant in progression and operated equally upon both types. Within a given reign no significant distinction in the quality of the various issues can be remarked.[38] With regard to the drachms the situation is entirely different. In the period of Mithradates I the obverse and the reverse displayed an approximately equivalent degree of artistry, but with the standardization of the reverse motif under Mithradates II a distinction developed in this regard which widened with each successive reign. The stereotyped design of the reverse dies came to be executed by men of little manual skill and little or no feeling for the symbolism which they were supposed to portray. Each copied the work of his predecessor, and the results departed farther and farther from the original concept. There is no relation whatsoever between the decrease in quality of the tetradrachms and that of the reverse of the drachms in respect to either the rate of decrease or the ultimate result. The obverse portraits on the drachms from the reign of Mithradates II to that of Phraates IV (38/37–2/1 B.C.) not only were similar in style to the design of the tetradrachms but, in most instances, maintained a general equivalence in the quality of execution. One must except, naturally, certain coins which were imitations of Parthian issues and which were struck beyond the Parthian borders.

With the reign of Phraates IV there becomes noticeable a change in the quality of the engraving of the royal portraits on the drachms. Though following the style of the tetradrachms, as a whole they suggest the efforts of copyists and on some the portraits become caricatures.[39] The tendency continued in the next reign, that of Phraataces, whose portrait on the drachms entirely lacks the individuality of that on the larger silver and represents a much lower quality of execution. In the reign of Vonones I which followed, the complicated design for the portrait which continued to characterize the tetradrachms was abandoned for the drachms. In its stead we find an extreme simplification

[38] A certain variation may occur even within a single issue, caused by a lack of uniformity in the dies. Some appear to have been the product of assistants rather than of master engravers. This tendency is particularly noticeable in the caches of tetradrachms and in the large groups of the autonomous bronze. There can be no question here of a plurality of mints.

[39] Wroth, Pls. XX, 6; XXII, 9–12; also others.

of design which required a minimum of strokes and which preferred straight lines to curves.[40] The hair was represented by vertical lines, and where curves were required, as for the loop of the diadem, they were large. This change in style can only have been an acknowledgment of reality. The mints for the drachms could no longer attempt even to copy the work of the engravers responsible for the tetradrachms. Therewith the quality of execution of the obverse types of the drachms fell to the level of that of the reverse, and this equivalence on a far lower standard than that of the tetradrachms was maintained throughout the rest of the Parthian period.[41]

The quality and the content of the legends

The quality of the Greek in the legends is nearly as significant as the quality of execution of the types in demonstrating the existence of essential distinctions between the tetradrachms and the drachms. We are not concerned with variations in the forms of letters consequent upon changes in standards of orthography which were general throughout the East, but with peculiarities in the formation of letters and in the spelling of words which indicate an ignorance of good contemporary Greek. Except during one definitely limited period the legends on the tetra-

[40] See above, p. 161.

[41] An explanation must be offered for the maintenance of a high standard of engraving for the royal portraits on the drachms until the reign of Phraates IV while, during the same period, the reverses for the most part were cut by mechanics and for the general equivalence of this standard to that of the tetradrachms. It cannot reasonably be assumed that both obverse and reverse dies for the drachms were prepared by the same hands or in the same mints. Orodes II, the predecessor of Phraates IV, had moved his principal capital from Iran to Ctesiphon. Both these kings, and most of their successors as well, were occupied in large measure by affairs in the west, whereas the eastern part of the empire demanded little attention. Presumably, in consequence, less of the royal time was spent in the east and less interest was taken in its administration. I suggest that it had previously been customary to prepare the dies for the obverse of all the royal coinage in Seleucia where the tetradrachms were struck and that so long as the kings were resident in Iran the obverse dies for issues intended to be struck in Iran were sent to the court for inspection and thence distributed to the various mints. Naturally some degree of variation would characterize each die within a given reign, but all would maintain a certain uniformity. I suggest further that, once the court was thoroughly established in the west with the reign of Phraates IV, the mints of the east were left to prepare the obverse dies of the drachms locally, that the local engravers copied the design for the portrait of Phraates from the tetradrachms but with indifferent success, and that with the accession of Vonones a simpler design was inaugurated for the drachms which was more in keeping with the capacity of provincial engravers.

drachms are entirely satisfactory from their inauguration under Mithradates I to the close of the reign of Volagases III, from about 141 B.C. to 192 A.D. Beginning with the latest issue of Orodes II, of 39/38 B.C. down to the latest issue of Artabanus II, of 27/28 A.D., a few blunders in spelling occur together with a more frequent use of debased forms for certain of the letters. This period is followed by the first revolt at Seleucia. With the first issues of Vardanes I, the successor of Artabanus, the quality of the legends again became entirely satisfactory according to contemporary standards.[42]

On the drachms debased forms of letters and blundered legends made their appearance as early as the reign of Mithradates II. Blunders and barbarities increased with each succeeding reign. It is evident that before the end of the first century B.C. the engravers of the drachms were for the most part ignorant of the Greek language. With the appearance of a legend in Pehlevi alongside the barbarous Greek in the second half of the first century A.D. one understands that the western characters had become only a part of a meaningless design. It is important to note that from the reign of Mithradates I through that of Volagases III debased and peculiar forms of letters which occur on one of the two denominations of silver are not found on contemporary examples of the other denomination. As has been stated above, these observations do not apply to such normal developments as the rectangular sigma and corresponding forms.

The variations in the content of the legends as between the two denominations of silver possess a significance, especially if regarded collectively. During the reigns of Mithradates I, Phraates II, and Artabanus I the legends of the tetradrachms consistently differed from those of the drachms. The title Philhellenos appears on most of the tetradrachms, but never on the drachms; the latter favor the term Theopatoros, which never occurs on the former. As usual, the drachms display a wider variation among themselves than do the tetradrachms. During the next reign, of Mithradates II, the legends are uni-

[42] On the issues for 43/44 and 44/45 A.D. the letter phi of Epiphanous has been omitted, a temporary slip which cannot be attributed to ignorance of Greek. The cause of the debasement in the legend during the particular period noted is discussed on pages 221–226. The change in the quality of the legend which followed the overthrow of Volagases III by Volagases IV is discussed on page 235.

form save for the appearance on the greater number of the drachms of the title King of Kings, absent from the tetradrachms. After the death of Mithradates II distinctions in the legends again became prevalent, with certain titles more generally characteristic of the one denomination than of the other. It is only with the later coinage of Orodes II, after his installation of the court at Ctesiphon, that a common legend for both drachms and tetradrachms was definitely determined and thereafter retained. These conditions require the conclusion that in the earlier period the form of the royal title on the coins was determined by local considerations in each principal division of the empire, and that distinctions which persisted over a considerable interval imply that the classes of coins so distinguished were struck in different areas. Uniformity was sought by such rulers as Mithradates II, the first Arsacid to attempt a serious organization of the central administration, and Orodes II, who continued the reorganization inaugurated by his father, Phraates III. This later enforced uniformity serves to emphasize the separation of the mints for tetradrachms and drachms in the early period.

The development of the term "King of Kings" during the reign of Mithradates II should be noted. His tetradrachms appear to have been struck during the early part of the reign, when Mithradates was engaged in the organization of the western part of the empire. The numerous drachms which bore the new title were first struck when the power of Mithradates reached its zenith, that is, after his reëstablishment of the Parthian frontiers in the east and the north. If it had been the Parthian practice to issue tetradrachms in the eastern provinces, where Mithradates undoubtedly maintained his headquarters at this time, certainly types of this, the more important denomination of silver, would have been struck in commemoration of the assumption of the paramount title.

The presence or the absence of dates

In the Parthian coinage dates first make their appearance in the latter part of the reign of Mithradates I on a series of tetradrachms and drachms struck at a common mint, probably Seleucia.[43] Another dated drachm assigned by Wroth to Himerus

[43] Wroth, pp. 14–15, Nos. 55–61. See also the discussion of the attribution of these coins on page 132.

is also of the Seleucia mint.[44] Aside from these two special issues of the Seleucia mint, no dated drachms are known for the entire Parthian period. In direct contrast with this the use of dates on the tetradrachms, irregular in the earlier reigns, became the regular practice with the reign of Phraates IV and, thereafter, they invariably form a part of the design.[45]

The character and the use of monograms

Of the various factors which demonstrate the fundamental dissimilarity of the two denominations of Parthian silver none, perhaps, affords such emphatic evidence as the usage in respect to monograms. On the tetradrachms monograms are numerous during the earlier reigns, prior to that of Orodes II. With this reign the issue of this class of silver became frequent, and with that of his successor the practice of placing dates on the tetradrachms became common. Coincident with these developments the use of monograms decreased sharply. Although both dates and monograms appear on a few issues, as a rule the latter are confined to those tetradrachms which lack the date. With the reign of Vardanes I monograms disappear entirely and thereafter are never found on the tetradrachms.[46] There can be no question but that the monograms on this class of silver represented the names of mint officials.

On the early drachms monograms appear at least as frequently as on the contemporary tetradrachms and with each succeeding reign during the early period their use became more common. The monograms which occur on the drachms up to the close of the reign of Phraates III (*c.* 70–57 B.C.) had a character similar to that of the monograms on the other silver, that is, they represented the names of individual mint officials. Although the use of monograms was so general on both classes of silver during this entire period, with one exception no monogram found on an example of the one class is known to occur on coins of the other class. The exception is constituted by the

[44] Wroth, p. 23, No. 2 and note 2. See also discussion on page 202.

[45] On one issue of Artabanus II (Wroth, p. 146, Nos. 2–7) no date can be distinguished, but it was apparently intended to be shown. See discussion on page 115, under No. 81. The purpose served by dates is discussed on page 147.

[46] With this same reign is inaugurated the practice of placing on the obverses of the tetradrachms a single letter or numeral, which did not stand for the name of an official but perhaps referred to an office in the mint.

series of tetradrachms and drachms of Mithradates I referred to above as the product of the Seleucia mint.[47] In contrast to the usage on the tetradrachms, after the reign of Phraates III the drachms almost without exception continued to show monograms to the end of the Parthian period. Their value, however, was now fundamentally changed. They cannot have represented individual officials, for on the drachms of each succeeding reign were reproduced the same monograms which had characterized those of the reign of Phraates III. With the passage of time some of the monograms disappeared, but they were not replaced by other new letter combinations. The steadily diminishing examples of the original group continued to serve all the drachms issued until for the latest reigns only one survived. We cannot escape the conclusion that the monograms on the drachms of the reigns which followed that of Phraates III had the value of mint marks. That is, each mint for the drachms was represented by a particular monogram. Since this practice was limited strictly to the one class of the silver coinage, the force of the evidence afforded by the monograms is readily seen.[48]

The relative abundance of tetradrachms and drachms

A comparison of the rates of issue of the two classes of silver at various periods serves not only the purposes of the present discussion but others of a more general historical nature.[49] A practical value is given such a comparison by the fact that it is based, in the case of Parthian coins, on the very large number of examples which have been published. In calculating the rates I have made use of those catalogs which for the most part are based on separate collections, and I believe that to a reasonable degree the figures are representative of the total issue of each

[47] See discussion on pages 167–168.

[48] In explanation of the change in the character of the monograms I suggest a fact which has often been proved true in the more backward parts of the present-day Orient — that the public objects seriously to any change in the appearance of the currency. It is very possible that a certain group of officials had been left in charge of the mints of the drachms over a long period, that the public became accustomed to the appearance of their initials in monogram, and that the administration decided to retain this set of monograms as the marks of the respective mints. It must be borne in mind that in Iran at that period few users of the currency would have been able to read the legend; to the great majority it was the monograms which indicated the authenticity of the coins.

[49] They are discussed on pages 219–221.

class of the silver in particular periods. The use of these data for our present purposes is based on the assumption that major changes in the rate of issue of currency at a time when the services of banks as we know them were unknown must have been caused by a corresponding expansion or contraction in the activity of commerce. A corollary assumption has been that, if the two classes of silver circulated in common areas, their rates of issue would respond in a similar manner both to the stimulus of economic change and to the repressive influence of internal strife.

From the inauguration of the issue of tetradrachms about 141 B.C., shortly after the occupation of Babylonia by Mithradates I, to a point in the reign of Orodes II (57–38/37 B.C.) this class of silver was struck only at irregular intervals and in extremely small quantities. Probably toward the close of the reign of Orodes what is called his second coinage introduced new and varied types, approximately contemporary, and at the same time the rate of issue advanced sharply. This trend culminated during the reigns of his successors, Phraates IV and Phraataces, from 38/37 B.C. to 4/5 A.D., in a rate approximately five times the average of that of the period prior to the second coinage of Orodes II. There followed a long period of intermittent civil strife which was brought to a close only about 130 A.D. As a result, during intervals the production of tetradrachms decreased and for as long as twenty-five consecutive years ceased entirely.[50] When, however, a particular royal administration was able to maintain its strength over a number of years, the rate of issue rose abruptly to figures apparently comparable to those of the peak. From about 130 A.D. to the period of final internal decline, which set in with the close of the reign of Volagases IV, about 208 A.D., the rate appears to have remained uniformly high, probably not appreciably under that of the earlier peak. It should be noted that in respect to the proportions in which they occur the tetradrachms found at Seleucia support the figures obtained from an analysis of the general body of material.

The coinage of Parthian drachms appears to have been inaugurated with the accession of Mithradates I about 171 B.C. From the beginning the issues were numerous and moderately

[50] The political events of this period are discussed on pages 229–234.

heavy. A slow steady increase marked the rate during the succeeding reigns until that of Phraates III. During this reign and that of his successors, Mithradates III and Orodes II, from about 70 to 38/37 B.C., the production of drachms was abruptly increased about three times. During the next reign, however, that of Phraates IV (38/37–2/1 B.C.), the rate dropped back to approximately the average level for the period prior to 70 B.C. Thereafter, to the close of the empire and without apparent reference to the conditions which affected the production of tetradrachms, the rate of issue of drachms remained uniform at a lower figure than that which had characterized the early period.

It is evident from this analysis that a graph of the rate of issue of the drachms has nothing in common with one based on the production of the tetradrachms. Both show periods of rapid expansion, but these were not contemporary and appear to have been produced by two different stimuli.[51] Natural causes tended to sustain the rate of production of the tetradrachms at a high level, although at times political forces operated to lower this level temporarily. On the other hand, the forces which had raised the level of production of the drachms for a period apparently ceased to function and the rate fell back to a new low, which does not appear to have been affected by the political factors which had influenced the rate of the tetradrachms. These distinctions in themselves would make unreasonable an assumption that the two denominations of silver circulated to a significant extent in common mint areas.

Of the eight principal factors of distinction between the tetradrachms and the drachms which have just been discussed, certain ones apply most significantly to the early period, others to the middle and the later periods. Taken together, the evidence afforded by these factors reveals, I believe, distinctions so fundamental and at the same time so comprehensive as to require the conclusion that the two classes of Parthian silver were not struck in common mints except for certain strictly limited exceptions.

As exceptions should be noted the series to which reference has already been made — tetradrachms with reverse of Hercules and drachms with reverse of Zeus Aëtophoros struck by Mithradates I near the close of his reign.[52] Because of their common

[51] The reasons for these major increases in circulation are discussed on pages 219–221.

[52] Wroth, pp. 12–15, Nos. 48–61.

monograms the two series must be assigned to the same mint. These tetradrachms are among the earliest struck under Parthian rule, and it is possible that this one series of the heavy silver was a product of the Ecbatana mint, though I can find no evidence to support such an assignment. It was issued just after the reoccupation of Seleucia which followed the defeat of Demetrius II — a particularly appropriate moment for an issue of coinage by the new administration in what had been the Seleucid capital in the East. The reverse motif of Hercules was a favorite one in Bactria, but no less so in Characene to the south of Seleucia;[53] it is of no assistance, that is, for a determination of the mint. The reverse type of the drachms, on the other hand, is closely similar to that of a group of autonomous coins of the Seleucia mint.[54] This fact, taken with the general evidence requiring the attribution of the tetradrachms to the local mint, has led me to assign this series of drachms to Seleucia. As the only additional exception I have tentatively attributed to the mint at Seleucia the group of drachms which Wroth assigned to Himerus and which have as reverse a Nike with palm.[55] Like the drachms of Mithradates I which have just been discussed, these coins differ in style from all other contemporary drachms. In addition, on the obverse the head is turned right, as on the contemporary tetradrachms, whereas all other drachms struck after the death of Mithradates I show the head turned left.

It will be well to consider here whether any evidence suggests that Parthian tetradrachms were struck in more than one mint. Several factors strongly support the contrary assumption. It has already been noted that mint marks were developed for the drachms with the close of the reign of Phraates III, about 57 B.C. If there had been more than one mint for the tetradrachms, it is reasonable to expect that they would have been distinguished in a corresponding manner. The absence of mint marks, that is, constitutes important evidence indicating a single source for this class of the silver. Mr. E. T. Newell has pointed out that in the Seleucid Empire certain provincial mints placed identifying marks on their issues, whereas the principal mint at Antioch

[53] S. W. Grose, *Catalogue of the McClean Collection of Greek Coins*, III, 407, Nos. 9685, 9687; 410, No. 9705; G. F. Hill, *Catalogue of the Greek Coins of Arabia, Mesopotamia and Persia*, pp. 289–302.

[54] See p. 94, No. 126.

[55] P. 23, No. 2.

did not. He noted further that the same practice prevails in the United States.[56] Under the Seleucidae, although the mint at Seleucia was active, at least in respect to the bronze coinage, it employed no identifying mark.[57] This may well have been due to the fact that the city was the second capital. Whatever its status in the early Parthian period, the Seleucia mint enjoyed the primacy by the close of the reign of Orodes II, when the principal capital was established in the west and the issue of tetradrachms assumed a major importance. The evidence indicating the fabrication of the obverse dies for the drachms at the mint of the tetradrachms during the early period and the special privileges enjoyed by Seleucia in respect to the autonomous coinage both suggest that from the beginning of the Parthian period a ranking position was accorded the local mint. Since in the development of their coinage the Arsacids drew upon Seleucid practice for many features, it is most likely that under the new administration the Seleucia mint continued its earlier practice and employed no distinguishing mark because its absence signified that this was the principal mint. This suggestion serves to explain the absence of mint marks from the tetradrachms and again points to their issue exclusively at Seleucia.

It has already been noted that monograms appear on the tetradrachms less frequently than on the drachms. Yet in one instance the former show a number of monograms within the same year. They occur on a type group of Artabanus II for the year 27/28 A.D.[58] and, taken by themselves, would suggest that the group represented the issues of several mints. One of the monograms is similar to that which served as one of the principal mint marks on the drachms, but this is probably due to an accidental similarity in initials. Although it was unusual to employ several different controllers for the issue of a single type group, this explanation of the plurality of monograms is preferable to an assumption that during one year of the entire Parthian period tetradrachms were struck in a number of centers which at no other time had possessed mints for this class of silver and only one of which was among the recognized mints for the drachms.

[56] *The Seleucid Mint at Antioch,* pp. 3–4.

[57] Very few Seleucid tetradrachms have as yet been recovered in the excavations.

[58] Wroth, pp. 148–149, Nos. 20–32. In a letter to the author Mr. E. T. Newell has offered the suggestion that the monograms on the coins of this group stand for various months, that is, they take the place of month dates. See Preface, p. viii.

During the reign of Phraates IV tetradrachms with variant reverse types appeared within the same year, in some instances within the same month.[59] This situation by itself would also suggest that at least during this period tetradrachms were struck in a number of mints. However, in no other respects do these coins show distinctions which would favor such a conclusion. If another reasonable explanation exists for the variation in types, the absence of anything in the nature of mint marks on the coins overweighs the suggestion in favor of a plurality of mints. The period of these coins is that marked by the rapid and very extensive increase in the minting of tetradrachms, which has been noted elsewhere.[60] Prior to the inauguration of this expansion in the last years of Orodes II the few tetradrachms which were struck had borne the reverse of the drachms.[61] The expansion and the appearance of a variety of new reverse types were coincident with the concentration of the interest of the Arsacids in the western part of the empire which aimed at an economic, and perhaps a military, penetration toward the Mediterranean.[62] Both these objectives required a large increase in the coinage of tetradrachms, the unit of silver preferred in Syria and its borderlands. At this same period there probably took place a renewal of what I have called the alliance between the Arsacids and the Greek commercial aristocracy of Seleucia.[63] The reverse motif which became the new standard for the tetradrachms — the city-goddess with her scepter offering a palm or a diadem to the reigning king — was intended, I believe, to portray this alliance. Beyond Seleucia this reverse, along with its variations and that other contemporary type which represented the king as Zeus Nikephoros, was more acceptable to the tastes and the traditions of the peoples outside the western border of Parthia than would have been the motif of the drachms. Considering these various factors one cannot well escape the conclusion that the apparent confusion in the selection of reverse types during the reign of Phraates IV was due (1) to the search for a type which would express the relationship between the dynasty and the powerful Greek element and which would be well received by the popula-

[59] See table on pages 184–186. Cf. p. 164, note 38, a reference to possible variations in the quality of engraving within a single mint.

[60] See pp. 169–171.

[61] See p. 162. [62] See pp. 219–220. [63] See pp. 220–221.

tion in the west who were just coming under Parthian influence and (2) to the necessity for a rapid expansion in the circulation of tetradrachms which could not wait for a final decision on the question of types.

Aside from the appearance at one period of variant reverse types within the same year and month, and, at another period, of a plurality of monograms within the same year, no characteristics of Parthian tetradrachms suggest that they were the product of more than one mint. The net evidence strongly supports the fact of their essential homogeneity. Even more conclusive is the evidence that the tetradrachms were not struck in the mints which issued the drachms. This consideration by itself appears to require the assumption that Seleucia was the sole mint for this class of silver. Additional and very practical evidence is afforded by a comparison of the characteristics of tetradrachms with those of the bronze struck at Seleucia. The issue of tetradrachms and of the autonomous coinage was inaugurated at the same time, shortly after the capture of Seleucia by Mithradates I, and the first three type groups of the one class are related to the corresponding three groups of the other class through common factors in their reverse motifs.[64] At a later period, when the civic types were giving way to the royal, the autonomous coinage borrowed two reverse types from the tetradrachms.[65] Again, during the early period tetradrachms and autonomous bronze of the period of Gotarzes I bore a common monogram.[66] The temporary debasement of the quality of the legend on the tetradrachms, which has been discussed above, was paralleled on the autonomous coinage during the same period and, apparently, owing to the same causes.[67] The word *ἔτους* used with the date appears in the entire coinage of the Parthian period only twice — on tetradrachms and autonomous coins of the approximately contemporary reigns of Vonones I and Artabanus II.[68] With respect to common elements in style, so far as it is possible to compare the civic types in bronze with the royal types in silver,

[64] See pp. 131–132, 133, 133–134.

[65] See p. 139, No. 138; p. 140, No. 139.

[66] See p. 133, No. 128. The absence of further examples of common monograms lacks significance in view of the fact that the poor condition of the greater part of the bronze has rendered obscure many of the details of the design.

[67] See discussion on pages 221–222.

[68] See p. 115, No. 81; p. 137, No. 134.

contemporary tetradrachms and autonomous coins display no dissimilarity.

The close relationship between the royal bronze struck at Seleucia and the contemporary tetradrachms has already been touched upon. Its evidence is decisive for the period beginning with 24 A.D. The invariable use of dates and the common treatment of the royal portrait characteristic of the two classes require their attribution to a single mint, Seleucia, and set them off as entirely distinct from the contemporary drachms and the rest of the Parthian bronze which followed the style of the drachms. The distinctions between the silver and the bronze of the Seleucia mint area and the silver and the bronze of the other Parthian mints which are so clear cut after 24 A.D. are no less real in the period prior to that date. The autonomous bronze of Seleucia is set off against the royal bronze of the other Parthian mints. The tetradrachms, related to the autonomous bronze by every factor of comparison which can be drawn, are in all significant respects entirely dissimilar to the drachms. Finally, the royal bronze of the period prior to 24 A.D., and in Iran later, followed the drachms through each development in style, technique, quality of execution in design and legend, and in the monograms used and the value which they possessed. All the factors involved, if carried to a natural conclusion, support the hypothesis advanced at the beginning of this discussion, that the Parthian tetradrachms were struck exclusively at the mint of Seleucia and that, with certain enumerated exceptions, the drachms were struck exclusively in the other mints of the empire.

This geographical separation of the two classes of silver harmonized entirely with the monetary traditions and the habits of the ancient East. The siglos, the larger silver unit of the Achemenid period, weighed on an average only 5.38 grams. Under the Seleucid kings the use of tetradrachms became general throughout the East, but by the close of the reign of Antiochus III, about 187 B.C., the drachm had surpassed in popularity the heavier silver.[69] This shift in the comparative rates of issue, which increasingly marked all subsequent Seleucid coinage in Iran, affords a definite indication that the economy of the country made the small unit more suitable. The earlier Bactrian

[69] This information I owe to the kindness of Mr. E. T. Newell, who, however, does not necessarily share my conclusions.

successors of the Seleucid line in the eastern portion of Iran continued to strike tetradrachms, but by the reign of Heliocles (*c.* 150–125 B.C.) the local units of currency had apparently regained favor.[70] This was only shortly after the organization of the currency system of Parthia. In southern Iran Persis inaugurated an independent currency which included tetradrachms until only about 150 B.C.[71] In the coinage of Elymais, lying between Persis and Babylonia, silver tetradrachms disappeared by the first century A.D.; in that of Characene, adjoining Elymais and Babylonia on the south, perhaps a little earlier.[72] To the west of Babylonia, in Syria and its adjoining territories, the use of tetradrachms continued late into the Roman period. Here was the center which throughout appears to have inspired a demand for the heavy silver. In Iran this demand was artificial, a creation of political ties. In Babylonia there was undoubtedly a local demand for tetradrachms, but beyond this they were a necessity if Seleucia was to compete successfully with Antioch and the other cities of the west for the trade of the great areas along the Euphrates and in northern Mesopotamia which lacked mints of their own. Before Parthian tetradrachms began to be struck in abundance Babylonia continued to use the stock of Seleucid tetradrachms which had been in local circulation and, in addition, those which undoubtedly were forced out of circulation in Iran with the development of the Parthian drachms. It will be shown in another section that Parthian tetradrachms began to be minted extensively only when relations with Syria took on an especial importance.[73] These various factors demonstrate that the limitation of the minting of drachms to the eastern provinces, and of tetradrachms to the western part of the empire, was in no sense arbitrary, but was rather the expression of a natural economic demand.

3. THE LIMITS OF THE MINT AREA

A word is necessary at this point with regard to the relationship between Seleucia and Ctesiphon. I find no evidence to indicate that Ctesiphon ever possessed a political entity distinct from that of Seleucia. In the Seleucid period it was a suburb,

[70] Grose, *op. cit.*, III, 409, No. 9702, and others.

[71] Hill, *op. cit.*, p. clxx.

[72] *Ibid.*, pp. 247–250, cxcviii.

[73] See discussion on pages 220–221.

important probably as a warehouse center where were unloaded the caravans from Iran and beyond, preparatory to the transfer of the merchandise across the river by boat. A similar district must have occupied the western suburbs of Seleucia to serve the caravans from Syria and Phoenicia. With the Parthian occupation it is doubtful if any immediate change took place in the status of Ctesiphon. Strabo has referred to the quartering of the troops there out of consideration for the sensibilities of the Seleucians.[74] That the court spent the winters there, as Strabo states, is probably not true of the period prior to the reign of Orodes II. It was undoubtedly a garrison center from the time of the Parthian occupation; that it was preferred in this respect over Seleucia was due to military rather than social considerations. Both exercises and actual operations, especially for an army which included a large proportion of mounted troops, must have been difficult to carry out in the area between the Tigris and the Euphrates, cut up as it was by a network of canals. This was true to a much less degree on the east bank of the Tigris. The topographical factors again must have played an important rôle when under Orodes II and thereafter the Arsacids found it necessary to concentrate their attention on the western portion of the empire. Not only was Ctesiphon better suited than Seleucia as a principal military headquarters but more space was there available for the peculiar needs of the royal court — spacious gardens and open country suitable for hunting from horseback.

There is no evidence to suggest that with the establishment of the court in Ctesiphon the east bank of the Tigris developed a political entity and in this respect became separated from Seleucia. One must think, I believe, in terms of a metropolis which occupied the two banks; in the course of time the newer sections inevitably gained in prestige at the expense of the older, but this involved no political separation. One group of the autonomous coins does in fact support an assumption that in the reign of Phraates IV, some time after 32/31 B.C., a union took place between Seleucia and Ctesiphon more formal than that which had previously characterized their relations.[75] The reverse type of the coins represents two city-goddesses probably clasping hands over an altar. This symbolism would scarcely have been em-

[74] xvi.1.16.

[75] See p. 100, No. 132.

ployed to express the union of two parties within Seleucia. This is the more unlikely since, at this period, party strife in the city was becoming more intense. I suggest that previously Ctesiphon had not shared in the privileges enjoyed by the *polis* of Seleucia, that indeed it had not possessed the status of a *polis*, and that in consequence of its increased political consciousness as the seat of the court the quarters on the east bank became amalgamated with those across the river as a single metropolitan unit, Seleucia-Ctesiphon. For our present purposes it should be noted that there is no indication of a transfer of the mint from Seleucia to Ctesiphon at any period. The apparent retention of certain branches of the administration in the older center in spite of the location of the principal royal palace and the military headquarters in the newer section harmonizes with this concept of one united metropolis.

It is important to examine the extent of the area served by the mint of Parthian Seleucia, that is, the area within which the tetradrachms and the autonomous and royal bronze were intended to circulate. It is obvious that coins are frequently carried beyond the boundaries of the territory which they were primarily intended to serve, but an essential difference in this respect exists between the silver and the bronze. The latter was employed almost exclusively in local trade, whereas the former played a certain part in interregional commerce, in maintaining a balance in the exchange of goods for goods, and must have been sought after, whatever the denomination, by those who hoarded precious metal. There were in addition important communities which lay along the border between two mint areas and enjoyed commercial relations with both centers. In such areas the medium of circulation was mixed, the proportions largely determined in each locality by the varying degree of proximity to the mint cities.

In Iran in the areas served by other Parthian mints occasional finds of tetradrachms have been made.[76] They serve only to illustrate the point made in the preceding paragraph, that under certain conditions silver was drawn beyond the areas in which

[76] Of particular importance is the so-called Teheran hoard discussed in part by E. T. Newell, "A Parthian Hoard," *The Numismatic Chronicle*, Fifth series, 4 (1924), 141–180. Mr. Newell has knowledge of still another hoard from Persia which contained numerous tetradrachms.

it was intended to circulate. In northern Mesopotamia some tetradrachms from Seleucia have come to light through native dealers, but the excavated material of which I have knowledge consists of drachms from Iran and tetradrachms struck at the mint of Roman Antioch. At Dura-Europos along the middle Euphrates Parthian tetradrachms and drachms have both been found, along with a number of autonomous coins and a few specimens of the royal bronze from Seleucia. The great bulk of the currency in that locality, however, was furnished throughout the Parthian period by the Antioch mint.[77] In eastern Mesopotamia the influence of Seleucia may have been stronger. A large number of autonomous bronze coins of the Seleucia mint have been found at Susa in Elymais.[78] So far as I have knowledge Parthian coins brought to light through excavations in Babylonia have all been of the mint at Seleucia. The sites include Babylon, Nippur, and Orchoi (Uruk) in the south and one near Tel Asmar to the northeast of Seleucia, probably along the highway which ran from Ctesiphon to Ecbatana.[79]

[77] Cf. R. H. Pfeiffer, "Excavations at Nuzi," *Bulletin of the American Schools of Oriental Research*, No. 34, April, 1929, p. 4; G. F. Hill, "A Hoard of Coins from Nineveh," *The Numismatic Chronicle*, Fifth series, 11 (1931), 160–170; E. T. Newell, *The Fifth Dura Hoard*, *Numismatic Notes and Monographs*, 58 (1933), 9; A. R. Bellinger, "The Coins," *The Excavations at Dura-Europos, Preliminary Report of Third Season of Work, November, 1929—March, 1930*, pp. 139–160; *idem*, "The Coins," *The Excavations at Dura-Europos, Preliminary Report of Fourth Season of Work, October, 1930—March, 1931*, pp. 259–282.

[78] A. Dieudonné, "La Mission de Suse," *Revue numismatique*, 4e série, 32 (1929), 32.

[79] Twenty-three autonomous coins were found at Babylon, apparently together. I have seen no description of their types, but they bore the ethnikon form of the name Seleucia and appear to have been associated with coins of Characene which had been overstruck with the types of Mithradates II. This suggests that they belonged to the close of the second century B.C. or the opening of the first. See A. de la Fuÿe, "Les Monnaies de l'Elymaïde," *Revue numismatique*, 4e série, 22 (1919), 74; cf. E. T. Newell, *Mithradates of Parthia and Hyspaosines of Characene: A Numismatic Palimpsest*, *Numismatic Notes and Monographs*, 26 (1925).

From Nippur have come five examples of the royal bronze struck at Seleucia during the early second century A.D., together with a specimen of our autonomous group No. 128 (see p. 96), which dates from about 122 to 83 B.C. This last coin (Nippur No. CBS 14555) has been described as an issue of the Seleucid king Alexander Bala, but an examination of the published photograph leaves no doubt as to its real character. See Leon Legrain, "Coins from Nippur," *The Museum Journal, University of Pennsylvania*, 15 (1924), 70–76.

At Orchoi there were found three autonomous coins in a very obscure condition and 196 tetradrachms of Gotarzes II (44–52 A.D.). The latter have been described

Although the evidence is as yet incomplete the outline of the Seleucia mint area can be distinguished with reasonable clearness. It embraced all of Babylonia and, probably, southern Mesopotamia. In the territories bordering on this area the coinage of Seleucia competed with that of other mints, in the north with that of Antioch and of one or more mints of Iran, and to the east with a mint of Iran, probably that of Ecbatana. Elymais presents an interesting problem which cannot be solved on the basis of extant knowledge. The fairly frequent occurrence in Susa of the autonomous coinage of Seleucia suggests rather close trade and social relations. This receives support from the fact that tetradrachms continued to be favored in Elymais after this class of coin had been discarded in central and northern Iran. The evidence of regional currency preferences throws light on another problem of cultural relationships. The fact that drachms circulated freely in northern Mesopotamia, but are not found in Babylonia, suggests that Iranian influence was stronger in the north than in the south. From the point of view of currency relationships we have one belt (the users of tetradrachms) extending from Syria down the Euphrates to Babylonia and thence across into southern Iran, and another (the users of drachms) stretching west from the solid block of central and northern Iran through into northern Mesopotamia as far west as the Euphrates. The relative influence of trade and of community of culture in establishing these relationships constitutes an important study which must wait on the discovery of more adequate evidence.

4. CHRONOLOGICAL TABLE OF THE COINS OF THE MINT

This table includes all the issues known to me of tetradrachms, of the autonomous coinage, and of the royal bronze

---

as of bronze, but the photographs reveal plainly the normal designs of the tetradrachms of this period. See J. Jordan, *Uruk-Warka, nach den Ausgrabungen durch die deutsche Orient-Gesellschaft,* pp. 70 and 39.

Dr. N. C. Debevoise of the Oriental Institute, The University of Chicago, has kindly permitted me to examine a number of coins found on the surface near Tel Asmar. They comprise examples of our Nos. 127, 128, 129, 130, and 132 of the autonomous coinage (see pp. 95, 96, 97, 98, 100), dating from as early as 137/36 to the interval from 32/31 to 2/1 B.C.; examples of the royal bronze from Seleucia for the reigns of Pacorus II (78–115/16 A.D.), Volagases II (105/06–148 A.D.), and Volagases III (148–192 A.D.); and a tetradrachm of Volagases IV (191–207/08 A.D.).

which replaced the autonomous coinage. Included also are two groups of drachms which were probably struck at Seleucia. The first column gives the date of each issue. The figures which appear in parenthesis are the estimated dates of coins on which the year of the issue does not appear. The second column is provided for those coins which are dated by the month as well as by the year. The third column gives the metal of the coins. The four occurrences of drachms are indicated by the letter *d*. In the fourth column the following abbreviations have been used in naming the successive kings: Mith. (Mithradates), Phra. (Phraates), Artab. (Artabanus), Sinat. (Sinatruces), Tirid. (Tiridates), Phra. V (Phraataces), Von. (Vonones), Vard. (Vardanes), Volag. (Volagases), Pac. (Pacorus). The autonomous issues are referred to as "autonom.," the revolt coinage of the city as "revolt." In the fifth column, with its references to the publication of each coin, I have cited the present volume in the case of all coins examples of which have been found in the excavations. In the case of tetradrachms the month dates of which have been obscured on the specimens from Seleucia but which are given in other publications, the reference to this volume follows the other in parenthesis. If several other authors have described the same coin, a reference to Wroth has been preferred. The following abbreviations have been used for the names of authors:

DeM.	De Morgan	M.	Markoff
G.	Gardner	N.a	Newell, "A Parthian Hoard"
Gr.	Grose	N.b	Newell, "A Numismatic Palimpsest"
H.	Hill	N.c	Newell (letter to author)
L.	Lindsay	P.	Petrowicz
Long.	Longpérier	P.-O.	Prokesch-Osten

The full titles of the works cited will be found in the Bibliography on page xiii. In his letter Mr. Newell has described coins of his collection. The first numerals in the fifth column refer to pages, the second to serial numbers. Certain authors have not numbered their coins; in these instances the page references stand alone. The last column gives an abbreviated description of the reverse types. In the case of some of the later bronze coins this has been accompanied by a description of the obverse types.

Year B.C.	*Mo.*	*Ml.*	*King*	*Reference*	*Type*
(141)[80]	..	AR	Mith. I	W. 10.29	Tyche Nikephoros (seated)
(c.140/39)[81]	..	AR	"	McD. 61.66	Hercules
(")[82]	..	AR d	"	W. 13.51	Zeus Aëtophoros
139/38	..	AR	"	W. 14.55	Hercules
"		AR d	"	W. 14.57	Zeus Aëtophoros
138/37	..	AR	"	W. 15.58	Hercules
"	..	AR d	"	W. 15.61	Zeus Aëtophoros
(c.140–137)[83]	..	Æ	Autonom.	McD. 94.126	"
(c.137/36)[84]	..	AR	Phra. II	W. 16	Apollo on omphalos
(c.129/28)[84]	..	AR	"	W. 23.1	Tyche Nikephoros (seated)
(c.137/36–123/22)[85]	..	Æ	Autonom.	McD. 95.127	Tripod
(c.125/24)[86]	..	AR	Artab. I	McD. 62.67	Tyche Nikephoros (seated)
124/23	..	AR	"	W. 20.1	"
(c.124/23)[87]	..	AR	Himerus	N.a 153.71	Dionysos Nikephoros
123/22	..	AR d	"	P.-O. 21.4	Nike
(c.122/21–121/20)[88]	..	AR	Mith. II	McD. 62.68	Arsaces on omphalos
121/20	..	Æ	"	N. b	Cornucopiae
(c.121/20–104/03)[89]	..	Æ	Autonom.	McD. 96.128	Tyche Nikephoros (seated)
103/02	..	Æ	"	"	"
102/01	..	Æ	"	"	"
99/98	..	Æ	"	"	"
96/95	..	Æ	"	"	"
95/94	..	Æ	"	"	"
(c.91/90)[90]	..	AR	Gotarzes I	W. 38.3	Arsaces on throne
88/87	..	Æ	Autonom.	McD. 96.128	Tyche Nikephoros (seated)
(c.86)[90]	..	AR	"Arsaces"	W. 38.2	Arsaces on throne
85/84	..	Æ	Autonom.	McD. 96.128	Tyche Nikephoros (seated)
84/83	..	Æ	"	"	"
(c.80)[90]	..	AR	Orodes I	W. 38.1,5	Arsaces on throne

[80] See p. 201. [81] See p. 112, No. 66.

[82] The drachm bears the monogram which appears on the tetradrachm and is probably contemporary. [83] See p. 131, No. 126.

[84] See pp. 201–202. The second type was assigned by Wroth to Himerus.

[85] See p. 133, No. 127.

[86] See p. 112, No. 67, and discussion of the value of dates, p. 147.

[87] See p. 202. [88] See p. 203. [89] See p. 133, No. 128.

[90] See pp. 206–210. The types were assigned by Wroth to an Artabanus II.

Year B.C.	*Mo.*	*Ml.*	*King*	*Reference*	*Type*
(*c.* 77) [91]	..	Æ	Sinat.	G. 35	Arsaces on throne
72/71	..	Æ	Autonom.	McD. 97.129	Cornucopiae
(*c.* 70) [92]	..	Æ	Phra. III	W. 45.1	Arsaces on throne
(*c.* 66) [92]	..	Æ	"	W. 48.25	The king as Zeus with Tyche
(*c.* 57) [93]	..	Æ	Orodes II	W. 68.1	Arsaces on throne
(*c.* 56) [93]	..	Æ	Mith. III	W. 58	"
(*c.* 54) [93]	10	Æ	Orodes II	W. 72.31 (McD. 69)	King r., Tyche kneeling
(*c.* 52) [94]	11?	Æ	"	W. 72.32	King r., Tyche and palm
(")	12	Æ	"	W. 73.33	"
42/41	..	Æ	Autonom.	McD. 98.130	Tyche and river god
41/40	..	Æ	"	"	"
(*c.* 40/39) [94]	..	Æ	Orodes II	McD. 63.70	The king as Zeus Nikephoros
39/38	..	Æ	"	W. 73.37	"
38/37	..	Æ	Autonom.	McD. 99.131	Tyche Nikephoros (standing)
37/36	3	Æ	Phra. IV	P. 77.1	King r., Tyche and diadem
"	4	Æ	"	W. 99.1	"
"	5	Æ	"	P. 77.3	"
"	6	Æ	"	P. 77.4	"
36/35	5	Æ	"	Long. 47	"
(One year for which no issues are known)					
34/33	1	Æ	Phra. IV	P. 78.5	King r., Tyche and palm
"	3	Æ	"	W. 99.2	"
"	4	Æ	"	P. 78.7	"
"	5	Æ	"	W. 100.4	"
"	6	Æ	"	P. 78.9	"
33/32	1	Æ	"	W. 100.5	"
"	5	Æ	"	P. 79.11	"
"	6	Æ	"	W. 100.6	"
32/31	1	Æ	"	P. 79.12	The king as Zeus Nikephoros
"	2	Æ	"	W. 100.8	"
"	2	Æ	"	P.-O. 36.10	King r., Tyche and palm
"	3	Æ	"	W. 101.9	The king as Zeus Nikephoros

[91] See p. 211.

[92] See pp. 211–212.

[93] See pp. 212–216. The coin here given to Mithradates III was assigned by Wroth to an Unknown King.

[94] See p. 216.

Year B.C.	*Mo.*	*Ml.*	*King*	*Reference*	*Type*
32/31	4	Æ	Phra. IV	N.c	The king as Zeus Nikephoros
"	5	Æ	"	W. 101.10	"
"	6	Æ	"	P. 79.15	"
"	11	Æ	"	P.-O. 36.8	King r., Tyche and palm
"	..	Æ	Autonom.	McD. 99.131	Tyche Nikephoros (standing)
(32/31–2/1)[95]	..	Æ	"	McD. 100.132	Two city-goddesses and altar
31/30	4	Æ	Phra. IV	W. 101.11	King r., Tyche and palm
"	6	Æ	"	P. 80.16	"
(One year for which no issues are known)					
29/28	1	Æ	Phra. IV	W. 101.12	King r., Tyche kneeling
"	6	Æ	"	P. 80.17	"
"	6	Æ	"	P.-O. 36.13	King r., Tyche and palm
28/27	2	Æ	"	P.-O. 37.4	King r., Athena and diadem
"	10	Æ	"	P. 80.18	King r., Tyche and diadem
27/26	?	Æ	"	M. 20.310	King r., Tyche and palm
"	1	Æ	"	W. 102.13	The king as Zeus Nikephoros
"	2	Æ	"	W. 102.14	"
"	12	Æ	"	P.-O. 37.9	"
26/25	1	Æ	"	W. 103.19	King r., Tyche and palm
"	2	Æ	Tirid. II	W. 135.2	"
"	5	Æ	Phra. IV	P. 82.26	"
"	6	Æ	"	McD. 64.71	"
"	8	Æ	"	W. 103.18	"
"	8	Æ	"	McD. 64.72	King r., Tyche and diadem
"	12	Æ	Tirid. II	W. 135.1	King r., Tyche and palm
25/24	2	Æ	Phra. IV	P.-O. 37.3	King r., Tyche and diadem
"	3	Æ	"	McD. 64.73	King r., Tyche and palm

95 See p. 136, No. 132.

Year B.C.	*Mo.*	*Ml.*	*King*	*Reference*	*Type*
25/24	7	Æ	Phra. IV	McD. 64.73	King r., Tyche and palm
"	7	Æ	"	W. 103.21	King r., Tyche and diadem
"	8	Æ	"	P. 83.29	King r., Tyche and palm
"	8	Æ	"	W. 104.24	King r., Tyche and diadem
"	9	Æ	"	W. 104.29	King r., Tyche and palm
"	9	Æ	"	W. 104.27	King r., Tyche and diadem
"	11	Æ	"	P.-O. 37.2	"
"	12	Æ	"	Long. 58	King r., Tyche and palm
"	Emb.	Æ	"	W. 104.31	King r., Tyche and diadem
24/23	1	Æ	"	W. 105.33	King r., Tyche and palm
"	2	Æ	"	W. 105.34	King r., Tyche and diadem
"	3	Æ	"	P. 84.35	King r., Athena and diadem
"	4	Æ	"	W. 105.35	"
"	5	Æ	"	W. 106.37	"
"	6	Æ	"	W. 106.39	"
"	12	Æ	"	W. 105.32	King r., Tyche and palm
23/22	4	Æ	"	W. 107.49	"
"	5	Æ	"	W. 107.50	"
"	6	Æ	"	W. 107.51	"
"	6	Æ	"	Long. 59	King r., Athena and diadem
"	7	Æ	"	P. 85.38	King r., Tyche and palm
"	8	Æ	"	W. 106.41	"
"	9	Æ	"	W. 106.42	"
"	10	Æ	"	W. 106.43	"
"	11	Æ	"	W. 107.45	"
"	12	Æ	"	W. 107.47	"
(22/21–2/1) [96]	1	Æ	"	W. 109.55 (McD. 75)	King r., Tyche and palm (variant)
(") [96]	1	Æ	"	McD. 65.74	The king as Zeus with bow

[96] See p. 222.

Year B.C.	*Mo.*	*Ml.*	*King*	*Reference*	*Type*
2/1	1?	Æ	Phra. V	W. 136.4	King r., Tyche and diadem
"	4	Æ	"	P. 100.1	"
"	5	Æ	"	P. 100.2	"
"	6	Æ	"	W. 136.1	"
1 B.C./1 A.D.	1	Æ	"	W. 137.5 (McD. 76)	Arsaces on throne
"	3	Æ	"	P.-O. 39.18	"
"	4	Æ	"	P. 101.5	"
"	5	Æ	"	P. 101.6	"
"	6	Æ	"	P. 101.7	"
"	7	Æ	"	P. 100.4	"
"	8	Æ	"	P.-O. 39.15	"
"	9	Æ	"	P.-O. 39.16	"
"	11	Æ	"	N.c	"
(One year for which no issues are known)					
2/3 A.D.	5	Æ	Phra. V	G. 46	"
"	12	Æ	"	P.-O. 40.3	Bust of the queen
3/4	..	Æ	"	McD. 66.77	Arsaces on throne
"	4	Æ	"	P.-O. 40.4 (McD. 78)	Bust of the queen
4/5	6	Æ	"	P.-O. 40.5	"
(2/1 B.C.–4/5 A.D.)[97]	..	Æ	Autonom.	McD. 101.133	Male deity, with lyre
(One year for which no issues are known)					
6/7	Emb.	Æ	Orodes III	G. 46.V.1.	The king as Zeus with bow
(Two years for which no issues are known)					
9/10	..	Æ	Von. I	W. 143.1	Nike
"	..	Æ	Autonom.	McD. 102.134	Draped figure on throne
(One year for which no issues are known)					
11/12	5	Æ	Von. I	W. 143.2	Nike
"	6	Æ	"	W. 143.3	Nike
"	..	Æ	Artab. II	McD. 67.80	King r., Tyche and palm
12/13	..	Æ	"	P.-O. 48.3	"
(")[98]	4	Æ	"	P. 105.2 (McD. 81)	"
(")[98]	5	Æ	"	P. 106.4	"
(")[98]	8	Æ	Von. I	P. 105.1	Nike
(11/12–15/16)[99]	..	Æ	Autonom.	McD. 102.135	Anchor
(Two years for which no issues are known)					

[97] See p. 137, No. 133. [98] See p. 115, No. 81. [99] See p. 138, No. 135.

Year A.D.	*Mo.*	*Ml.*	*King*	*Reference*	*Type*
15/16	5	Æ	Autonom.	H. 145.41	Female bust with kalathos
“	6	Æ	“	McD. 103.136	“
“	8	Æ	“	“	“
“	9	Æ	“	“	“
“	10	Æ	“	“	“
“	11	Æ	“	“	“
“	12	Æ	“	“	“
“	..	Æ	“	McD. 104.137	A monogram as type
16/17	1	Æ	“	McD. 103.136	Female bust with kalathos
“	3	Æ	“	“	“
“	10	Æ	“	“	“
“	..	Æ	“	McD. 104.137	A monogram as type
(17/18) [100]	..	Æ	“	McD. 104.138	The king as Zeus Nikephoros
18/19	..	Æ	“	McD. 105.139	King l., Tyche and diadem
(One year for which no issues are known)					
20/21	..	AR	Artab. II	W. 147.8	King, Tyche and subject
(Two years for which no issues are known)					
23/24	1	AR	Artab. II	W. 147.11 (McD. 82)	“
“	6	AR	“	W. 147.12	“
“	12	AR	“	Long. 93	“
“	..	Æ	Autonom.	McD. 105.140	King seated l. on throne
24/25	..	AR	Artab. II	P. 110.6 (note)	King, Tyche and subject
“	..	Æ	“	McD. 69.84	Bust of Tyche
25/26	..	Æ	“	“	“
“	..	Æ	“	McD. 69.85	The king as Zeus Nikephoros
26/27	..	Æ	“	McD. 69.84	Bust of Tyche
27/28	..	AR	“	McD. 69.83	King mounted, Tyche and palm
(One year for which no issues are known)					
29/30 ?	..	Æ	Artab. II	McD. 70.86	Bust of Tyche
30/31 ?	..	Æ	“	“	“
(Approximately five years for which no issues are known)					
(c. 36–40) [101]	..	Æ	Revolt	McD. 106.141	Humped bull
40/41	..	Æ	Autonom.	McD. 107.142	Nike with palm
41/42	..	Æ	“	“	“

[100] See p. 139, No. 138.

[101] See p. 141, No. 141.

Year A.D.	*Mo.*	*Ml.*	*King*	*Reference*	*Type*
42/43	..	Æ	Autonom.	McD. 107.142	Nike with palm
"	3	AR	Vard. I	W. 153.1 (McD. 87)	King r., Tyche and palm
"	4	AR	"	W. 153.3	"
"	5	AR	"	P. 113.3	"
"	6	AR	"	W. 154.5	"
"	7	AR	"	P.-O. 53.2	"
"	8	AR	"	P.-O. 53.3	"
"	9	AR	"	P.-O. 53.4	"
"	10	AR	"	P.-O. 53.5	"
"	11	AR	"	P.-O. 53.7	"
"	12	AR	"	P.-O. 53.9	"
43/44	..	Æ	Autonom.	N.c(McD. 142)	Nike with palm
"	..	Æ	"	McD. 108.143	The deified king
"	2	AR	Vard. I	P.-O. 53.10 (McD. 87)	King r., Tyche and palm
"	3	AR	"	P.-O. 53.12	"
"	4	AR	"	W. 154.9	"
"	5	AR	"	W. 154.12	"
"	6	AR	"	W. 155.13	"
"	8	AR	"	W. 154.6	"
"	9	AR	"	W. 154.7	"
"	11	AR	"	W. 154.8	"
"	..	Æ	"	McD. 71.88	Veiled head (with kalathos?)
"	..	Æ	"	McD. 71.89	Boule
44/45	1	AR	"	W. 155.19	King r., Tyche and palm
"	2	AR	"	P. 114.7	"
"	3	AR	"	P.-O. 53.21	"
"	3	AR	Gotarzes II	De M. 299.224	King r., Tyche and diadem
"	4	AR	Vard. I	McD. 70.87	King r., Tyche and palm
"	6	AR	"	N.c	"
"	7	AR	"	W. 155.17	"
"	8	AR	"	W. 155.18	"
"	10?	AR	"	N.c	"
"	..	Æ	"	McD. 71.89	Boule
"	10	AR	Gotarzes II	De M. 299.224	King r., Tyche and diadem
45/46	1	AR	Vard. I	P.-O. 53.23	King r., Tyche and palm
"	3	AR	"	P.-O. 53.24	"
"	4	AR	"	P.-O. 53.25	"

Year A.D.	*Mo.*	*Ml.*	*King*	*Reference*	*Type*
45/46	..	Æ	Vard. I	McD. 71.89	Boule
"	10	AR	Gotarzes II	W. 161.2	King r., Tyche and diadem
46/47 [102]	1	Æ	"	McD. 73.92	Bust of Tyche
"	2	Æ	"	"	"
"	3	Æ	"	"	"
"	4	AR	"	W. 161.3	King r., Tyche and diadem
"	4	Æ	"	McD. 73.92	Bust of Tyche
"	5	AR	"	W. 162.5	King r., Tyche and diadem
"	5	Æ	"	McD. 73.92	Bust of Tyche
"	6	AR	"	W. 162.6	King r., Tyche and diadem
"	6	Æ	"	McD. 73.92	Bust of Tyche
"	7	AR	"	W. 162.7	King r., Tyche and diadem
"	7	Æ	"	McD. 73.92	Bust of Tyche
"	..	AR	"	W. 162.10	King r., Tyche and diadem (with name of king)
47/48	..	AR	"	W. 162.11	As above (with name)
"	1	AR	"	McD. 72.90	King r., Tyche and diadem
"	2	AR	"	P.-O. 54.9	"
"	3	AR	"	P.-O. 54.11	"
"	4	AR	"	W. 163.15	"
"	7	AR	"	W. 163.16	"
"	8	AR	"	W. 163.12	"
"	11	AR	"	W. 163.13	"
"	12	AR	"	P.-O. 54.7	"
"	..	Æ	"	McD. 73.92	Bust of Tyche
48/49	10	AR	"	P.-O. 54.14	King r., Tyche and diadem
"	11	AR	"	W. 163.21	"
49/50	2	AR	"	W. 164.23	"
"	3	AR	"	W. 164.24	"
"	4	AR	"	P.-O. 54.17	"
"	6	AR	"	P.-O. 54.18	"
"	7	AR	"	W. 164.25	"
50/51	1	AR	"	P.-O. 54.22	"
"	2	AR	"	P.-O. 54.23	"

[102] Beginning with the opening of this year I have assumed the insertion of an extra intercalary month, which brings Xandikos rather than Artemisios into correspondence with Nisannu as the first month of the Babylonian year. See pp. 151–153.

Year A.D.	*Mo.*	*Ml.*	*King*	*Reference*	*Type*
50/51	9	AR	Gotarzes II	P.-O. 54.21	King r., Tyche and diadem
51/52	2	AR	"	P.-O. 55.7	"
"	3	AR	"	W. 164.31	"
"	6	AR	Volag. I	Long. 110	King l., Tyche and diadem
"	7	AR	"	W. 178.1	"
"	9	AR	Gotarzes II	P. 118.11	King r., Tyche and diadem
52/53	2	AR	Volag. I	P.-O. 58.2	King l., Tyche and diadem
"	3	AR	"	W. 179.4	"
"	5	AR	"	W. 179.5	"
"	9	AR	"	W 179.3	"
"	10	AR	"	P.-O. 57.1	"
"	12	AR	"	P.-O. 58.1	"
53/54	11	AR	"	P.-O. 58.5	"
54/55	7	AR	"	P.-O. 58.7 (McD. 93)	"
"	12	AR	"	P.-O. 58.6	"
55/56	..	AR	"	N.c	"
56/57	5	AR	"	W. 180.15	"
"	7	AR	"	P. 130.1	"
"	9	AR	"	P.-O. 62.1	"
"	10 ?	AR	"	N.c	"
57/58	3	AR	"	W. 181.21	"
"	9	AR	"	W. 181.20	"
58/59	2	AR	"	L. 185.68	"
"	4	AR	"	L. 185.69	"
"	11	AR	"	W. 181.27	"
(59/60) [103]	..	Æ	Revolt	McD. 109.144	Eagle
"	..	Æ	"	McD. 109.145	Artemis
(60/61) [104]	..	Æ	"	"	Artemis
61/62	..	Æ	"	"	Artemis
"	..	AR	Volag. I	P.-O. 63.10	King l., Tyche and palm
62/63	..	AR	"	P. 133.1	"
63/64	1	AR	"	W. 185.58	"
64/65	6	AR	"	L. 185.7	"
65/66	6	AR	"	W. 185.62	"
66/67	1	AR	"	P.-O. 63.14	"
"	7	AR	"	L. 185.73	"
"	11	AR	"	W. 186.63	"
"	12	AR	"	W. 186.65	"

[103] See p. 143, No. 144.

[104] See p. 144, No. 145.

Year A.D.	*Mo.*	*Ml.*	*King*	*Reference*	*Type*
67/68	1	AR	Volag. I	P.-O. 63.15	King l., Tyche and palm
68/69	1	AR	"	P.-O. 63.17	"
69/70	..	AR	"	L. 185.76	"
"	..	Æ	"	McD. 75.95	Bust of Tyche
"	..	Æ	Revolt	McD. 110.146	Humped bull
"	..	Æ	Autonom.	McD. 111.147	Tyche seated l. on column
(") [105]	..	Æ	"	McD. 111.148	Nike with wreath
"	..	Æ	Volag. I	McD. 75.96	"
70/71	..	Æ	"	"	"
(One year for which no issues are known)					
72/73	..	Æ	Volag. I	McD. 75.96	Nike with wreath
73/74?[106]	..	AR	"	L. 185.77	King l., Tyche and palm
"	..	Æ	"	McD. 75.96	Nike with wreath
74/75?[106]	..	AR	"	L. 185.78	King l., Tyche and palm
75/76	..	Æ	"	McD. 75.96	Nike with wreath
(One year for which no issues are known)					
77/78?[106]	..	AR	Volag. I	L. 185.80	King l., Tyche and palm
"	..	Æ	"	McD. 75.96	Nike with wreath
"	..	Æ	"	McD. 76.97	Eagle
78/79	1	AR	Pac. II	W. 193.2	King l., Tyche and diadem
"	3	AR	Volag. I	P. 136.3	"
"	..	Æ	"	McD. 75.96	Nike with wreath
"	3	AR	Pac. II	W. 194.3	King l., Tyche and diadem
"	4	AR	"	N.c	"
"	6	AR	"	W. 194.4	"
"	12	AR	"	W. 193.1	"
79/80	2	AR	"	P.-O. 66.3	"
"	3	AR	Volag. I	P.-O. 64.4 (McD. 94)	"
"	10	AR	Pac. II	McD. 76.98	"
"	10	AR	Volag. I	P. 136.4	"
"	Emb.	AR	"	G. 56	"
80/81	..	AR	Pac. II	W. 194.11	"
"	..	Æ	"	McD. 77.99	Male bust r.

[105] See p. 146, No. 148.

[106] Some doubt attaches to the correctness of Lindsay's reading of these coins. His No. 79, said to bear the date 75/76, has not been included in the table.

Year A.D.	*Mo.*	*Ml.*	*King*	*Reference*	*Type*
80/81	..	Æ	Pac. II	P. 147.15	Bust of Tyche
"	6	AR	Artab. III	N.c	King l., Tyche and diadem
81/82	1	AR	"	W. 203.3	"
"	3	AR	"	P. 143.2	"
"	8	AR	"	W. 203.1	"
"	9	AR	"	W. 203.2	"
82/83	7	AR	Pac. II	W. 195.14	King mounted, Tyche and subject
83/84	11	AR	"	W. 197.33	"
"	..	Æ	"	McD. 77.100	Bust of Tyche
84/85	..	Æ	"	"	"
85/86	..	AR	"	W. 198.36	King mounted, Tyche and subject
"	..	Æ	"	P. 147.18	Bust of Tyche
(One year for which no issues are known)					
87/88	..	Æ	Pac. II	Long. 131	Bust of Tyche
(Five years for which no issues are known)					
93/94	3	AR	Pac. II	W. 200.45	King l., Tyche and diadem
"	4	AR	"	P.-O. 68.1	"
"	6	AR	"	P.-O. 68.2	"
"	..	Æ	"	L. 208.100	Bust of Tyche
94/95	10	AR	"	P. 148.24	King l., Tyche and diadem
95/96	4	AR	"	P.-O. 68.6	"
96/97	12	AR	"	P.-O. 68.7	"
(Eight years for which no issues are known)					
105/06	..	Æ	Volag. II?	McD. 82.111	Bust of Tyche
(One year for which no issues are known)					
107/08	..	Æ	Volag. II?	McD. 82.111	Bust of Tyche
108/09	..	Æ	"	"	"
109/10	..	Æ	Osroes	P. 150.3	Bust of Tyche (obv.: head bare)
110/11	..	Æ	"	W. 205.8	"
(One year for which no issues are known)					
112/13	..	Æ	Volag. II	McD. 82.112	Tyche seated l.
"	..	Æ	Osroes	P. 151.5	Bust of Tyche (obv.: head bare)
113/14	..	Æ	Volag. II	McD. 82.112	Tyche seated l.
"	..	Æ	Osroes	McD. 78.102	Bust of Tyche (obv.: head bare)
114/15	..	Æ	"	"	"
115/16	..	Æ	Volag. II	P. 141.40a	Tyche seated l.
"	..	Æ	Pac. II	McD. 78.101	Bust of Tyche

Year A.D.	*Mo.*	*Ml.*	*King*	*Reference*	*Type*
(For the year 116/17 no Parthian issues are known, but at Seleucia coins of Trajan circulated.)[107]					
117/18	..	Æ	Osroes	McD. 78.102	Bust of Tyche (obv.: head bare)
118/19	..	Æ	"	"	"
"	..	Æ	"	McD. 79.103	Bust of Tyche (obv.: spiked headdress)
"	..	Æ	"	McD. 79.104	Bust of Tyche (obv.: head facing)
119/20	..	Æ	"	McD. 78.102	Bust of Tyche (obv.: head bare)
"	..	Æ	"	McD. 79.103	Bust of Tyche (obv.: spiked headdress)
"	..	Æ	"	McD. 79.104	Bust of Tyche (obv.: head facing)
"	..	Æ	Volag. II	McD. 83.113	Bust of Tyche
120/21	..	Æ	"	"	"
121/22	..	Æ	Osroes	P. 152.15	Bust of Tyche (obv.: head bare)
"	..	Æ	"	McD. 79.105	Bust of Tyche (obv.: spiked headdress)
122/23	4	Ꞓ	Volag. II	McD. 82.110	King l., Tyche and diadem
"	9	Ꞓ	"	L. 186.87	"
"	11	Ꞓ	"	McD. 81.109	"
"	..	Æ	Osroes	P. 152.16	Bust of Tyche (obv.: head bare)
"	..	Æ	Volag. II	W. 216.54	Bust of Tyche
123/24	4	Ꞓ	"	P. 137.12	King l., Tyche and diadem
"	8	Ꞓ	"	W. 211.15	"
"	..	Æ	"	W. 216.55	Bust of Tyche
"	..	Æ	Osroes	McD. 80.106	Bust of Tyche (obv.: head bare)
124/25	4	Ꞓ	Volag. II	P.-O. 75.1	King l., Tyche and diadem
"	8?	Ꞓ	"	W. 211.19	"
"	..	Æ	"	P.-O. 75.9	Bust of Tyche
125/26	..	Ꞓ	"	W. 212.23	King l., Tyche and diadem
"	8	Ꞓ	"	N.c	"
"	..	Æ	Osroes	McD. 80.106	Bust of Tyche (obv.: head bare)

107 See pp. 232–233.

Year A.D.	*Mo.*	*Ml.*	*King*	*Reference*	*Type*
126/27	4	AR	Volag. II	P.-O. 75.5	The king l., Tyche and diadem
"	..	Æ	"	P.-O. 75.10	Bust of Tyche
"	..	Æ	Osroes	McD. 80.106	Bust of Tyche (obv.: head bare)
127/28	..	Æ	"	"	"
128/29	..	Æ	Volag. II	W. 216.56	Tyche seated l. (obv.: helmet flap curved)
"	..	Æ	Osroes	McD. 80.107	Bust of Tyche (obv.: head helmeted)
"	..	Æ	"	McD. 81.108	Tyche standing r.
129/30	..	Æ	Volag. II	McD. 83.114	Tyche seated l. (obv.: helmet flap curved)
(Two years for which no issues are known)					
132/33	9	AR	Volag. II	L. 186.97	King l., Tyche and diadem
"	..	Æ	"	McD. 83.114	Tyche seated l. (obv.: helmet flap curved)
133/34	..	Æ	"	McD. 84.115	Bust of Tyche (obv.: helmet flap curved)
(Two years for which no issues are known)					
136/37	..	AR	Volag. II	P. 139.24	King l., Tyche and diadem
137/38	..	AR	"	P. 139.25	"
138/39	1	AR	"	N.c	"
"	8	AR	"	McD. 81.109a	"
"	..	Æ	"	P. 142.49	Bust of Tyche (obv.: helmet flap curved)
139/40	9	AR	"	P.-O. 75.7	King l., Tyche and diadem
140/41	9	AR	"	W. 212.29	"
141/42	..	AR	"	P. 139.27	"
142/43	9	AR	"	L. 186.100	"
143/44	9	AR	"	P. 139.28	"
(Two years for which no issues are known)					
146/47	8	AR	Volag. II	W. 213.30	King l., Tyche and diadem
147/48	8	AR	"	W. 213.31	"
148/49	2	AR	Volag. III	McD. 85.116a	"
"	3	AR	"	"	"
"	4	AR	"	"	"
"	8	AR	"	"	"
"	..	Æ	"	McD. 87.117	Tyche seated l. (obv.: head facing)
149/50	8	AR	"	McD. 85.116a	King l., Tyche and diadem

Year A.D.	*Mo.*	*Ml.*	*King*	*Reference*	*Type*
149/50	..	Æ	Volag. III	P. 165.51	Tyche seated l. (obv.: head facing)
150/51	4	Ꜳ	"	W. 224.3	King l., Tyche and diadem
"	8	Ꜳ	"	McD. 85.116a	"
"	9	Ꜳ	"	P.-O. 75.11	"
"	..	Æ	"	McD. 87.117	Tyche seated l. (obv.: head facing)
151/52	8	Ꜳ	"	W. 224.4	King l., Tyche and diadem
"	9	Ꜳ	"	McD. 85.116a	"
152/53	9	Ꜳ	"	"	"
153/54	3	Ꜳ	"	"	"
"	4	Ꜳ	"	P.-O. 75.16	"
"	8	Ꜳ	"	Gr. 403.9668	"
"	9	Ꜳ	"	McD. 85.116a	"
"	..	Æ	"	McD. 87.117	Tyche seated l. (obv.: head facing)
154/55	8	Ꜳ	"	McD. 85.116a	King l., Tyche and diadem
"	..	Æ	"	P. 166.54	Tyche seated l. (obv.: head facing)
155/56	8	Ꜳ	"	McD. 85.116a	King l., Tyche and diadem
"	..	Æ	"	McD. 87.117	Tyche seated l. (obv.: head facing)
156/57	3	Ꜳ	"	P.-O. 76.2	King l., Tyche and diadem
"	8	Ꜳ	"	McD. 85.116a	"
157/58	8	Ꜳ	"	"	"
158/59	8	Ꜳ	"	"	"
"	9	Ꜳ	"	P.-O. 76.4	"
159/60	9	Ꜳ	"	W. 226.19	"
"	10	Ꜳ	"	N.c	"
"	..	Æ	"	P.-O. 77.19	Tyche seated l. (obv.: head l.)
160/61	9	Ꜳ	"	McD. 85.116a	King l., Tyche and diadem
161/62	8	Ꜳ	"	"	"
162/63	8	Ꜳ	"	W. 226.22	"
"	9	Ꜳ	"	P.-O. 76.8	"
163/64	8	Ꜳ	"	McD. 85.116a	"
164/65	9	Ꜳ	"	"	"
"	..	Æ	"	McD. 88.118a	Bust of Tyche
165/66	9	Ꜳ	"	McD. 85.116a	King l., Tyche and diadem

Year A.D.	*Mo.*	*Ml.*	*King*	*Reference*	*Type*
165/66	..	Æ	Volag. III	McD. 88.118a	Bust of Tyche
166/67	8	AR	"	P. 160.20	King l., Tyche and diadem
167/68	8	AR	"	P.-O. 76.13	"
168/69	5	AR	"	W. 227.26	"
"	12	AR	"	N.c	"
169/70	4	AR	"	N.c	"
"	8	AR	"	P.-O. 76.15	"
"	12	AR	"	W. 227.27	"
"	..	Æ	"	McD. 89.118b	Bust of Tyche
170/71	6	AR	"	W. 227.28	King l., Tyche and diadem
"	..	Æ	"	McD. 89.118b	Bust of Tyche
171/72	4	AR	"	P. 161.24	King l., Tyche and diadem
172/73	3	AR	"	P.-O. 76.17	"
"	5	AR	"	P.-O. 76.18	"
"	6	AR	"	W. 227.29	"
"	10	AR	"	N.c	"
"	..	Æ	"	P. 166.57	Bust of Tyche
173/74	8	AR	"	P. 161.26	King l., Tyche and diadem
"	..	Æ	"	McD. 90.119	Tyche standing r.
"	..	Æ	"	P. 166.58	Tyche seated l. (obv.: head l.)
174/75	8	AR	"	N.c	King l., Tyche and diadem
"	..	Æ	"	McD. 89.118b	Bust of Tyche
"	..	Æ	"	McD. 90.120	Tyche seated l. (obv.: head l.)
175/76	4	AR	"	W. 227.31	King l., Tyche and diadem
"	8	AR	"	P.-O. 76.20	"
"	..	Æ	"	McD. 89.118b	Bust of Tyche
"	..	Æ	"	McD. 90.120	Tyche seated l. (obv.: head l.)
176/77	8	AR	"	P.-O. 76.21	King l., Tyche and diadem
"	..	Æ	"	McD. 90.120	Tyche seated l. (obv.: head l.)
177/78	1	AR	"	N.c	"
"	3	AR	"	P.-O. 76.22	King l., Tyche and diadem
"	6	AR	"	W. 228.34	"
"	11	AR	"	L. 187.114	"

Year A.D.	*Mo.*	*Ml.*	*King*	*Reference*	*Type*
177/78	12	Æ	Volag. III	W. 227.33	King l., Tyche and diadem
"	..	Æ	"	McD. 90.120	Tyche seated l. (obv.: head l.)
178/79	3	Æ	"	P.-O. 76.23	King l., Tyche and diadem
"	4	Æ	"	N.c	"
"	9	Æ	"	McD. 84.116	"
"	10	Æ	"	N.c	"
179/80	2	Æ	"	P.-O. 76.25	"
"	4	Æ	"	W. 228.36	"
"	5	Æ	"	P.-O. 76.26	"
"	11	Æ	"	W. 228.35	"
180/81	4	Æ	"	W. 228.38	"
"	9	Æ	"	P.-O. 76.27	"
"	..	Æ	"	McD. 91.121	Bust of Tyche (with arms)
181/82	4	Æ	"	W. 228.40	King l., Tyche and diadem
"	6	Æ	"	P.-O. 76.28	"
"	12	Æ	"	W. 228.39	"
182/83	2	Æ	"	P.-O. 76.32	"
"	6?	Æ	"	W. 228.41	"
"	9	Æ	"	P.-O. 76.30	"
183/84	1	Æ	"	P.-O. 76.33	"
"	4	Æ	"	P.-O. 76.34	"
184/85	1	Æ	"	N.c	"
"	2	Æ	"	W. 229.44	"
"	4	Æ	"	W. 229.45	"
"	6	Æ	"	N.c	"
"	8	Æ	"	W. 228.43	"
185/86	3	Æ	"	P.-O. 76.38	"
"	7	Æ	"	N.c	"
186/87	2	Æ	"	W. 229.48	"
"	8	Æ	"	P.-O. 76.39	"
187/88	6	Æ	"	P.-O. 76.40	"
188/89	3	Æ	"	N.c	"
"	5	Æ	"	P.-O. 77.1	"
"	12?	Æ	"	W. 229.51	"
189/90	..	Æ	"	P. 163.42	"
190/91	1	Æ	"	P.-O. 77.5	"
"	4	Æ	"	W. 229.52	"
191/92	6	Æ	Volag. IV	W. 237.1	" (obv.: head facing)
"	12	Æ	Volag. III	W. 229.53	"

Year A.D.	*Mo.*	*Ml.*	*King*	*Reference*	*Type*
192/93	7	Æ	Volag. IV	W. 237.3	King l., Tyche and diadem (obv.: head facing)
(*c.* 192/93)[108]	..	Æ	"	McD. 93.123	Bust of Tyche (obv.: head facing)
193/94	2	Æ	"	McD. 91.122	King l., Tyche and diadem
"	4	Æ	"	"	"
"	5	Æ	"	P.-O. 77.22	"
"	6	Æ	"	McD. 91.122	"
"	9	Æ	"	"	"
"	11	Æ	"	"	"
"	12	Æ	"	"	"
194/95	1	Æ	"	"	"
"	4	Æ	"	"	"
195/96	1	Æ	"	"	"
"	2	Æ	"	"	"
196/97	10	Æ	"	"	"
197/98	..	Æ	"	"	"
198/99	..	Æ	"	"	"
199/200	..	Æ	"	W. 238.11	"
200/01	..	Æ	"	W. 238.12	"
201/02	..	Æ	"	McD. 92.122a	"
202/03	..	Æ	"	"	"
203/04	10?	Æ	"	W. 239.13	"
204/05	..	Æ	"	W. 239.14	"
205/06	..	Æ	"	W. 239.16	"
206/07	..	Æ	"	P. 169.14	"
207/08	..	Æ	"	P. 170.15	"
208/09	..	Æ	Volag. V	W. 241.1	King l., Tyche and diadem
209/10	..	Æ	"	McD. 93.124	"
210/11	11	Æ	"	P.-O. 81.3 (McD. 124)	"
211/12	11	Æ	"	P.-O. 81.4 (McD. 124)	"
212/13	11	Æ	"	P.-O. 81.5 (McD. 124)	"
213/14	11	Æ	"	P.-O. 81.6 (McD. 124a)	"
214/15	11	Æ	"	P.-O. 81.7 (McD. 124a)	"
"	..	Æ	"	McD. 95.125	Tyche standing r.

[108] See p. 130, No. 123.

Year A.D.	Mo.	Ml.	King	Reference	Type
215/16	..	AR	Volag. V	P. 173.7	King l., Tyche and diadem
"	..	Æ	"	McD. 95.125	Tyche standing r.
216/17	..	AR	"	P. 173.8	King l., Tyche and diadem
217/18	..	AR	"	P. 173.9	"
218/19	..	AR	"	P. 173.10	"
219/20	..	AR	"	W. 242.16	"
220/21	..	AR	"	W. 243.17	"
221/22	..	AR	"	P. 173.13	"
222/23	..	AR	"	W. 243.18	"
(Five years for which no issues are known)					
228/29	..	AR	Artavasdes?	Long. 157 G. 59	"

CHAPTER VII

THE COINS IN RELATION TO EVENTS IN THE WESTERN PROVINCES

I. THE REIGN OF MITHRADATES I THROUGH THAT OF ORODES II

SELEUCIA probably was occupied by Mithradates I along with the rest of Babylonia in 141 B.C. By the spring of 139 Demetrius II had been captured and the western provinces reoccupied.[1] Immediately thereafter Mithradates began the issue of the tetradrachms which were struck during the years 140/39, 139/38, and 138/37. To the interval in 141 during which Seleucia was in Parthian hands I have tentatively assigned the issue of undated tetradrachms with reverse of Tyche Nikephoros. The attribution is based on the distinction in the style of the portrait as compared with that of the later issues of Mithradates and on the complete absence of evidence linking the issue with some mint other than that at Seleucia. The reverse type, borrowed from the contemporary Seleucid coinage, recurs on issues of Phraates II and Artabanus I which appear to be of the Seleucia mint. The exact date for the death of Mithradates and the accession of Phraates II is not known. Rawlinson suggested the year 136, and Wroth, confused by his use of the Macedonian calendar in computing the dates on the coins, the year 138.[2] It is probably accurate to count 138/37 as the last calendrical year for the reign of Mithradates and 137/36 as the first of the next reign. There is little doubt that, beginning with Phraates II, the accession of each king was normally marked by the issue of tetradrachms. Two groups of this denomination are attributed to Phraates, one with reverse of Apollo, the other with reverse of Tyche Nikephoros.[3] The obverse of

[1] W. W. Tarn, "Parthia," *The Cambridge Ancient History*, IX, 581–582.

[2] H. C. Rawlinson, *The Sixth Great Oriental Monarchy*, p. 83; W. Wroth, *Catalogue of the Coins of Parthia*, p. xxi.

[3] The second group was assigned by Wroth to Himerus, but later writers have not concurred. See M. Dayet, "Un Tétradrachme arsacide inédit," *Aretheuse*, I (1925),

the former represents the king as somewhat youthful, whereas the obverse of the latter shows him as a mature man. Antiochus VII of Syria was defeated by Phraates in the spring of 129 B.C., and shortly thereafter the Arsacid left for the eastern provinces, where he was killed in battle with the Scythians.[4] It is reasonable to assign the first issue to the year of the accession of Phraates, 137/36, and the second to the interval after the defeat of Antiochus before the departure of Phraates to the east, that is, 129/28 B.C. At this time the king was in the western provinces and was in communication with the administration of Seleucia. The late date is required by the differences in the two obverse portraits. The circumstances suggest that the issue of the second group, after an interval of about seven years, was not necessarily a matter of routine mint policy, but may have been the result of the momentary interest in the western provinces experienced by the royal administration at this particular time.[5]

So far as the literary sources afford evidence, Artabanus I throughout his reign was occupied by the threat of the invasion of Parthia by the Steppe peoples from the northeast. He met his death during a campaign in those regions, probably in 124/23. It is possible that he visited the western provinces in connection with his preparations for this campaign, say in 125/24, when his initial issue of tetradrachms was inaugurated, but there is no evidence for this. Both the issues of tetradrachms of Artabanus, therefore, were probably struck under the orders of Himerus, who was the viceroy in the West.

The relations of Himerus with Seleucia have been discussed elsewhere.[6] Appointed as governor-general of the western provinces under Phraates II, he appears to have made himself independent during the latter part of the reign of Artabanus. The tetradrachms of Himerus are undated, but one of his two issues of drachms at Seleucia bears the date 123/22. This implies that the other issue was struck in 124/23, to which date we may also assign the tetradrachms.[7] Since the latest coins

63–65; also E. T. Newell's chapter on coins in Mr. A. U. Pope's forthcoming *Survey of Persian Art and Archaeology*.

[4] Tarn, *op. cit.*, p. 581. [5] See pp. 217–218. [6] See p. 219.

[7] See the discussion of the value of dates on page 147. Dayet (*loc. cit.*) assigns these tetradrachms to Phraates II. I do not feel, however, that his evidence over-

of Artabanus are of the same date, it is to be presumed that the open revolt took place toward the close of the year.

The separatist and nationalist movement in Babylonia of which Himerus was the formal head was crushed by Mithradates II, who succeeded to the throne upon the death of Artabanus. The date for the accession can best be placed at 123/22 B.C. Bronze coins have been found in Babylonia which had been issued by Hyspaosines, king of Characene, and had been overstruck with the types of Mithradates II in the year 121/20 (by the Babylonian calendar).[8] By this date, then, Parthian sovereignty had been reëstablished in Babylonia. Since the campaign against Characene must have followed the overthrow of Himerus, the latter event can be placed in 122/21. This agrees with the date for the issue of the latest coins of Himerus, which must have taken place toward the close of 123/22.

The drachms of Mithradates II comprise five successive series. Details of the reverse design, the style, and the form of the legend demonstrate that his tetradrachms constituted one series approximately contemporary with the first, or earliest, series of the drachms.[9] None of his tetradrachms bear dates, which implies again that they formed a single group, all struck at approximately the same time.[10] Under the circumstances it may be assumed that their issue was inaugurated upon the occupation of Seleucia by Mithradates in 122/21, but was continued for only a short time thereafter. Mithradates appears to have left Babylonia for the east very soon after his reorganization of the administration, probably by 120 B.C.[11] Subsequent to his departure no tetradrachms were struck during the rest of his reign, a period of thirty years.

In the previous twenty years, since tetradrachms were first struck under Mithradates I, ten issues had appeared. After

---

weighs the argument adduced by Mr. Newell upon the initial publication of the type, "A Parthian Hoard," *The Numismatic Chronicle*, Fifth series, 4(1924), 141–180.

[8] E. T. Newell, *Mithradates of Parthia and Hyspaosines of Characene: A Numismatic Palimpsest, Numismatic Notes and Monographs*, No. 26 (1925).

[9] E. T. Newell, "A Parthian Hoard," *The Numismatic Chronicle*, Fifth series, 4 (1924), 165–166.

[10] It should be noted, however, that the issue was very large. This is indicated by the variety of the dies represented by examples of the issue which formed part of the Teheran hoard. See Newell, *op. cit.*, p. 165.

[11] Tarn, *op. cit.*, p. 584.

the close of the thirty-year period, for the subsequent period of about fifty years, eleven issues were struck at intervals, the greatest of which approximated ten years. Thereafter the striking of tetradrachms each year was the normal practice, interrupted only by periods of civil commotion. During the generation which passed without the issue of silver at Seleucia the issues of drachms in Iran were numerous and large, and the autonomous bronze of Seleucia appeared at fairly frequent intervals and in large quantities. It follows that in the East a policy was pursued not only of continued displacement of the Seleucid currency by Parthian types but of support of national prestige and of trade through an increase in the coinage of silver, which served also to commemorate the assumption by Mithradates of the new title "King of Kings." In Seleucia the extensive coinage of autonomous bronze reveals an active civic consciousness. To what, then, may be ascribed the failure to issue silver in Babylonia?

It is to be understood, of course, that silver continued to circulate in the western provinces. The extant issues of Parthian tetradrachms, although insufficient to displace, served to supplement the older Seleucid coinage. It is very likely that Seleucid tetradrachms, forced out of general circulation in Iran, found their way into the channels of western trade. In addition, drachms from Iran passed into Mesopotamia, which probably was also served at this period, as later, by the mint at Antioch.[12] It is clear, therefore, that no drastic stoppage in interregional and international trade took place. Very possibly the controlling elements in Seleucia, the Greek bankers and traders, so profited by the displacement of Seleucid tetradrachms in the East that they were opposed to the issue of additional silver by the Seleucia mint. Although obviously only a hypothesis, this solution alone appears to satisfy the conditions. Political turmoil in Syria at this time would not have permitted Antioch to supplant Seleucia as the banking center of the western part of the Parthian Empire. An assumption that Mithradates intentionally throttled the commercial life of Seleucia by forbidding the coinage of silver there would be opposed by the strong indications of an alliance between the dynasty and the Greeks throughout the Parthian period.[13] Nor, again, can it be assumed

[12] See pp. 179–180.

[13] See pp. 216–221.

that during the reign of Mithradates conditions were so disturbed in Babylonia as to prevent the entry of bullion for the mint or the passage of trade which would serve to place the resulting currency in circulation. Although our literary sources are silent, cuneiform tablets reveal that in Babylonia, as in Iran, Mithradates was recognized first as king, later as "King of Kings," and the heavy issue of bronze coins reflects a healthy economic situation in and around Seleucia.

Although the long interruption in the minting of silver at Seleucia does not point either to a political or to an economic breakdown locally, it does demonstrate, I believe, that at this time the Parthian royal administration valued but little its prestige in the west and the political and economic importance of the western provinces, especially Babylonia. Only on this hypothesis can one well explain its failure to displace the Seleucid currency and to commemorate with issues of tetradrachms the assumption of the paramount title by Mithradates II. Actually the attitude of mind was one to be expected at this time. The Parthian dynasty and nobles were much more indifferent toward Babylonia than is, perhaps, generally recognized. In this respect Greek and Roman writers frequently perpetuated the wrong impression, owing to the fact that this province and Seleucia, with Ctesiphon, were better known to them than was Iran with its principal city, Ecbatana. The chief pleasure of the Parthian nobles lay in hunting from horseback, and cavalry formed their reliance in war; it is not to be expected, therefore, that Babylonia, cut up as it was by a network of canals large and small, would have appealed to them. There is as yet no evidence to indicate that the culture of Babylonia during the Parthian period was significantly influenced by the introduction of North Iranian elements.

It is apparent that Mithradates I had realized the importance to the development of his empire of the Greek commercial and banking class which had its center at Seleucia, and in time his views appear to have become part of the normal dynastic policy. Notwithstanding this, to an extent at all times but especially during the early period, it is to be presumed that the military aristocracy which formed the nucleus of Parthian expansion and the basis of Parthian power better understood and more willingly supported that economic system which relied upon the acquisition of agricultural and pastoral lands suitable to their tastes and the erection thereon of feudal fiefs. To these nobles and kindred of the royal family fundamental governmental policy was undoubtedly largely limited to, first, the protection of the lands already won from the inroads of later arrivals from the Steppes and, secondly, the expansion of the Parthian boundaries into the naturally rather than artificially fertile lands of northern Mesopotamia and Armenia. The campaigns of Mithradates II into Central Asia resulted in the stabilization of the frontiers on the east. Our fragmentary sources afford glimpses of subsequent Parthian aggression in Armenia and northwestern Mesopotamia. Under these conditions throughout the greater part of the reign of Mithradates II Babylonia and the Greeks of Seleucia appear to have been left to their own devices.[14]

One of the latest acts of Mithradates was the sending of an embassy to the Roman, Sulla. This, I believe, was due neither to Parthian fear of Tigranes nor to Parthian ability to read the future of Roman policy in the Orient,[15] but to Parthian plans for further expansion in Armenian territory which might be facilitated by an ally in western Asia. It is possible, however, that the embassy also involved the question of the trade routes between Seleucia and the Mediterranean which later was to become an important factor in Parthian policy. In any event the death of Mithradates soon after prevented any more concrete display of interest in the development of the western portion of his empire.

In the table tetradrachms have been attributed to a Gotarzes for the year 91/90 B.C., an "Arsaces" for the year 86, and an Orodes for the year 80. These coins were all assigned by Wroth to an Artabanus II. The insertion of this ruler in the Parthian king list between Mithradates II and Sinatruces, with a reign which is supposed to have extended from about 88 to 77 B.C., is based on a reconstruction of the text in Justin by the German historian, Gutschmid.[16] Otherwise a king of this name in the general period with which we are concerned is not known.

Since the publication of the work by Gutschmid cuneiform tablets from Babylon have come to light which name as kings

[14] It is to be noted that the campaigns of Mithradates in Central Asia served to open, perhaps without intention, the road to commercial relations with China from which Seleucia greatly profited. See pp. 217–221.

[15] Rawlinson, *op. cit.*, p. 134; Tarn, *op. cit.*, p. 586.

[16] *Geschichte Irans*, p. 81.

a Gotarzes, from 90 through 87; another called simply "Arsaces," from 86 through 81; and an Orodes, in 80 B.C.[17] The fact that they are not mentioned by name in our literary sources has delayed their inclusion in the Parthian king list. Actually, strictly contemporary documents, which these tablets are, must be given their face value. The omission of the names of these kings from our incomplete literary sources is of no significance, especially in view of the short duration of their reigns and the dominant position held by Armenia during this interval. Although the tablets naturally are not concerned with the geographical limits of their power, they do establish the existence of three successive kings in a part of the Parthian Empire. Certain modern writers have assumed the existence at various periods of "joint kings" within Parthia. A careful study of the literary sources fails to support this hypothesis, and the evidence of the coins is opposed to it. In rare instances "local kings" were recognized on the borders of Parthia, but there is nothing to suggest that Parthian Babylonia ever possessed such dynasts. The formulas in the tablets of the three reigns of the interval 91–80 B.C. differ in no significant respects from those in the tablets of the reign of Mithradates II. In the absence of conclusive evidence suggesting the existence during this period of rulers in other parts of the empire,[18] it is only reasonable to assume that Gotarzes, "Arsaces," and Orodes were acknowledged kings of all Parthia.

[17] The tablets have been brought together by Minns ("Parchments of the Parthian Period from Avroman in Kurdistan," *The Journal of Hellenic Studies*, 35 [1915], 34–36).

[18] The sole possibility is that Mithradates II continued to live until 88 B.C. So far as I know, the only evidence which favors this possibility is afforded by Professor Minns' dating of the well-known Avroman parchments and by a passage in Josephus. Minns (*op. cit.*, pp. 22–65) argued that the documents are dated by the Seleucid Era and in consequence assigned the earliest to the year 88. Since the parchment refers to the reigning king by the title "King of Kings" it would follow that Mithradates was still alive in that year. However, there are strong and, to my mind, convincing reasons for dating the Avroman documents by the Arsacid Era and thereby assigning the earliest to the reign of Phraates IV. These reasons have been clearly set forth by Professor M. I. Rostovtzeff (M. I. Rostovtzeff and C. Bradford Welles, "A Parchment Contract of Loan from Dura-Europos on the Euphrates," *Yale Classical Studies*, II, 41–42). It should be noted in addition that the use of the Seleucid Era on the coins has no bearing on the dating of the parchments, for the latter were composed in Iran whereas the practice of placing dates on coins was limited to the Seleucia mint.

In connection with an account of affairs in Syria Josephus wrote that after Demetrius III had been captured by a confederated force which included Parthians,

It has long been recognized that statements in certain of the classical authors suggest the existence of several short reigns during the period with which we are concerned.[19] Justin, on the authority of Trogus Pompeius, stated that *many* kings ruled between Mithradates II and the Orodes (II) who came to the throne about 57 B.C.[20] The reigns of two kings, Sinatruces and Phraates III, completely occupied the period from about 77 to 57 B.C. The passage in Justin, therefore, not only supports but requires the insertion in the "king list" between 91 and 77 B.C. of the three kings Gotarzes I, "Arsaces," and Orodes I. Plutarch remarked that Parthia lacked the strength to withstand the attacks of Tigranes of Armenia because of internal as well as external welfare.[21] In the passage cited above, Justin refers also to the "varied succession" of the many kings. This Rawlinson takes as an indication of strife in the succession.

In this connection it is interesting to note the possibility that Gotarzes, "Arsaces," and Orodes may have been sons of Mithradates II. It is difficult to doubt that by the close of his reign Mithradates had at least three grown sons. The strife of brothers over the succession all too frequently marred Parthian history and constituted a threat at all times. The portrait on the tetradrachm assigned to Gotarzes shows a strong family resemblance to that on the coins of Mithradates, and the legends on the coins of the three reigns include the title "Theopator."

---

he was sent to "Mithridates who was then king of Parthia," at whose court he remained until his death (*Ant. Jud.*, xiii.14.3). The battle took place about 88 B.C., and it has been assumed that the Parthian king was Mithradates II. The assumption, however, presupposes that, though the latter was unable to enforce the normal form of royal administration in Babylonia — near the center of Parthian power — he maintained his own governor (Josephus has ἔπαρχον in the extreme northwestern portion of Mesopotamia, who had the strength to interfere in Syrian affairs. Whatever the weakness of Josephus as an authority, he is generally accurate in his direct references to affairs in Babylonia. I would accept, therefore, his statement that Demetrius III ended his life as a prisoner of a Mithradates, king of Parthia. The passage in question, however, does not require the assumption that this Mithradates was on the throne at the date of the battle. It will be suggested below that the "Arsaces" who reached the throne in the year 86 was a son of Mithradates II, who may well have borne the personal name of his father. I suggest here that he may be the king referred to by Josephus. While only a hypothesis, the suggestion, unlike the assumption of the survival of Mithradates II until 88 B.C., is not opposed by contemporary documents and does not entail improbable corollaries.

[19] Rawlinson, *op. cit.*, pp. 137–138; Tarn, *op. cit.*, p. 587.

[20] *Prologue*, p. xlii.

[21] *Lucullus*, xxxvi.6.

Previously the term had appeared only on issues of Phraates I and Artabanus I, sons of Phriapatius, and of Phraates II, son of Mithradates I, and it is difficult to imagine its use during the period under consideration by anyone other than a son of the second Mithradates. The references in the literary sources, therefore, and the shortness of the reigns can well be explained by the assumption that the sons of Mithradates disputed the succession until, at last, the third was displaced by Sinatruces, who represented some collateral branch of the Arsacid family. A Parthian rock carving at Behistun in Persia portrays Mithradates II attended by a small group of principal figures, one of whom is named in the accompanying legend as "Gotarzes, Satrap of Satraps." It is difficult to believe that anyone other than the heir apparent would have been permitted to employ this title, which appears to have been inspired by the royal title "King of Kings," itself at this period a relatively new concept. It has already been suggested by recent writers that the Gotarzes of the inscription and the Gotarzes of the tablets are one;[22] I would suggest further that he was the eldest son of Mithradates II. The "Arsaces" who brought to a close the short reign of Gotarzes I in 86 B.C. is not distinguished in the tablets by his personal name. We know that the Arsacids followed the practice of bestowing the father's name on one of the sons other than the eldest. As a hypothesis, therefore, intended to harmonize the passage in Josephus discussed above with the evidence of the tablets, I suggest that this prince was a younger son of Mithradates II, named after his father but, like him, known to the temple scribes by the dynastic name.

The insertion by Gutschmid of an Artabanus in the Parthian king list between 88 and 77 B.C. won support on the part of Wroth because of the existence of groups of tetradrachms, drachms, and bronze which form a fairly homogeneous whole and clearly belong to this period, but which cannot well be assigned either to Mithradates II or to Sinatruces. The similarity of the tetradrachms applies to their use of a common reverse and legend and a superficially common style in the representation of the hair on the obverse portraits. This style — the indication of the hair by formal rows — was followed on practically all

[22] E. Herzfeld, *Am Tor von Asien*, p. 35. See also N. C. Debevoise, *A Political History of Parthia* (to be published shortly by The University of Chicago Press).

subsequent tetradrachms, but hitherto had only been hinted at. The tetradrachms fall into three clear-cut classes in respect to the degree of development of the style; that assigned to Gotarzes shows the least development, whereas on those attributed to Orodes the formalism is pronounced. On the obverses differences are to be noted also in the style of portrayal of the diadem and the tunic. These distinctions in the tetradrachms transcend the variations which normally result within a single reign from a change in the dies or in the engraver. Mr. E. T. Newell has kindly informed me that an examination of the coins themselves, rather than of the plates, reveals greater similarity than dissimilarity in the features of the portraits. This factor taken alone would require the assumption that the coins were struck within a single reign. However, the various factors of dissimilarity in portraiture and in style, together with the fact that the coins must have been struck at Seleucia within the relatively short period between the death of Mithradates II and the accession of Sinatruces, and the unquestioned existence during this period of three kings in Babylonia appear to me to require the assumption that the similarities in the portraiture are due to the kinship of the subjects, and that the tetradrachms were struck by the three kings, Gotarzes, "Arsaces," and Orodes.

The series of tablets which name Gotarzes as king start with the last month of the year 91/90, about March, 90 B.C. They had been preceded by a long series which referred to an Arsaces, King of Kings, and came to a close about October, 91 B.C. The reference can have applied only to Mithradates II, whose death, therefore, and the accession of Gotarzes must be presumed to have taken place during the winter of 91/90 B.C. Since the issue of tetradrachms upon the accession of each new king appears to have been customary, the tetradrachms of Gotarzes have been assigned to this same date. These tablets cease in 87/86 and are followed in the year 86/85 by a series in which the ruler is called simply "Arsaces, King." To 86 B.C., therefore, I assign the accession of this Arsaces, who perhaps was called Mithradates, and the issue of his tetradrachms. The latest tablet of this series is of 81/80 and is followed in the year 80/79 by one which names Orodes as king. His accession and the issue of his tetradrachms can best be assigned to the year 80 B.C.

Note should be taken of the drachms which are associated

with the tetradrachms of Gotarzes, "Arsaces," and Orodes. So far as it is possible to attempt an identification of the portraits, it is likely that the majority are of the reign of Gotarzes. One group, the so-called campaign coins, does not appear to me to have more than a superficial relationship to the others.[23] Additions to the normal legends on these coins require their assignment to a campaign in the provinces of the northeastern frontier of Parthia. As a result efforts have been made to attribute them either to Mithradates II, who alone of the Arsacids of this period can be connected with an aggressive policy in that area, or to a co-king, for whom no basis can be established by fact or through analogy.[24] On numismatic grounds, however, the coins cannot reasonably be assigned to the reign of Mithradates II. The portrait of their obverses approaches that of the coins of Sinatruces. Aside from this and from the addition to the legends the coins are closely similar to those of Gotarzes. It is known that Sinatruces was not in the regular line of succession and gained the throne with the aid of the Steppes people.[25] I suggest, therefore, that instead of representing a campaign on the part of the royal government against this element — an assumption which presents great difficulties — the coins were struck in the areas named on them to support the campaign of Sinatruces to gain the throne. It would be natural for these coins, issued in the haste of the campaign, to follow the style of the drachms then in circulation. This solution, I believe, satisfies the conditions which have made difficult the identification of the coins and is warranted by the relationship of their obverse portrait to that on the subsequent coinage of Sinatruces. It should be noted that the rate of issue of drachms during the years between the death of Mithradates II and the final succession of Sinatruces appears to be distinctly lower than that maintained both prior to and after this period. Although possibly without significance, this fact suggests that in Iran conditions were disturbed.

The exact date cannot be established, but Sinatruces is supposed to have gained the throne by about 77 B.C., and to this year his issue of tetradrachms has been tentatively assigned. He was succeeded about 70 B.C. by Phraates III, to whom two

[23] Wroth, *op. cit.*, p. 40, Nos. 23–25 and note 1. [24] Tarn, *op. cit.*, p. 585.
[25] *Ibid.*

issues of tetradrachms are generally attributed. On the obverse of one the head is bare and in style is related to the tetradrachms of Orodes I. On the obverse of the other the king is shown helmeted and on the reverse he is pictured as Zeus Aëtophoros crowned by the city-goddess. This is supported by the legend, which bears the new title *Theos*. It is probable that the one group represents a routine issue in connection with the accession of Phraates, and it has been assigned the date 70 B.C. The second group appears to have been struck upon some especial occasion.[26] Although conclusive evidence as to the date of its issue is lacking, a tentative determination is suggested by various factors. The drachms of Phraates III are numerous and, like the tetradrachms, fall into two classes according to whether the obverse head is bare or is helmeted.[27] The first class is small, the second large; the collection in the British Museum gives a proportion of about one to four. If, as appears likely, the first class was inaugurated with the accession of Phraates, it covered the first fourth or third of the reign. On this basis the second class might be presumed to have been inaugurated in 67 or 66 B.C. Now, according to the literary sources, about the year 66 Phraates opened a campaign against Armenia in alliance with the Romans.[28] The circumstances may well have required the issue of additional coinage, and the occasion was suitable for the representation of the king wearing a helmet. The correspondence warrants, I believe, the tentative choice of the date 66 B.C. as the initial year of issue of the second class of his coinage, including the tetradrachms on which the king is shown associated with the city-goddess.

Phraates III was succeeded by his sons Mithradates (III) and Orodes (II). Some confusion attends the accounts in the literary sources, and a decided difference of opinion exists among modern writers as to the order in which they came to the throne. Although the evidence of the coins is not final, it supports the conclusion that Mithradates directly followed Phraates, after a short interval was succeeded by Orodes, later regained the throne, and, after a somewhat longer period, was again defeated by Orodes, who thereafter retained the diadem. To Mithradates

[26] The possible significance of the reverse type is discussed on page 219.

[27] I include those doubtfully assigned to Phraates by Wroth (*op. cit.*, pp. 51–55).

[28] Dio Cassius, xxxvi.45.3; Rawlinson, *op. cit.*, p. 143.

can be attributed one issue of tetradrachms and two classes of drachms. The coinage of Orodes consists of numerous classes, but we are immediately concerned with two issues of tetradrachms and four classes of drachms.[29] The first class of drachms of Mithradates, comprising a limited number of issues, is distinguished by the frontal position of the obverse head, includes in the legend the term *Theopator*, and represents all the principal mints of Iran, but has associated with it no issue of tetradrachms from Seleucia. In the second class the obverse shows the head in profile; for *Theopator* we have *Philopator;* the class is again representative of all the eastern mints and, because of the similarity in style and in the legend, the issue of tetradrachms must be assumed to have been contemporary with it. Of the first four classes of drachms of Orodes the earliest is distinguished by the title "Great King" and the term *Theos Eupator*, the second by the title "Great King of Kings" and the same term, the third by the title "King of Kings" and the term *Philopator*, and the fourth (as well as those which succeed it) by the title "King of Kings" unaccompanied by a reference to the father. Each of the four classes is representative of the principal mints of Iran. The first issue of tetradrachms of Orodes bears the peculiar combination of "Great" with the title "King of Kings" and hence is contemporary with the second class of drachms. The second issue of tetradrachms duplicates the legend of the fourth class of drachms and, therefore, is not of an earlier date.

This issue of tetradrachms shows on the reverse the city-goddess kneeling before Orodes and, presumably, was struck to commemorate the surrender of the city in connection with the final defeat of Mithradates.[30] The expression *Theos Eupator* appears nowhere in the Parthian coinage except on the first and second classes of drachms of Orodes. If Orodes himself had assumed the title *Theos*, it is unlikely that it would have been omitted from the numerous issues which succeeded. It is more reasonable to associate it with *Eupator* as a reference to Phraates

[29] It is now rather generally agreed that the coins assigned by Wroth to an unknown king (*op. cit.*, pp. 56–60) actually constitute the coinage of Mithradates, whereas those attributed to the latter by Wroth (*op. cit.*, pp. 61–67) represent the two earliest classes of drachms of Orodes. See in particular Mr. Newell's forthcoming survey of the Parthian coinage. (See p. 201, note 3.)

[30] Tarn, *op. cit.*, p. 604.

III. It must be borne in mind that the brothers had murdered their father, and that each would seek, on his early coinage at least, to proclaim his own innocence. The introduction of the new term suggests that it was intended as a counterblast to the use of *Theopator* on the first issues of Mithradates which, on this assumption, it followed. The assumption is supported by the fact that on his second coinage Mithradates discarded the term *Theopator* in favor of still another, *Philopator*. With the issue of the third class of the drachms of Orodes he, in turn, dropped the title *Theos Eupator* in favor of *Philopator*. The second and third classes of drachms of Orodes are extensive, and both, along with the first class, can scarcely have occupied the period prior to the second coinage of Mithradates. It must be presumed, therefore, that the use of *Philopator* on the third class of Orodes was borrowed from the second coinage of Mithradates and, hence, succeeded it. On the basis of these various factors the evidence of the coins may be said to suggest strongly that the first coinage of Mithradates immediately succeeded the death of Phraates III and was followed shortly by the first class of drachms of Orodes, then by the second class of drachms with the first issue of the tetradrachms of Orodes. Similarly, the second coinage of Mithradates was followed in turn by the third class of drachms of Orodes, his second issue of tetradrachms, and the fourth class of his drachms. The presence of mint marks on the drachms confirms the fact that at no interval did the brothers divide the empire between them.

The literary sources provide only four significant references to the struggle between Mithradates and Orodes. Dio Cassius and Appian mention it casually in discussing criticism in Rome of the conduct of Gabinius, Roman proconsul in Syria. That is, their accounts represent statements very much abridged.[31] The former says that, after Phraates had been murdered by his sons, Orodes succeeded to his kingdom and drove out Mithradates, who was ruling Media. The latter, fleeing to Gabinius, persuaded him to aid his restoration to the throne. Media was the largest and richest province of Iran, contained the principal Parthian capital, Ecbatana, and was better known to westerners than were the other provinces of Iran. The earlier kingdom of Media, which included a large portion of Iran, was well known

[31] Dio Cassius, xxxix.56.2; Appian, *Roman History*, xi.8.51.

to western writers. I suggest, therefore, that the term was employed by Dio in reference to Iran. There are no grounds in reason for the assumption sometimes made that the original plan of the brothers had provided for a division of the empire, Mithradates taking the province of Media, Orodes as paramount king, the rest. For Media was the geographical as well as the political center and, at this period, Babylonia, with Seleucia and Ctesiphon, was of secondary importance. It is clear also that Mithradates was ruling "Media" when Orodes succeeded to the kingdom. The passage in Appian, which applies to the same episode, reads as follows: "Mithradates, king of the Parthians, having been driven out of the kingdom by Orodes his brother, persuaded him [Gabinius] to turn his forces against the Parthians." Plutarch in describing the character of the chief of the Surens clan, who defeated Crassus, recounts a later episode in the civil war.[32] He says that Orodes was once expelled from the kingdom and that the chief brought him back to Parthia and captured Seleucia for him. Justin describes the same event in more detail,[33] but omits the inconclusive capture of Seleucia: "Mithradates, king of the Parthians, after his war with the Armenians was banished by the Parthian senate for cruelty. His brother, Orodes, who took possession of the vacant throne, besieged Babylon, whither Mithradates had fled." He continues with the statement that Mithradates surrendered and was executed.

The events of the civil war and the relation of the coins to the events may be stated as follows. About 57 B.C. Mithradates III succeeded Phraates III in Iran but, after a very short interval and before he had been able to occupy Babylonia, was driven out by Orodes II. During this interval in Iran he struck drachms which bore the term *Theopator*. Within the same year Orodes established himself in Iran and issued the first class of his drachms, with *Theos Eupator*. He then extended his administration to Babylonia, proclaimed himself King of Kings, and struck the first issue of his tetradrachms and the second class of his drachms, still with *Theos Eupator*. Sometime in 56 B.C. Mithradates returned from Syria, drove out Orodes, and occupied Babylonia and Iran. At this interval he struck his second coinage, of tetradrachms and of drachms, which bore the term

[32] *Crassus*, 21.7.

[33] xlii.4.

Philopator. He appears not to have assumed the paramount title, perhaps because of an obligation to Roman influence. His campaign against Armenia must have been of short duration. A group of Parthian nobles, led by the chief of the Surens clan, revolted and brought back Orodes to the principal capital, Ecbatana. Mithradates fled to Seleucia and probably at this moment Orodes struck his third class of drachms, which borrowed the term *Philopator*. Seleucia was captured and Mithradates fled south to Babylon, which was besieged. Upon the surrender of Mithradates and his death, perhaps early in 54 B.C., Orodes caused to be struck at Seleucia his second issue of tetradrachms, which picture the kneeling city-goddess. This was soon followed in Iran by the issue of his fourth class of drachms which, since the question of the succession had been settled, omit all reference to Phraates III.

Four further issues of tetradrachms of Orodes II are known. One is dated in the last year of his reign, 39/38 B.C. Another, which has the same types, probably immediately preceded it [34] and may be assigned, therefore, to about the year 40/39. Since in this year the Parthians inaugurated a campaign into Syria, where tetradrachms would be required, it is very possible that the coins were struck in connection with the campaign. The remaining two issues of tetradrachms have a common type, but lack a year date. They were probably struck in a single year, in the eleventh and twelfth months. On the grounds that a campaign into Syria would increase the demand for tetradrachms, I have tentatively assigned them to the year 52, when for the first time the Parthian armies entered the Mediterranean coastlands. This gives us a period of about twelve years during which no tetradrachms were struck, although in Iran the issue of drachms appears to have been uninterrupted. Certain factors suggest that during this period there was internal dissension in Seleucia as well as in other parts of the Empire.[35]

2. SELEUCIA AND THE PARTHIAN DYNASTY

The history of party strife within Seleucia parallels to an extent the course of the disturbances which mark Parthian political history from the close of the first century B.C. to the rise

[34] See the discussion of the value of dates, p. 147.

[35] See pp. 221–222.

of the Sassanids. The operation of the mint at Seleucia naturally was affected by disorders and revolt within the city, and such conditions are reflected in the rate of issue. It is possible, I believe, to draw further evidence as to political conditions from the character and the quality of the designs and the legends on the coins, both royal and autonomous. Certain types and certain elements in the legends find a reasonable explanation only in the assumption that they were intended to commemorate new developments in the relationship between the paramount power, the dynasty, and the local political unit which issued the coins, the city. During certain intervals a deterioration in the quality of the Greek of the legends took place, but disappeared as rapidly as it had developed. The variations can well be explained only by the assumption that during these periods the personnel of the mint was less well acquainted with, and more indifferent to, the usages of good contemporary Greek than were those who preceded and succeeded them.

It is not possible to discuss in this volume the origin and history of party strife in Seleucia. It may be summarized, however, as follows. Seleucia was founded to serve as the principal center in the East for Hellenic culture and trade. It became the greatest city of its time because it controlled the transit trade between the Mediterranean area and Iran and Farther Asia. The dominant group in the city, its aristocracy, was composed largely of traders and bankers of Hellenic extraction. The majority of the population, however, undoubtedly consisted of Babylonians drawn originally from Opis and Babylon. Jews comprised a third important element. The popular party, in opposition to the Hellenic and Hellenized aristocratic party, appears to have been principally representative of the native Babylonians, with whom the Jews were at times associated. The statement is generally made by present-day writers that Seleucia was hostile to the Parthians. This is inexact. Throughout the greater portion of Parthian history what may be called the legitimate succession within the dynasty was supported by the aristocratic party, whereas rival claimants for the throne were frequently aided by the popular party.

The affiliation was natural. At an earlier period the commercial elements in the Greek cities of Asia Minor had preferred the security and the avenues of trade offered by the Persians to the obligations of kinship and culture represented by the Athenians. At a later date the conservative elements in Antioch called in Tigranes of Armenia to suppress the disorders into which the intradynastic strife of the Seleucids had degenerated. The lifeblood of Seleucia's wealth and power flowed along the single great artery of trade which passed through the center of Iran. A hostile power in control of that highway could throttle the transit trade, whereas a friendly power in Iran, possessed of military capacity, could protect and extend the eastern branches of the artery as far as India and China. Toward the west the situation was entirely different; a number of alternate routes led to the sea, and when one was blocked by disorder or a hostile frontier, another was usually available. The Arsacids, in turn, by this alliance gained a large, regular, and easily controlled source of revenue and the services of highly trained Greeks for the administration of their dominions. Beyond these factors it must be borne in mind that the military aristocracy which we call the Parthians was as alien as the Greeks to the great mass of their subjects, not only the Semitic elements of the west but the more settled Iranians of the east. The Parthian Empire was not a reaction against Hellenism. Throughout its course it protected and made use of Hellenism against Oriental nationalism, and it was the persistence in this policy by the later Arsacids which permitted the rise to power of the Sassanids.

When Mithradates I defeated Demetrius II of Syria, instead of placing some penalty upon Seleucia, the eastern capital of the Seleucids, he granted the city an autonomy which was not only much greater than that enjoyed previously but which remained as an outstanding example of civic liberty in the ancient world.[36] At the same time he caused to be placed on the royal silver struck at Seleucia the term *Philhellenos*, hitherto never used as a royal title and indicative, therefore, of an especial relationship between the dynasty and the Hellenic elements of the empire which had their center in Seleucia. The absence of delay in conferring these benefits, together with the fact that Seleucia,

[36] For the relationship between Seleucia and the Seleucids see R. H. McDowell, *Stamped and Inscribed Objects from Seleucia on the Tigris*, pp. 171–172. Of Seleucia under the Parthians Lucius Ampelius says (l): "Rerum publicarum tria genera sunt, regium, optimatum, populare. Aut enim sub regum sunt potestate, ut Seleucia Parthorum."

although a notable stronghold, appears to have offered no resistance to the Parthians, suggests that Mithradates and the Greeks may have come to an agreement prior to the occupation.

The title *Philhellenos* appears only sporadically on the coins of the early successors to Mithradates, and it is very possible that the true value of the Greek commercial class was not again recognized until the reign of Phraates III, when the period of expansion and of the stabilization of the eastern frontiers had come to an end.[37] In any case the Greeks appear to have remained loyal. When Antiochus VII invaded Parthia the native princes deserted to him, whereas it was in the cities, more influenced by Hellenism than the countryside, that the plot was executed which led to the destruction of the Syrian army.[38] Himerus, a rebel against the Arsacid dynasty, was notorious for his persecution of the Hellenic elements in Babylonia.[39] His strength, therefore, must have been based on the non-Greek elements.

Phraates III caused to be struck, about the year 66 B.C., an issue of tetradrachms on which he is portrayed as Zeus Aëtophoros in the act of being crowned with a wreath by the city-goddess of Seleucia. After a short interruption this association of the reigning Arsacid and the city-goddess, the latter grasping a scepter, became the standard motif for Parthian tetradrachms. Its inauguration commemorates, I believe, a renewal of the alliance between the dynasty and the Hellenic elements within the empire. This resulted from a shift in the direction and character of Parthian expansion. It is very possible that Mithradates I and Phraates II had planned to continue the Parthian sweep westward until it reached the limits of the Seleucid Empire, but the subsequent series of invasions from the Steppes had afforded their successors little occasion to renew their policy. As Tarn has stated,[40] with the reign of Phraates III the west became the principal front. The immediate task, performed by this ruler and by Mithradates III, was the restoration in the west of Parthian administration and prestige, which had fallen to a particularly low ebb. This was followed under Orodes II by a series of efforts to push the Parthian frontiers to the Mediterranean. The urge behind the program was primarily

[37] See the next paragraph.

[38] Justin, xxxviii.10.

[39] *Ibid.*, xlii.1.3; Diodorus Siculus, xxxiv.18.

[40] *Op. cit.*, p. 587.

economic. The old land hunger of the Parthian nobles presumably had its influence. But beyond this there was, I believe, a new realization of the importance of the transit trade and its control. About 115 B.C. the joint efforts of Mithradates II and of the Han emperor in China had resulted in the opening of trade communications through Central Asia. During the period from about 70 to about 40 B.C. the mints of Iran appear to have abruptly and very markedly increased their issue of silver.[41] This can be reasonably explained only by the assumption that by the period in question trade between Iran and Central Asia, China, and India had become of major importance. Full advantage of the trade, from the point of view of its value for revenue purposes, could be enjoyed only if Parthia controlled an outlet to the Mediterranean.

Such appears to have been the basis of the renewed alliance between the Greek commercial aristocracy and the Arsacids. The latter had come to appreciate the value of this source of revenue; the former benefited to the extent that their goods were protected, and taxed, by the minimum number of fiscal agencies. Beyond this, however, I suggest that the new reverse motif of the tetradrachms reveals another factor in the alliance. The Arsacids possessed no claims to power beyond their military organization. No national groups of importance recognized them. In Persis, Elymaïs, and Armenia local dynasties did in increasing measure receive such support. The Seleucid predecessors of the Arsacids had based their right to rule not alone on force but on two theories, that the Hellenic groups transplanted into Asia represented the Macedonian people and by their acclamation conferred the succession from Alexander the Great, and that the apotheosis of the kings permitted the "free" cities within their borders to accept the royal administration. Recognition of the Arsacids as the successors of the Seleucid dynasty would at all times and in all parts of the Empire possess a certain value. It was particularly important if Parthia was to make effective her administration of Mesopotamia and was to advance her boundaries into territory from which the last of the Seleucid dynasty had only lately been driven by the Romans. Seleucia traditionally was the center of Hellenism beyond the Euphrates, and in the west it enjoyed a great renown. Under

[41] See pp. 170–171.

these conditions it cannot have been chance that led to the selection of the new type for that unit of the Parthian currency which in particular would circulate in areas where Hellenic influence was still strong. The representation of the city-goddess of Seleucia in the act of crowning the deified Phraates commemorates, I believe, a formal assumption of that claim to kinship with Alexander the Great and Seleucus Nikator which became the boast of later Parthian kings. It may well have been due in part at least to this act of policy that the Parthian armies a few years later were so readily received from Palestine to Asia Minor. Even though their military capacity did not permit the Parthians to retain their political hold on the west, the remarkable increase in the rate of issue of tetradrachms which persisted after 40 B.C.[42] suggests that a satisfactory outlet had been arranged for the transit trade.

The rôle of Seleucia during the civil war between Mithradates III and Orodes II is obscure. It will be seen in a later instance that the pro-Roman candidate to the Parthian throne was supported by the native-popular party, and this may well have been true at this time. Mithradates had sought Roman aid, and his rapid success thereafter suggests that, in some form, it had been extended. Since he retired to Babylon in defeat and since that city underwent a siege in his behalf, it is not unlikely that his principal support was afforded by the native Babylonians. The fact that on the first issue of tetradrachms after the defeat of his brother, Orodes is shown accepting the hand of the kneeling city-goddess suggests that only slight blame attached to Seleucia for her part in the revolt, limited, perhaps, to a division of allegiance.

During the period between 50 and 40 B.C. Parthia failed to interfere in Syrian affairs and struck no tetradrachms. Whether this was due to internal weakness is not known. The literary sources are silent, but the autonomous coins indicate that at least during the years 42/41 to 39/38 B.C. the native party had gained control of Seleucia. The bronze struck during these years for the first time bears the place name rather than the ethnikon — always employed by cities with Hellenic traditions — and shows a quality of execution noticeably inferior to that of the preceding and succeeding issues.[43] Control of the city by the native party would not necessarily imply a state of revolt. On

[42] See p. 170. [43] See p. 98, No. 130.

the latest issue of tetradrachms of Orodes II, in 39/38, the Greek of the legend has errors in spelling, but on the tetradrachms of Phraates IV which begin in the year 37/36 the legends are correctly formed. An issue of autonomous bronze struck in 38/37 has the ethnikon, and the quality of execution is again equivalent to that of early issues. The conditions suggest that the murder of Orodes and the succession of Phraates were accompanied by a transfer of the control of Seleucia from the native-popular party to the Greek-aristocratic party. At what period the popular party had assumed power cannot be determined.

Of some significance in the reign of Phraates IV was the attempt by one faction among the Parthian nobles to replace him by an avowedly pro-Roman candidate, Tiridates. Two issues of tetradrachms can be assigned to this prince, one of about May, 26 B.C., the other of about March, 25 B.C. Issues of Phraates are known for approximately April, August, September, and November, 26, and for May, 25 B.C. Tiridates struck no drachms. On the evidence of the coins it appears that the revolt consisted of two successive spring offensives, probably launched from the Roman border of Mesopotamia, which reached Babylonia but failed to win Iran. The latest dated tetradrachms of Phraates IV were struck in the year 23/22, the earliest of his successor, Phraataces, in 2/1 B.C. Two groups of this denomination, on which no dates can be distinguished, were assigned by Wroth to the period 27–26 B.C. I find no adequate grounds, however, for not attributing them to the period for which we have no examples with dates. If they were not intended to show dates it is to be assumed that each represented a single issue, separated by an interval from those which preceded and succeeded. The slackened rate of issue of tetradrachms during the final twenty years of the reign of Phraates is to be noted, although no particular significance appears to attach to it. Two issues of autonomous bronze, one of 32/31, the other assigned to the period from 32/31 to the end of the reign of Phraates, bear the ethnikon and reveal the quality of execution which associate them with earlier issues of the aristocratic party. This is true also of the issue of bronze assigned to the reign of Phraataces, 2/1 B.C. to 4/5 A.D.

The short reign of Orodes III, marked by an issue of tetradrachms in 6/7 A.D., was preceded and succeeded by years in which no silver was struck. The absence of drachms indicates that his power either failed to extend into Iran or was effective there for a very short interval. His successor, Vonones I, inaugurated his issue of tetradrachms in 9/10 A.D. For this same year we have an issue of autonomous bronze which is poorly executed and which bears the place name rather than the ethnikon; it appears, that is, to have been struck by the native party. This indication of a shift in party rule at Seleucia coincident with the accession of Vonones suggests that his partisans included the native Babylonians. He had been brought from Rome by one party among the Parthian nobles, whereas another faction put forward Artabanus, who had been king of Media (Atropatene). The appearance of the personal name of Vonones on his first issues of tetradrachms and drachms points to the presence of Artabanus in the field, already an open claimant to the throne. Both classes of silver show Nike as reverse type. In addition, the drachms bear a legend which refers to a victory over Artabanus. These factors point to a battle in the year 9/10, somewhere in Iran, in which Artabanus was defeated.[44] Vonones continued to rule at least until about September, 11 A.D. Sometime during 11/12 Artabanus II issued his first tetradrachms, presumably between September, 11, and April, 12 A.D. He remained in control of Seleucia until at least August, 12 A.D., but in November of this year we find Vonones again issuing tetradrachms in Seleucia. The drachms of Vonones, and his rule over Media, belong to the opening of his reign.

Artabanus II struck no more tetradrachms until the year 20/21, but for the years 15/16 and 16/17 we have two issues of autonomous bronze, related by their use of common monograms, which were struck under the authority of the aristocratic party. It is to be assumed that during the two preceding years, when the mint was inactive, the native party had been overthrown and that Vonones, who had received their support, had been obliged to flee.[45] On this group of autonomous coins all reference to the

[44] The mint mark which distinguishes the greater part of the drachms is probably that of Ecbatana. It is likely that in Iran the rule of Vonones was effective only in Media.

[45] One of the issues of bronze, that for 15/16, bears month dates and presents an uninterrupted series from the fifth through the twelfth month. It is very possible that the victory of the aristocratic party, therefore, should be dated only from about August, 15 A.D.

city was discarded. On the second issue the monograms which had appeared on the first in normal position occur as the reverse types, accompanied by the word *βουλῆς*, in reference to the aristocratic council of Seleucia. Three other issues of autonomous bronze, on none of which the city name occurs, followed in the years 17/18, 18/19, and 23/24. The first was probably struck by the aristocratic party, but the last two, to judge from the coarseness of their design, by the popular party. During the next year the royal bronze of the Seleucia mint was inaugurated; thereafter civic types reappeared only during periods of revolt. I believe that the revocation of the right to employ an autonomous currency marks also the end of the city's autonomous rights. I suggest, further, that this was decided upon at a time when the aristocratic party was in control, in 15/16, when the name of the city was dropped from the design of the coins, and that it received the approbation of this group.[46] Tacitus states that at some time during this particular period Artabanus had betrayed the people of Seleucia into the power of the aristocrats.[47] The correspondence of this act with the apparent withdrawal of autonomy can be reasonably explained only by the supposition that by this time the native party had become more powerful than the Greek party and that to maintain their position the aristocrats, with their ally Artabanus, superseded the forms of self-government by the armed force of the royal administration. During the years 20/21, 23/24, and 24/25 tetradrachms were struck which show on the reverse Artabanus seated, the city-goddess standing, and a male in native costume kneeling. I take this as commemorative of the formal submission of the native elements in the city who, as we have seen, had again come into power during 18/19 and who had probably offered resistance to the proposed change in the constitution. This was consummated in 24/25, which saw the initial issue of the royal bronze.

With the aid of Roman intrigue certain elements in Parthia turned against Artabanus and welcomed in his place the Roman

[46] The use of the personal monograms of mint controllers as the type suggests that the initial issue, which lacked the familiar city name, was not well received and that the controllers were men of such standing in the community that their initials served as a guarantee of the authenticity of the succeeding issue, which was probably first struck at the very close of the year 15/16. The remaining three issues borrowed their motifs from the tetradrachms with which the public was familiar.

[47] *Annales*, vi.42.

candidate, Tiridates. The native party in Seleucia was evidently associated with the revolt, for an account has been preserved of its extravagant reception of Tiridates and his transfer to it of the power which Artabanus had conferred upon the aristocratic party.[48] This took place about 36 A.D. For several years previously no coinage had been struck in Seleucia. The inactivity is probably to be associated with the condition of anarchy in Babylonia which Josephus has described.[49] About June, 42 A.D., the issue of tetradrachms was resumed in the name of Vardanes I, a son of Artabanus, who had meanwhile succeeded to the throne. During this interval there had taken place the so-called revolt of Seleucia which, according to Tacitus, occupied seven years.[50] It is important to bear in mind that, contrary to the impression left by nearly all modern commentators, this "revolt" was only a detail in the civil war which was raging throughout Parthia. The native party in control of Seleucia under the authority of Tiridates simply continued his administration. After the flight of Tiridates Artabanus was probably so occupied with the continued dissension among the nobles that he was unable to concentrate an important force to retake the city. Upon his death, probably about 40 A.D., the civil war was continued in the rivalry between his sons Vardanes (I) and Gotarzes (II). At one time the former attacked Seleucia, but was driven off by a counter thrust on the part of Gotarzes.[51] Effectively there was an interregnum after about 36 A.D. During this period the native party struck an extensive series of bronze, which again bore the city name, was of a very inferior execution, and had on the reverse the characteristic Oriental motif of the humped bull. It was displaced in the year 40/41 by a new series without the city name, well engraved and showing on the reverse Nike with a palm. These coins continued to be struck from 41/42 to 43/44. In 43/44 there was struck a new issue of bronze with civic types, without the city name and well executed, and two issues of royal bronze. The more important of the latter bore on the obverse the portrait of Vardanes; on the reverse, a personification of the

[48] *Ibid.* This passage taken out of its context has been employed as evidence that Seleucia as a unit was anti-Parthian and pro-Roman.

[49] *Antiquities of the Jews*, xviii.9.

[50] *Annales*, xi.9. Cf. Gutschmid, *op. cit.*, pp. 121–125.

[51] Tacitus, *Annales*, xi.8.

Boule, the aristocratic council of Seleucia, accompanied by the legend Βουλή. The "Victory" coins of the years 40/41–43/44 are closely related to this royal bronze in respect to both style and quality.

These successive series of bronze permit of but one conclusion. In 40/41 the aristocratic party overthrew the popular party and took over the administration of the city. Only in the spring of 42 did Vardanes arrive again in the vicinity; he was voluntarily received into the city and about June began the issue of a continuous series of tetradrachms.[52] The first issues of royal bronze commemorate the alliance between Vardanes and the aristocratic party. The one small issue of civic bronze which immediately preceded the royal bronze and was struck alongside the tetradrachms suggests that there was some question of retaining that class of coinage.

On the evidence of the coins it is apparent that in the civil war between the two brothers Vardanes inherited the policy and the partisans of his father, Artabanus.[53] Prokesch-Osten had read on a tetradrachm of Gotarzes the date equivalent to 41/42, but Petrowicz has demonstrated that the correct reading gives the year 48/49.[54] The literary sources state that upon the death of Artabanus Vardanes laid hands on the "adjoining provinces," which in this period must refer to the western part of the Empire, whereas they associate Gotarzes with the East. This division is supported by the large number of drachms and bronze coins of the latter struck in Iran, where Vardanes can have retained possession of little more than Media — and that for a short period only. It may be assumed also that the native party in Seleucia and Babylonia looked to Gotarzes to break the domina-

[52] It should be noted that Tacitus, our only literary source on the "revolt," states simply that, when Vardanes had previously attacked Seleucia, it had been in anger at the revolt against Artabanus (that is, at the native party for their loyalty to Tiridates) and that later the city gave itself up to him (*Annales*, xi.8–9). The victory of the aristocratic party in 40/41 appears to represent the conclusion of the incident related by Josephus to the effect that the natives in Seleucia had overthrown the Greeks with the aid of a group of Jewish refugees and that later the Greeks and the natives became reconciled and joined in a massacre of the Jews, upon whom the blame was conveniently cast (*Antiquities of the Jews*, xviii.9.9). Cf. Gutschmid, *op. cit.*, p. 121.

[53] This supports the testimony of Josephus that Artabanus had chosen Vardanes as his successor, as against the generally accepted interpretation of Tacitus to the effect that Gotarzes immediately succeeded (*Antiquities of the Jews*, xx.3.4; *Annales*, xi.8).

[54] *Op. cit.*, p. 118, note.

tion of the Greek aristocratic party supported by Vardanes. In the course of the continued civil war Gotarzes twice occupied Seleucia, about June, 44, and about January, 45 A.D., before he was able to make himself master. The latest tetradrachms of Vardanes were struck about July, 45. We have an issue of Gotarzes of about January, 46, followed in July of that year by the inauguration of an uninterrupted series which continued to the close of his reign. The unique series of royal bronze dated in each of the first seven months of 46 A.D. suggests strongly that the administration of Gotarzes was established in Seleucia just prior to the opening of that year.

The issues of tetradrachms in 46/47 and 47/48, probably in consecutive months, bear the personal name of Gotarzes and indicate that at this period some rival laid claim to the throne. Such a rival existed in the person of a pro-Roman candidate, Meherdates, but the date 49 A.D. generally assigned to his campaign presents difficulties.[55] According to Tacitus,[56] Gotarzes died of an illness and was succeeded by a Vonones, king of Media (Atropatene), who in turn died after a short reign and was succeeded by his son, Volagases. Josephus,[57] on the other hand, states that Gotarzes was killed as a result of a conspiracy and was followed by his brother, Volagases. The coins demonstrate the essential accuracy of the Jewish historian. No coins exist which can be assigned to Vonones, who, aside from the mention in Tacitus, is unknown. Volagases I came into control of Seleucia and struck tetradrachms about September and October, 51 A.D.; Gotarzes regained possession of the mint in December of this year, and the uninterrupted series of tetradrachms of Volagases date only from about May, 52. It is clear that there was an open revolt led by Volagases, in the course of which Gotarzes appears to have been assassinated during the late winter or early spring of 52 A.D. Josephus as a Jew enjoyed closer relationships with Babylonia than did contemporary western writers, and his narrative of Parthian history, especially as it concerns Babylonia and Mesopotamia, deserves more credence than is generally accorded to it. In this instance it is reasonable to assume that he is correct in making Volagases the brother of Gotarzes.

[55] See Gutschmid, *op. cit.*, p. 127.

[56] *Annales*, xii.14.

[57] *Antiquities of the Jews*, xx.3.4.

Vardanes I, who received the support of the aristocratic party in Seleucia, had been overthrown by Gotarzes II, probably supported by the popular-native party. Volagases, who took the throne from Gotarzes, appears to have represented again the political forces which had supported Vardanes and, before him, Artabanus II. During the early years of his reign occurred the short-lived revolt of his son, Vardanes II, to whom may rightfully belong some of the tetradrachms here assigned to Volagases I.[58] Again, for the years 59/60 and 60/61 no tetradrachms exist. During this interval and a part of the succeeding year there were struck two groups of bronze with civic types, Oriental in motif and of poor execution. Thereafter silver continued to be issued into the year 69/70. For this single year we have, besides the issue of tetradrachms, two issues of royal bronze and three issues of bronze with civic types. One of these, No. 146 in the table, is related by the character of the motif and by style and execution to the civic types struck in the interval 59/60–61/62, and repeats the reverse type of the revolt coinage struck during the interval 36–40 A.D. The other two issues with civic types for 69/70 are dissociated from the first by their execution, style, and fabric; on the basis of these characteristics they are related to the succeeding issue of royal bronze. The latter repeats the reverse type of one of the two issues and the monogram which appears on the other. These successive issues of bronze can be explained only on the assumption that a revolt of the native party became overt in Seleucia in the year 59/60, was temporarily broken up in 61/62, presumably by royal forces, broke out again in 69/70, and was almost immediately crushed by a counter movement of the loyalist party in the city. It appears, further, that the royal administration was temporarily unable to resume control, with the result that the loyalist party issued its own coinage in commemoration of the disaster of the revolt (the city-goddess seated on a broken column in an attitude of mourning) and of the subsequent victory (Nike with wreath). Before the close of the year, however, the central government again became effective and continued the issue of the "Victory" coinage, but with the royal portrait on the obverse.

[58] Wroth, *op. cit.*, pp. l–lii. See also the forthcoming survey of Parthian coins by Mr. E. T. Newell, cited on p. 201, note 3. A bronze coin from Seleucia, found too late to include in the catalog of the present volume, appears to reproduce on the obverse the facing portrait of Vardanes II.

The temporary weakness of the central administration in Babylonia during the year 69/70 may well have been due to more general disturbances in Parthia. About 58 A.D. there had broken out in the eastern provinces a revolt which appears to have continued, perhaps intermittently, until approximately 75 A.D., when Hyrcania, at least, obtained its independence.[59] The two outbreaks by the native party in Seleucia, therefore, can reasonably be assumed to have formed part of a general nationalistic reaction against the Parthian overlordship encouraged, to some extent, by the Romans. The relationships of the coins demonstrate that Volagases supported the Greek-aristocratic party and was opposed by the native-popular party. His reign, that is, represents the domination of the group in Babylonia, and probably in Parthia as a whole, which had formerly been headed by Artabanus II and Vardanes I. It is very possible, therefore, that the disturbances which marked the reign of Volagases constituted a continuation of the struggle for power by those elements in Parthia which had previously supported Gotarzes II. Volagases is credited by Pliny with the construction of a new metropolis, Volageisias, intended to destroy the position in commerce hitherto held by Seleucia.[60] The continued disloyalty of the native groups in Seleucia, with the consequent disruption of the transit trade, may well have resulted at this time in a decision on the part of both the central administration and the leading merchants and bankers of Seleucia to erect a new center through which commerce could flow under the more facile control of the royal government.

3. THE ROMAN CAMPAIGNS AND THE DECLINE OF PARTHIA

The disturbed conditions which marked the reign of Volagases I were accentuated in those of his immediate successors. Parthia became again an effective unity, for a time at least, only with the final defeat of Osroes by Volagases II about 130 A.D. A revolt against Volagases I broke out under the leadership of Pacorus II in the spring of 78. To judge from his portrait, the prince was closely related to Volagases, a son or a nephew. Although evidence is lacking, it is not unreasonable to attribute

[59] Rawlinson, *op. cit.*, pp. 270–271 and 271, note 1; p. 286 and note 2.

[60] *Nat. Hist.*, vi.123, where it is called Vologesocerta.

the revolt to the same groups in Parthia which had been responsible for earlier disturbances. In the course of the movement Seleucia and the mint changed hands repeatedly until the tetradrachms of Volagases came to an end early in the year 80, to which date, in the entire absence of evidence in the literary sources, the death of this ruler may be assigned.[61] The new administration was almost at once attacked by another prince, Artabanus III, who issued tetradrachms at Seleucia in the fall of 80 and the greater part of 81. Since he appears to have struck no drachms, his rule must have been effective only within the confines of Babylonia and Mesopotamia. Between 82/83 and 96/97 A.D., when the tetradrachms of Pacorus ceased to be issued, there was a consecutive period of seven years, 86/87 to 92/93 inclusive, for which no issues of silver are known and during which unrest may well have prevailed. For a period of twenty-five years after the spring of 97 A.D. no tetradrachms were struck and the mint at Seleucia was entirely inactive until 105/06. The abundant bronze coinages during the period between 105/06 and 129/30 vividly illustrate the bitter struggle between Volagases II and Osroes for control of Seleucia, interrupted only by short occupations on the part of Pacorus and the Roman army in 115–116. The status of Seleucia during the interval between 97 and 105/06 is not known; presumably the city was under the nominal rule of Pacorus, and the conditions of practical anarchy prevented the operation of the mint. During this and later intervals the effective rule of Pacorus seems to have been limited to northern Mesopotamia.[62] Osroes, another claimant for the paramount power, appears to have hailed from Elymaïs, adjacent to Babylonia on the southeast.[63] These conditions require the assumption that the third contestant, Volagases II, made his headquarters somewhere in northern Iran, near its western borders. The close relationships between the

[61] It should be borne in mind that in this volume a group of tetradrachms has been assigned to Volagases I which were attributed by Wroth to a "First Reign" of Volagases II. See p. 119, No. 94.

[62] This is suggested by the fact that he controlled Armenia through his son Exidares, that he sold the principality of Edessa at some time about 110 A.D., and that he was engaged in border disputes with the Romans.

[63] It was pointed out by Percy Gardner (*Parthian Coinage*, p. 19) that the name Osroes is "Persian" (that is, South Iranian), as is the peculiar style of hairdressing which marks his coin portraits. As Osroes retired before the advance of Trajan, instead of making for Media he moved first to Babylon, then to Susa in Elymaïs. The daughter

coin portraits of Volagases I, Pacorus II, and Volagases II suggest that the last two may have been brothers, and sons of Volagases I. The fact that Pacorus revolted against Volagases I suggests further that Volagases II may have been the rightful heir, who was forced to wait before asserting his claims until the power of Pacorus had abated.

The general assumption by historians that Osroes was recognized as paramount king of Parthia lacks a basis in fact. To the east of the Zagros during this period only western Iran appears to have remained under Parthian control; the center of the kingdom lay to the west. Yet Osroes struck no tetradrachms, the principal medium of exchange in the west. His issues of drachms and bronze outside Seleucia are very limited. His letter to Trajan, which may have led Roman writers to think of him as effectively King of Kings, represents necessarily nothing more than a bid for Roman support. The answer of Trajan — that the friendship of kings depends on deeds, not words — suggests that the emperor was well aware of the real status of Osroes. This situation explains also the cavalier treatment accorded by Trajan to Parthamasiris, Osroes' candidate for the Armenian throne.[64] The reign of Osroes represents essentially an antidynastic reaction on the part of Elymaïs and Babylonia.

Volagases II appears to have been responsible for the issue of bronze in Seleucia from 105/06 through 108/09. Presumably he had advanced from Media and driven out the administration of Pacorus — if Pacorus still exercised any control on the borders of Babylonia. The occupation of Seleucia by Osroes in 109/10 was, I suggest, part of a campaign which carried him north from Elymaïs to Armenia, where he deposed Exidares, the son of Pacorus, and installed Parthamasiris. To this period must be assigned the few drachms of Osroes, struck probably in Ecbatana. Presumably Volagases was pushed back to the outlying parts of Media, while Pacorus retired on western Mesopotamia. The

---

and the throne of Osroes were captured in Susa by the Romans, who followed his flight. Contrary to the impression left by modern commentators, I find in the sources no evidence which connects Osroes by name with Ctesiphon or which requires the assumption that he was the brother of Pacorus. Dio (18.19.4) states simply that Osroes was the uncle of the sons of Pacorus; in other words, the relationship may well have been one of marriage.

[64] For a general discussion of these events see Rawlinson, *op. cit.*, pp. 301–305.

sale of Edessa by the latter about 110 A.D. may well have been for the purpose of raising troops. During the years 112/13 through 114/15 Osroes was chiefly engaged in contesting with Volagases the possession of Seleucia and, presumably, Ctesiphon. This explains the failure of either to aid materially in resistance to the Roman aggression in northern Mesopotamia.[65] During 115/16, the year in which Trajan occupied Babylonia,[66] Volagases and Pacorus both struck bronze in Seleucia.

Of the considerable number of Roman coins found at Seleucia nearly all can be connected with one of the campaigns to Babylonia. The thirteen bronze coins of Trajan which have been recovered fall within this class; most of them are dated "XX TRIB POT," which is also the latest date. This is equivalent to the period from October/December, 115, to October/December, 116. Since it is not likely that they were struck in Seleucia, it is reasonable to assume that the Roman occupation of the city covered the latter part of this period only, and may in part have been subsequent to it. The accounts of the campaign in our sources fail to mention any occupation of Seleucia prior to the later uprising against the Romans. They do describe, however, what superficially appears to be an extraordinary maneuver on the part of Trajan — an advance down the Euphrates to Babylon, leaving the Roman left flank and rear exposed to an attack from Seleucia or Ctesiphon.[67] Both these factors become intelligible if it can be assumed that Seleucia had been occupied by a friendly force prior to the Roman advance, and that Babylon rather than Ctesiphon was the headquarters of the particular Parthian prince against whom the Roman drive on Babylonia was directed. I suggest, therefore, that Pacorus headed the pro-Roman elements in Mesopotamia and Babylonia, and that as an ally of Trajan he advanced down the Euphrates ahead of the Roman army[68] to take Seleucia from the hands of Volagases II who, presumably, retired on Ctesiphon, whence he could maintain contact with Media. Since Volagases had al-

[65] The evidence of the coins is supported by the direct statement in Dio Cassius, lxviii.26.

[66] R. P. Longden, "Notes on the Parthian Campaign of Trajan," *The Journal of Roman Studies*, 21 (1931), Part I, 8.

[67] Dio Cassius, lxviii.26.

[68] In view of the fact that our source material for this period is only fragmentary, the absence of specific reference to Pacorus in this connection has no significance.

ready issued coins in Seleucia after April of 115, the occupation by Pacorus must have taken place in the summer or fall. Osroes, who had been forced out of Seleucia by Volagases, probably in the winter of 114/15, can have retired in only one direction, south on Babylon, whence ran the main highway to Susa in Elymaïs.

During the Roman campaign in Mesopotamia it was Osroes rather than Volagases who had been the nominal source from which resistance proceeded. This follows from the fact that he had been conducting an aggressive campaign in those regions just prior to the Roman advance. It was natural, therefore, for Trajan to seek battle with him rather than with Volagases, and the presence of Pacorus in Seleucia, guarding the crossing from Ctesiphon, made it safe for the Roman army to break up the forces of Osroes around Babylon before seeking to occupy Ctesiphon. Upon the flight of Osroes to Susa, where certain of the Romans who followed him captured his throne and his daughter,[69] Trajan appears to have passed by Seleucia without entering the city, and occupied Ctesiphon, from which Volagases II fled without resistance.[70] Following the evidence of the coins I suggest that Seleucia remained in the hands of Pacorus and the pro-Roman party until the uprising against the Romans in the winter of 115/16, after which it presumably was garrisoned by Trajan until the time of his retreat.[71]

After the retreat of the Romans Osroes occupied Seleucia and struck coins in 117/18 while Volagases appears again only after two more years. This may indicate that the "puppet king," Parthamaspates, set up by Trajan had been able to maintain himself during this interval. There is nothing in the literary sources to invalidate such a conclusion. It is very possible also that during the period from 117 to 119 Volagases had been preoccupied with the reëstablishment of Parthian control over

[69] Spartianus, *Hadrian*, 12; Capitolinus, *Antoninus Pius*, 9.

[70] It was only surmise on the part of Rawlinson which led him to describe the flight of Osroes from Ctesiphon (*op. cit.*, p. 312). Longpérier has noted that the literary sources give no information concerning the Parthian prince from whom Trajan took the capital (*Mémoires*, p. 138).

[71] Although the excavations have not yet revealed definite evidence, we know that the Great House suffered a severe conflagration between 115 and about 120 A.D., and the remains of a very heavy fire in trial trench 4, in the temple area, can be assigned to this general period.

Mesopotamia, evacuated by the Romans under the orders of Hadrian. Such a reopening of the trade routes between Seleucia and the highlands to the north would explain the ability of Volagases to reinaugurate the issue of tetradrachms in 122/23. Although Osroes continued to dispute his control of Seleucia, probably from a base in southern Babylonia, the issues of bronze reveal the constantly increasing strength of Volagases. The latest issue of Osroes at Seleucia is of 128/29, but he may have continued to control Elymaïs for some years after this date.

Although Volagases II reëstablished Parthian unity in the western provinces, with their consequent commercial prosperity reflected in the almost unbroken sequence of tetradrachms struck during the rest of his reign and that of his successor, a series of drachms struck in Iran by another prince, who must have been a contemporary, proves that the old empire no longer existed.[72] The comparatively few Parthian drachms of the late period which have been recovered suggest that only small areas in Iran were under effective Parthian rule and that even in those regions there was a low level of prosperity.

The latest issue of Volagases II is of 147/48; the earliest of Volagases III was struck about May, 148. This was the first instance of a succession to the Parthian throne unaccompanied by civil war, revolt, or parricide since about 70 B.C., when Phraates III, so far as we have knowledge, inherited peacefully the rights of his father, Sinatruces. The apparently prosperous reign of Volagases III was interrupted by the invasion of Babylonia and the capture of Seleucia on the part of the Roman, Avidius Cassius. A number of caches of coins of this period have been described in the catalog.[73] The latest date on such coins is always the ninth month of the year 165/66, or about December, 165. Tetradrachms were again struck about November, 166, and continue thereafter with no apparent decrease in the rate of issue of either silver or bronze. The evidence of the coins, amply supported by the results of the excavations themselves, demonstrates that the damage inflicted by the Romans was not so extensive as the literary sources suggest.

The reign of Volagases III appears to have been brought to a close by a revolt of which the literary sources have left no record. He struck tetradrachms in about April and July, 190;

[72] Wroth, *op. cit.*, pp. 217–233.

[73] See pp. 85–88.

for about September, 191, there appears an issue by his successor, Volagases IV. Volagases III was in control of the mint again about March, 192, but in October of the same year the series of Volagases IV was resumed. The quality of the engraving and of the Greek of the legends on the tetradrachms of Volagases III was maintained without noticeable variation throughout his reign. From the outset those of the new king, on the other hand, are markedly inferior in regard to both these characteristics. It must be concluded, therefore, that the revolt introduced a new group of engravers to the Seleucia mint. The hairdressing pictured on the coin portraits of Volagases IV is closely similar to that characteristic of Osroes, that is, South Iranian in style. I suggest, therefore, that the reign of Volagases IV represents a period during which Elymaïs once more sought the paramount power. During this period Babylonia was again attacked by the Romans, under Septimius Severus. To this occasion must be assigned a cache of tetradrachms, the latest of which is dated in 198/99. No month dates can be distinguished.[74] There was no break at this time in the annual issue of the silver, which continued without interruption upon the accession of the next king, Volagases V, until the year 222/23. Another son of Volagases IV, Artabanus IV, ruled during a part of this period in what was left of Parthian Iran, where he struck a series of drachms, probably at Ecbatana.[75] The issue of the royal bronze at Seleucia appears to have reached a close in the year 215/16, and the regular issue of tetradrachms apparently ceased in 222/23, probably the year of the death of Volagases V. A tetradrachm exists, however, which, on the authority of both Gardner and Longpérier, bears a date equivalent to 228/29 A.D.[76] It was struck by an Artavasdes, perhaps a son of Artabanus IV, who must be assumed to have been ruling in some part of Iran, where he issued drachms. The tetradrachm probably marks a temporary occupation of Seleucia by this prince.

The evidence of the coins [77] demonstrates that the site of Seleucia continued to be inhabited from the outset of the Sassanian occupation of Babylonia, but apparently on a much-

[74] See p. 91, No. 122. [75] Wroth, *op. cit.*, pp. 247–250.

[76] Gardner, *op. cit.*, p. 59; Longpérier, *op. cit.*, p. 157.

[77] Fairly numerous Sassanian coins have been found among the surface débris at various parts of the mounds, and a few in burials.

reduced scale. The important Sassanian town of Weh-Ardashir covered the southeast portion of the complex of mounds; a large villa appears to have existed during this period at the north-central extremity (trial trench 4); but what had been the principal residential section until the close of the Parthian period reveals only scattered burials of Sassanian times.

Seleucia probably ceased to be the center for the transit trade after the foundation of Volageisias during the troubled reign of Volagases I.[78] It is likely that this change was accompanied and followed by a major shift in the population, the gradual transfer to the new site of that important element in the older metropolis which was directly dependent upon interregional commerce. The evident local prosperity which had marked the relatively peaceful reign of Volagases III was perhaps made possible by the residue of accumulated capital which had not been directly connected with this form of trade. Besides local trade agriculture may be presumed to have occupied a large share of the population of Seleucia as of other cities in the Orient, both ancient and modern. The seizure of power by Volagases IV must have drawn yet closer the bonds which had long linked Seleucia with Susa in Elymaïs.[79] This in turn may well have facilitated the Sassanian occupation. The dominant element in the city, however, remained the native Babylonian which, boring from within during the course of generations, finally succeeded in entirely destroying the Hellenic blood and tradition to which the commercial greatness of Seleucia had been due. Weh-Ardashir appears to have been a local Babylonian emporium, in its economic relationships probably very similar to the earlier Babylonian Opis which, as an individual entity, had so abruptly disappeared when the genius of Seleucus I and Antiochus I created Hellenic Seleucia.

[78] See p. 229.

[79] See pp. 181 and 231.

LIST OF PARTHIAN KINGS

The table which follows comprises those rulers who appear to have struck coins at the mint of Seleucia within the Parthian period. The two columns of figures give the earliest and the latest dates to which such coins of each of the successive rulers have been assigned in this volume.

King	B.C.
Mithradates I	141–138/37
Phraates II	137/36–129/28
Artabanus I	125/24–124/23
Himerus	124/23–123/22
Mithradates II	122/21–121/20
Gotarzes I	91/90
"Arsaces"	86
Orodes I	80
Sinatruces	77
Phraates III	70–66
Mithradates III	56
Orodes II	57/56–39/38
Phraates IV	37/36–2/1 (?)
Tiridates II	26/25
Phraataces	2/1 B.C.–4/5 A.D.
	A.D.
Orodes III	6/7
Vonones I	9/10–12
Artabanus II	11–30/31 (?)
Vardanes I	42–45
Gotarzes II	44–51
Volagases I	51–80
Pacorus II	78–115/16
Artabanus III	80/81
Volagases II	105/06–148
Osroes	109/10–128/29
Volagases III	148–192
Volagases IV	191–208/09
Volagases V	208/09–222/23
Artavasdes	228/29

INDEXES

I. INDEX OF TYPES

II. INDEX OF SYMBOLS AND PARTICULAR OBJECTS IN TYPES

III. INDEX OF VARIANT FORMS OF GREEK CHARACTERS

1	(A)	A	First occurrence, p. 64, No. 73
2	(A)	A	Pages 66–67, Nos. 76–78
3	(A)	Λ	Pages 67–69, Nos. 80–83
4	(B)	K	First occurrence, p. 74, No. 93
5	(E)	⊏	Pages 64, 66–67, 67–69, 106, Nos. 72, 76–78, 80–83, 141
6	(E)	Є	Page 78, No. 102 (as numeral)
7	(Θ)	⊙	Page 81, No. 109a (as numeral)
8	(M)	⊓	Page 70, No. 86 (as numeral)
9	(N)	N	Pages 68, 91, 103, 109, Nos. 82, 122, 136, 144
10	(Ξ)	⌯	Page 73, No. 92 (as numeral)
11	(O)	□	First occurrence, p. 67, No. 80
12	(O)	•	Page 98, No. 130 (as numeral)
13	(Σ)	⊏	First occurrence, p. 63, No. 70
14	(Υ)	V	First occurrence, p. 63, No. 70
15	(Φ)	+	First occurrence, p. 63, No. 69
16	(Ω)	ω	Page 18, No. 41
17	(Ω)	Ш	First occurrence, p. 70, No. 87
18	(Ϛ)	⊏	Page 104, No. 137 (the numeral stigma)

IV. GENERAL INDEX

PLATES

PLATE I

Monograms

The pages on which the various monograms are mentioned and the type groups to which they belong are listed below

1. p. 3, No. 1
2. p. 3, No. 1
3. p. 3, No. 1
4. p. 4, No. 2
5. p. 5, No. 6
6. p. 6, No. 9
7. p. 7, No. 10
   p. 7, No. 12
   p. 10, No. 19
   p. 11, No. 22
   p. 16, No. 36
   p. 17, No. 37
8. p. 7, No. 10
9. p. 7, No. 11
10. p. 7, No. 11
11. p. 7, No. 12
12. p. 9, No. 16
13. p. 9, No. 16
    p. 11, No. 20
14. p. 9, No. 16
15. p. 9, No. 16
16. p. 9, No. 16
    p. 10, No. 18
17. p. 9, No. 16
    p. 10, No. 18
    p. 10, No. 20
18. p. 10, No. 20
19. p. 10, No. 20
20. p. 11, No. 20
21. p. 11, No. 21
22. p. 12, No. 24
23. p. 13, No. 27
24. p. 13, No. 28
25. p. 14, No. 30
26. p. 14, No. 30
    p. 15, No. 31
27. p. 15, No. 31
28. p. 15, No. 32
    p. 15, No. 33
    p. 16, No. 34
    p. 16, No. 35
    p. 16, No. 36
29. p. 17, No. 38
    p. 18, No. 39
    p. 18, No. 40
30. p. 19, No. 43
31. p. 19, No. 43
32. p. 20, No. 45
33. p. 21, No. 46
    p. 62, No. 67
34. p. 62, No. 67
35. p. 62, No. 68
36. p. 63, No. 69
37. p. 65, No. 74
38. p. 65, No. 74
39. p. 65, No. 75
40. p. 67, No. 79
41. p. 73, No. 92
42. p. 75, No. 95
    p. 111, No. 147
43. p. 75, No. 96
44. p. 96, No. 128
45. p. 96, No. 128
46. p. 98, No. 130
    p. 99, No. 131
47. p. 101, No. 133
    p. 102, No. 134
    p. 109, No. 145
48. p. 102, No. 134
49. p. 103, No. 136
    p. 104, No. 137
50. p. 103, No. 136
51. p. 104, No. 137
52. p. 106, No. 141
53. p. 109, No. 145
54. p. 109, No. 145
55. p. 110, No. 146

PLATE II

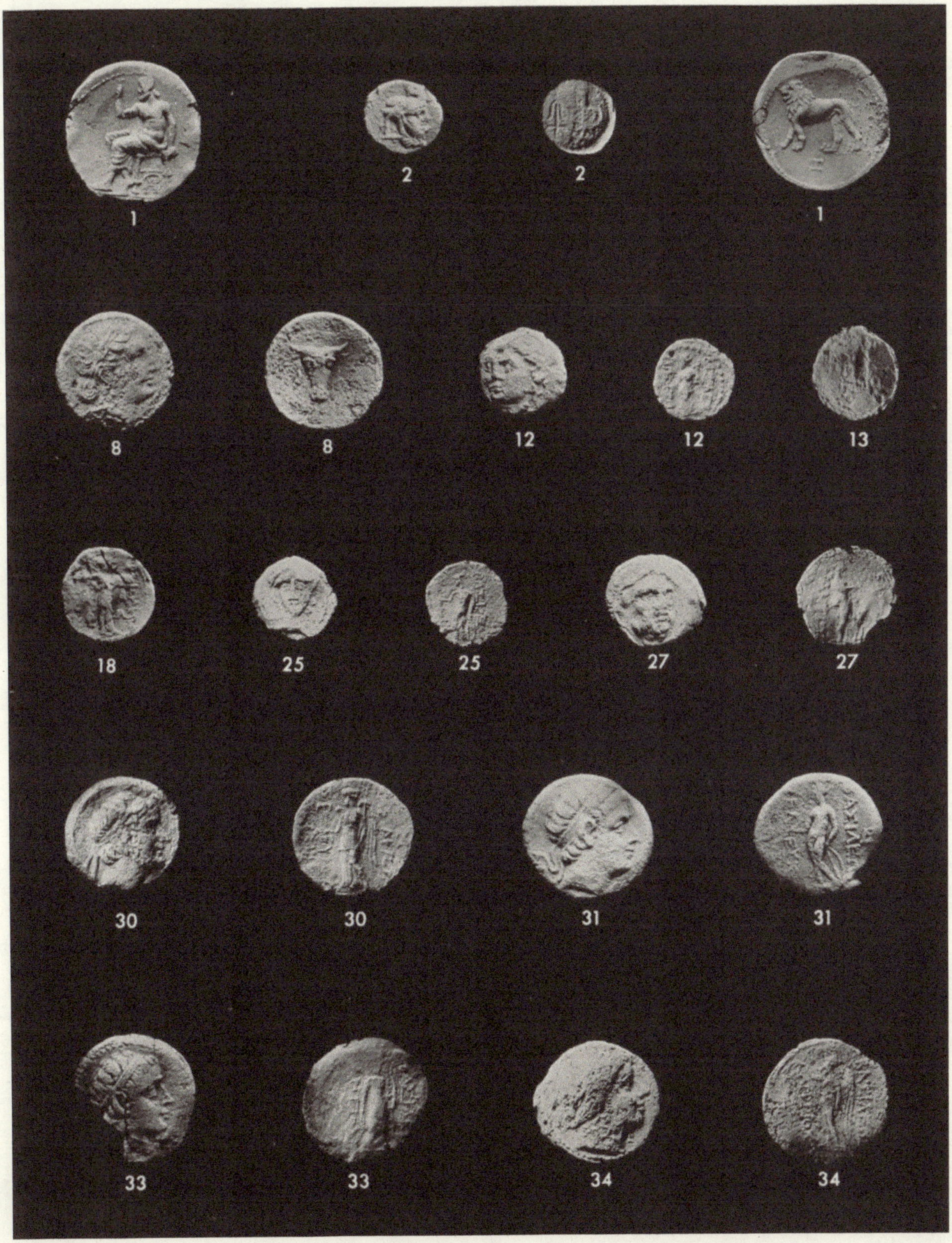

Seleucid coins (pp. 4–16)
(The catalog numbers of coins are retained in all plates)

PLATE III

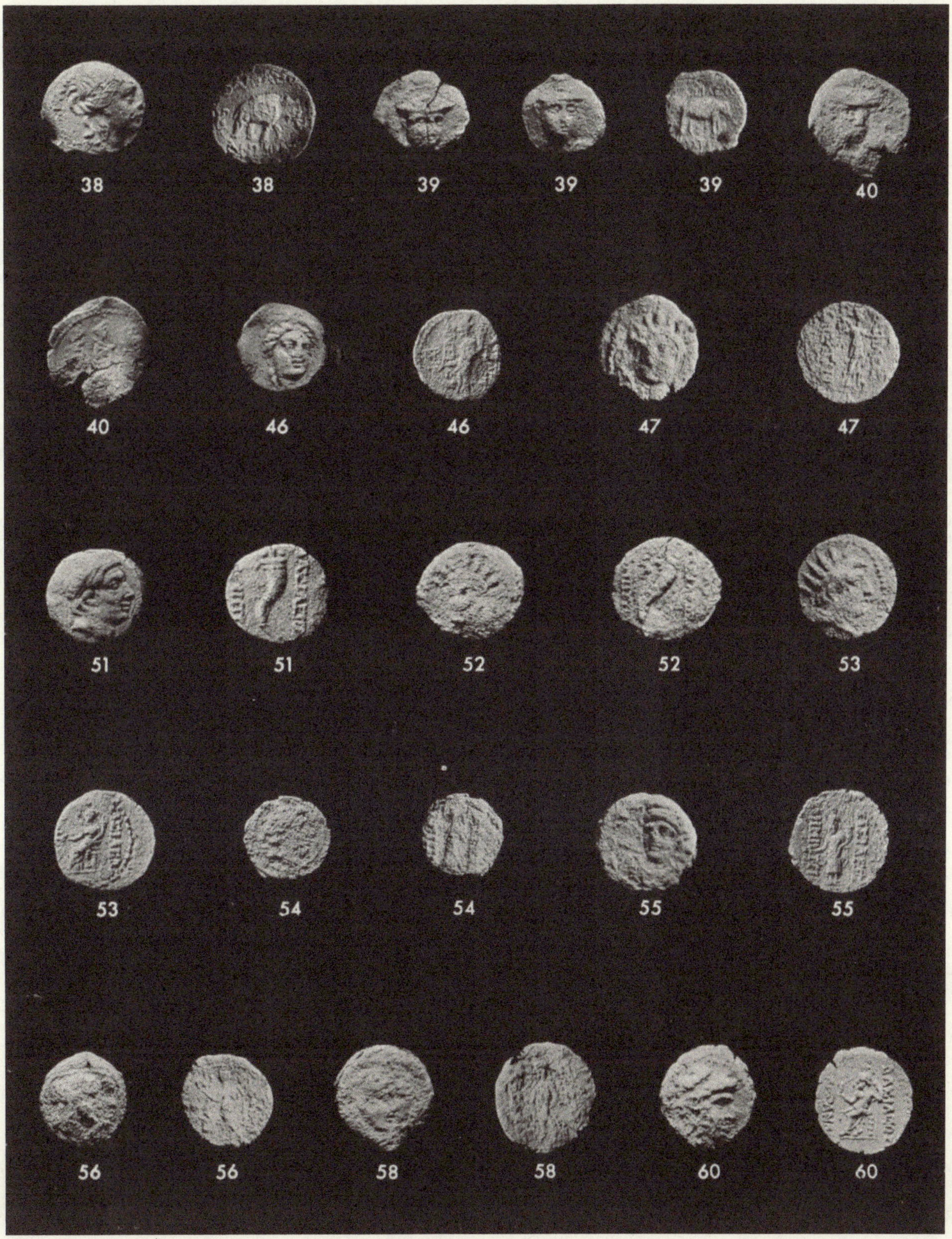

Seleucid coins (pp. 17–25)

PLATE IV

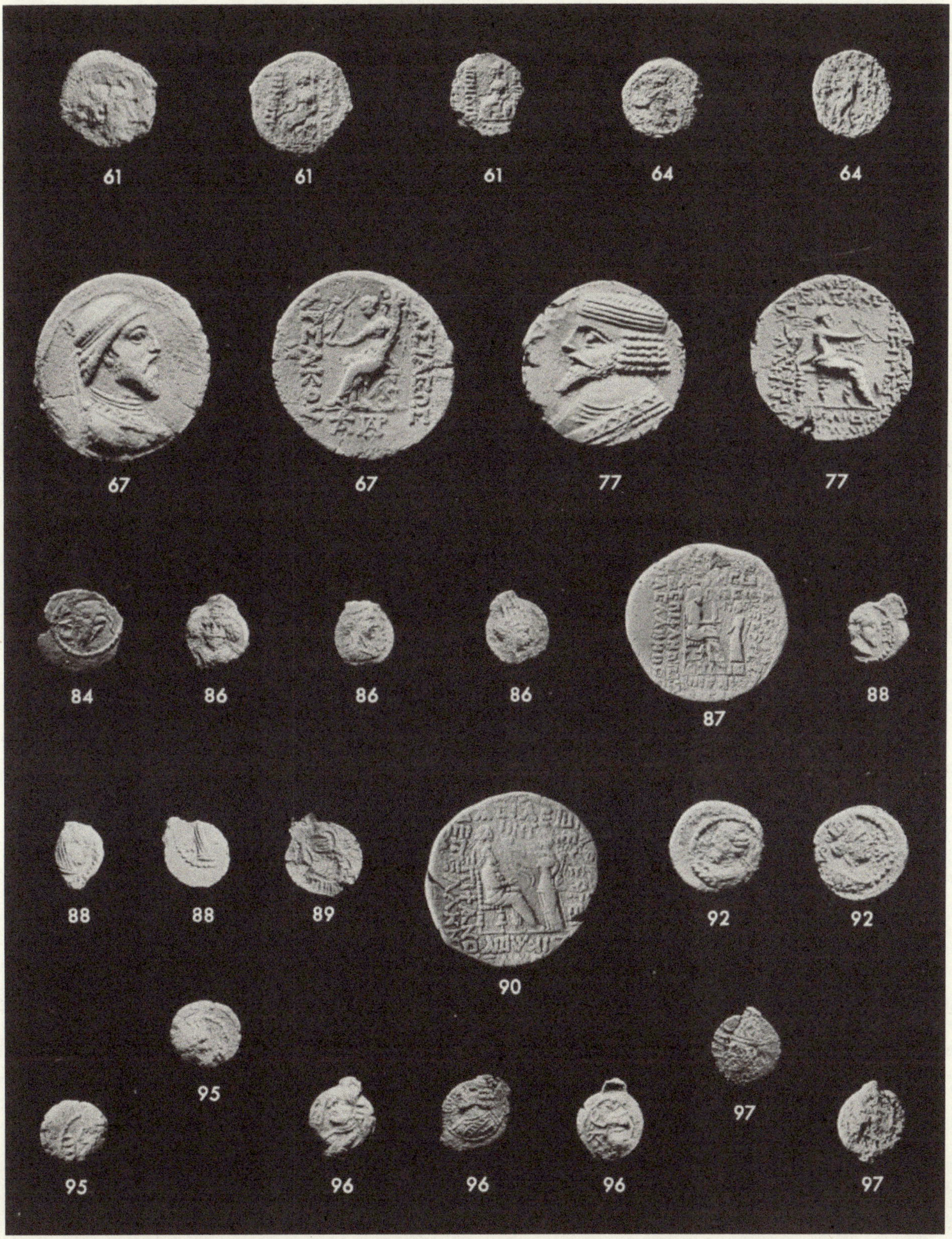

Seleucid coins in first row (pp. 26–27); Parthian royal coins in other rows (pp. 62–76)

PLATE V

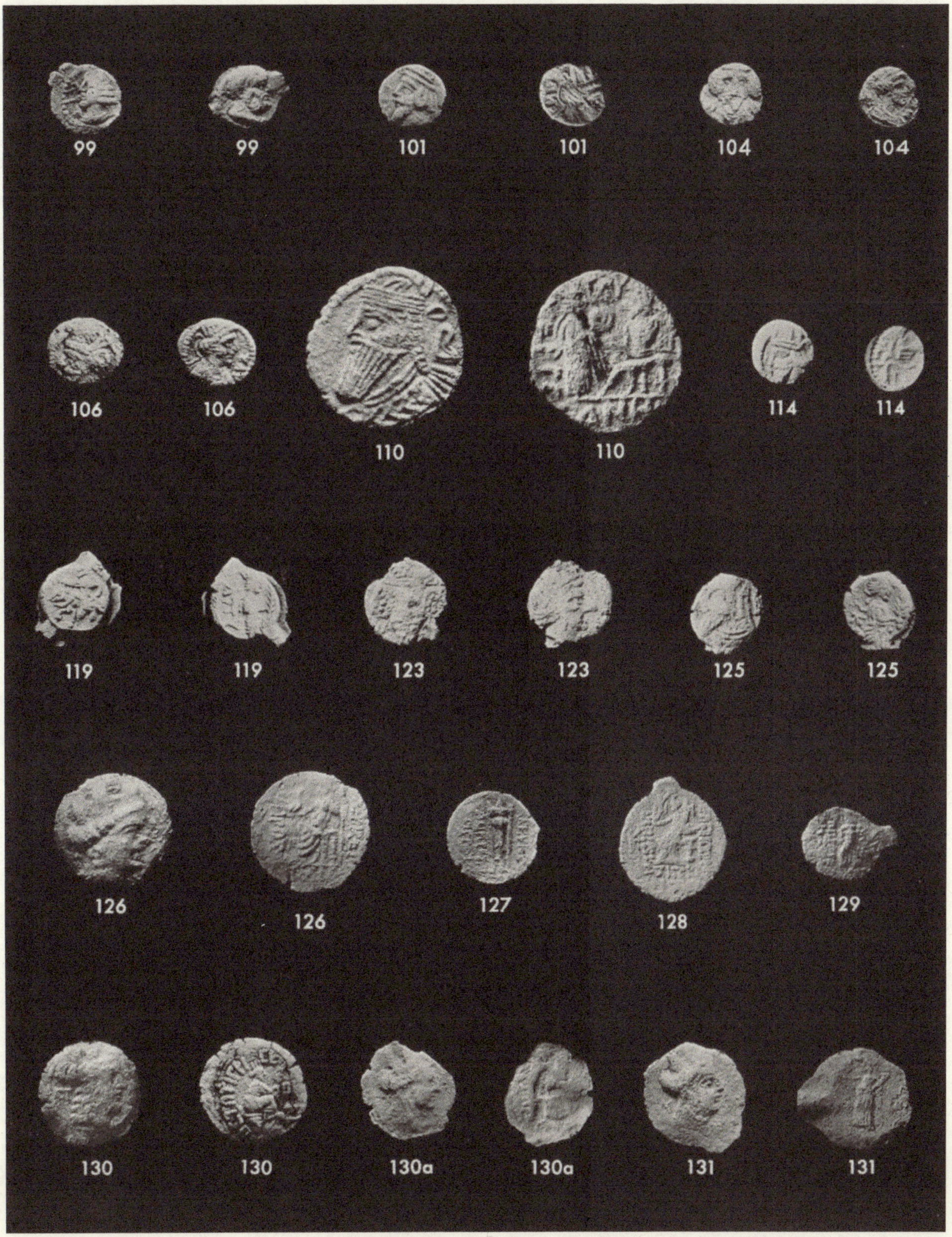

Parthian royal coins in first three rows (pp. 77–94); autonomous coins of Seleucia in last two rows (pp. 94–99)

PLATE VI

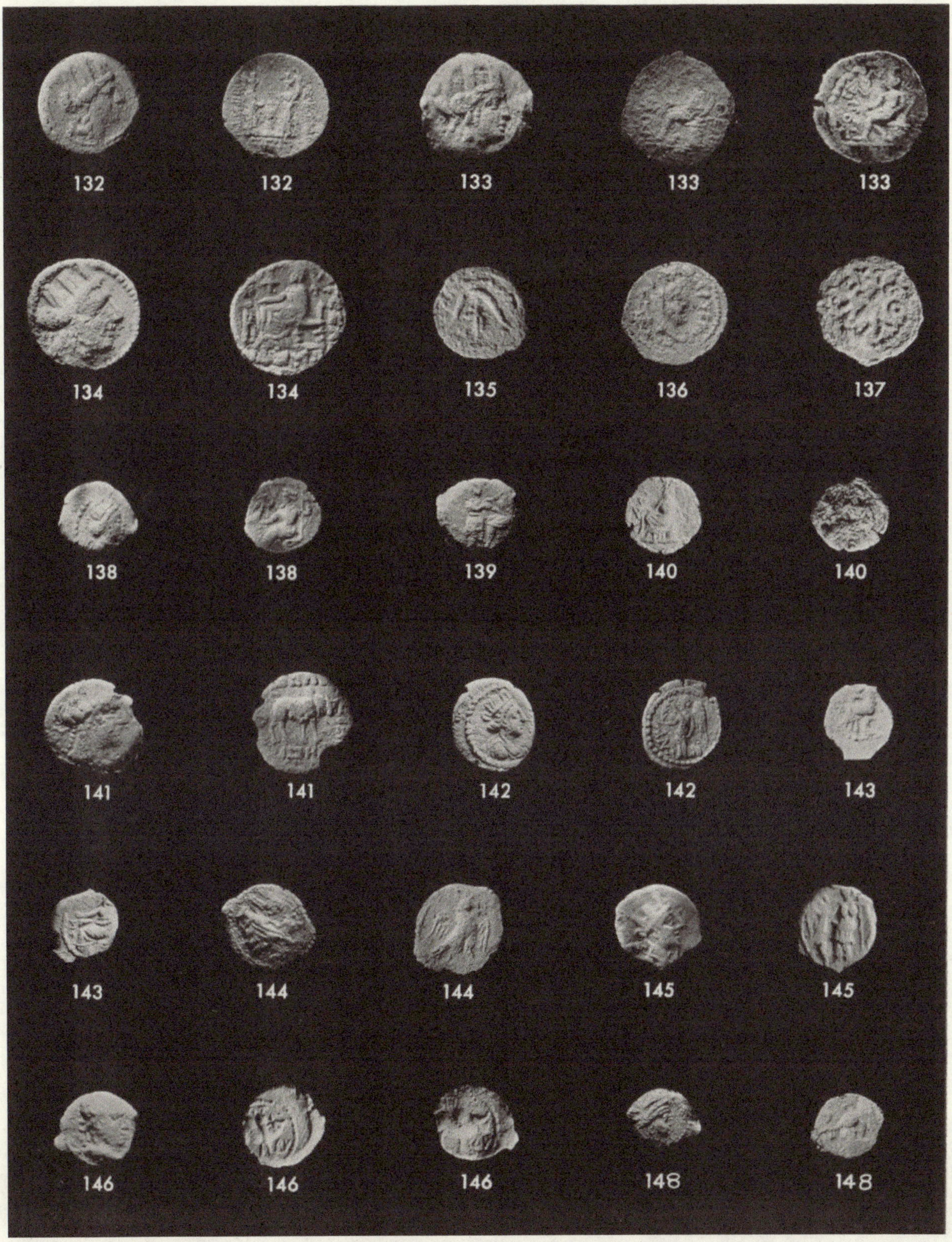

Autonomous coins of Seleucia (pp. 100–111)

University of Michigan Studies

HUMANISTIC SERIES

General Editors: JOHN G. WINTER, HENRY A. SANDERS, and EUGENE S. McCARTNEY

Size, 22.7 × 15.2 cm. 8°. Bound in cloth.

VOL. I. ROMAN HISTORICAL SOURCES AND INSTITUTIONS. Edited by Henry A. Sanders. (*Out of print.*)

VOL. II. WORD FORMATION IN PROVENCAL. By Edward L. Adams. Pp. xvii + 607. $4.00.

VOL. III. LATIN PHILOLOGY. Edited by C. L. Meader. (*Out of print.*)

Parts I, II Available in Paper Covers:

Part I. THE USE OF IDEM, IPSE, AND WORDS OF RELATED MEANING. By C. L. Meader. Pp. 1–112. $0.75.

Part II. A STUDY IN LATIN ABSTRACT SUBSTANTIVES. By M. A. Stewart. Pp. 113–178. $0.40.

VOL. IV. ROMAN HISTORY AND MYTHOLOGY. Edited by Henry A. Sanders. (*Out of print.*)

Parts I, III Available in Paper Covers:

Part I. STUDIES IN THE LIFE OF HELIOGABALUS. By Orma F. Butler. Pp. 1–169. $1.25.

Part III. ROMAN LAW STUDIES IN LIVY. By A. E. Evans. Pp. 275–354. $0.40.

VOL. V. SOURCES OF THE SYNOPTIC GOSPELS. By C. S. Patton. Pp. xiii + 263. $1.30.

Size, 28 × 18.5 cm. 4°.

VOL. VI. ATHENIAN LEKYTHOI WITH OUTLINE DRAWING IN GLAZE VARNISH ON A WHITE GROUND. By Arthur Fairbanks. Pp. viii + 371. $4.00.

VOL. VII. ATHENIAN LEKYTHOI WITH OUTLINE DRAWING IN MATT COLOR ON A WHITE GROUND. By Arthur Fairbanks. Pp. x + 275. $3.50.

VOL. VIII. THE OLD TESTAMENT MANUSCRIPTS IN THE FREER COLLECTION. By Henry A. Sanders. Pp. x + 357. $3.50.

Parts Sold Separately in Paper Covers:

Part I. THE WASHINGTON MANUSCRIPT OF DEUTERONOMY AND JOSHUA. Pp. vi + 104. $1.25.

Part II. THE WASHINGTON MANUSCRIPT OF THE PSALMS. Pp. viii + 105–357. $2.00.

Orders should be addressed to The Librarian, University of Michigan, Ann Arbor, Michigan.

Vol. IX. The New Testament Manuscripts in the Freer Collection. By Henry A. Sanders. Pp. x + 323. $3.50.

Part II Available in Paper Cover:

Part II. The Washington Manuscript of the Epistles of Paul. Pp. ix + 251–315. $1.25.

Vol. X. The Coptic Manuscripts in the Freer Collection. By William H. Worrell. Pp. xxvi + 396. $4.75.

Parts Sold Separately in Paper Covers:

Part I. The Coptic Psalter. Pp. xxvi + 112. $2.00.

Part II. Two Coptic Homilies and a Magical Text in the Freer Collection. Pp. 113–396. $2.50.

Vol. XI. Contributions to the History of Science. By Louis C. Karpinski and John G. Winter. Pp. xi + 283. $3.50.

Parts Sold Separately:

Part I. Robert of Chester's Latin Translation of the Algebra of Al-Khowarizmi. With an Introduction, Critical Notes, and an English Version. By Louis C. Karpinski. Pp. vii + 164. $2.00.

Part II. The Prodromus of Nicolaus Steno's Latin Dissertation on a Solid Body Enclosed by Process of Nature within a Solid. Translated into English by John G. Winter. Pp. vii + 169–283. $1.30.

Vol. XII. Studies in East Christian and Roman Art. By Charles Morey and Walter Dennison. (*Out of print.*)

Vol. XIII. Fragments from the Cairo Genizah in the Freer Collection. By Richard Gottheil, and William H. Worrell. Text, with Translation, Notes and an Introduction. Pp. xxxi + 273. $4.00.

Vol. XIV. Two Studies in Later Roman and Byzantine Administration. By Arthur E. R. Boak and James E. Dunlap. Pp. x + 324. $2.25.

Part II Available in Paper Cover:

Part II. The Office of the Grand Chamberlain in the Later Roman and Byzantine Empires. By James E. Dunlap. Pp. 161–324. $1.00.

Vol. XV. Greek Themes in Modern Musical Settings. By Albert A. Stanley. (*Out of print.*)

Parts Sold Separately in Paper Covers:

Part I. Incidental Music to Percy Mackaye's Drama of Sappho and Phaon. Pp. 1–68. $0.90.

Orders should be addressed to The Librarian, University of Michigan, Ann Arbor, Michigan

Part II. Music to the Alcestis of Euripides with English Text. Pp. 71–120. $0.80.

Part III. Music for the Iphigenia among the Taurians by Euripides, with Greek Text. Pp. 123–214. $0.75.

Part IV. Two Fragments of Ancient Greek Music. Pp. 217–225. $0.30.

Part V. Music to Cantica of the Menaechmi of Plautus. Pp. 229–263. $0.50.

Part VI. Attis: A Symphonic Poem. Pp. 265–384. $1.00.

Vol. XVI. Nicomachus of Gerasa: Introduction to Arithmetic. Translated into English by Martin Luther D'Ooge, with Studies in Greek Arithmetic by Frank Egleston Robbins and Louis C. Karpinski. (*Out of print.*)

Vols. XVII–XX. Royal Correspondence of the Assyrian Empire. Translated into English with a Transliteration of the Text and a Commentary. By Leroy Waterman.

Vol. XVII. Translation and Transliteration. Pp. x + 492. $4.50.

Vol. XVIII. Translation and Transliteration. Pp. iv + 524. $4.50.

Vol. XIX. Commentary. Pp. x + 377. $4.00.

Vol. XX. Supplement and Indexes. (*In preparation.*)

Vol. XXI. The Minor Prophets in the Freer Collection and the Berlin Fragment of Genesis. By Henry A. Sanders and Carl Schmidt. Pp. xii + 436. $3.50.

Vol. XXII. A Papyrus Codex of the Shepherd of Hermas, with a Fragment of the Mandates. By Campbell Bonner. Pp. x + 137. $3.00.

Vol. XXIII. The Complete Commentary of Oecumenius on the Apocalypse: Now printed for the first time from Manuscripts at Messina, Rome, Salonika and Athos. By H. C. Hoskier. Pp. viii + 260. $4.00.

Vol. XXIV (= Michigan Papyri, Vol. I). Zenon Papyri in the University of Michigan Collection. By C. C. Edgar. Pp. xiv + 211. $3.50.

Vol. XXV. Karanis: Topographical and Architectural Report of Excavations during the Seasons 1924–28. By A. E. R. Boak and E. Peterson. Pp. viii + 69. $2.00.

Vol. XXVI. Coptic Sounds. By William H. Worrell. With an Appendix by Hide Shohara. Pp. xviii + 186. $3.00.

Orders should be addressed to The Librarian, University of Michigan, Ann Arbor, Michigan.

Vol. XXVII. Athenian Financial Documents of the Fifth Century. By B. D. Meritt. Pp. xiv + 192. $3.50.

Vols. XXVIII–XXIX (= Michigan Papyri, Vols. II–III). Papyri from Tebtunis. By A. E. R. Boak.

Vol. XXVIII (= Michigan Papyri, Vol. II). Pp. xvi + 259. $3.50.

Vol. XXIX. (*In preparation.*)

Vol. XXX. Karanis: The Temples, Coin Hoards, Botanical and Zoölogical Reports, Seasons 1924–31. Edited by A. E. R. Boak. Pp. xii + 93. With 37 plates, 16 plans, and 4 diagrams. $2.50.

Vol. XXXI. Ancient Textiles from Egypt in the University of Michigan Collection. By Lillian M. Wilson. Pp. x + 77. With 23 plates. $2.50.

Vol. XXXII. Parthian Pottery from Seleucia on the Tigris. By Neilson C. Debevoise. Pp. xiv + 132. With 14 plates. $3.00.

Vol. XXXIII. The Athenian Assessment of 425 b.c. By B. D. Meritt and A. B. West. Pp. xiv + 112. With 2 plates and 17 figures. $2.50.

Vols. XXXIV–XXXV. Greek Ostraca in the University of Michigan Collection. By Leiv Amundsen.

Vol. XXXIV. Part I. Texts. Pp. xx + 232. $3.50.

Vol. XXXV. Part II. Commentary. (*In preparation.*)

Vol. XXXVI. Stamped and Inscribed Objects from Seleucia on the Tigris. By R. H. McDowell. Pp. xviii + 272. With 6 plates. $3.50.

Vol. XXXVII. Coins from Seleucia on the Tigris. By R. H. McDowell. Pp. vii + 248. With 6 plates. $3.50.

Vol. XXXVIII. A Third-Century Papyrus Codex of the Epistles of Paul. By Henry A. Sanders. Pp. xii + 127. $3.00.

THE JEROME LECTURES

Life and Letters in the Papyri. By John G. Winter. Pp. viii + 308. $3.50.

SCIENTIFIC SERIES

Size, 28 × 18.5 cm. 4°. Bound in cloth.

Vol. I. The Circulation and Sleep. By John F. Shepard. Pp. ix + 83, with an Atlas of 63 plates, bound separately. Text and Atlas. $2.50.

Orders should be addressed to The Librarian, University of Michigan, Ann Arbor, Michigan.

Vol. II. Studies on Divergent Series and Summability. By Walter B. Ford. Pp. xi + 194. $2.50.

Size, 23.5 × 15.5 cm.

Vol. III. The Geology of the Netherlands East Indies. By H. A. Brouwer. Pp. xii + 160. With 18 plates and 17 text figures. $3.00.

Vol. IV. The Glacial Anticyclones: The Poles of the Atmospheric Circulation. By W. H. Hobbs. Pp. xxiv + 198. With 3 plates and 53 figures. $2.75.

Vols. V–VIII. Reports of the Greenland Expeditions of the University of Michigan (1926–31). W. H. Hobbs, Director.

Vol. V. Aërology, Expeditions of 1926 and 1927–29. Pp. x + 262. With 23 plates and 30 text figures. $6.00.

Vol. VI. Aërology, Expeditions of 1930–31. (*In preparation.*)

Vol. VII. Meteorology. (*In preparation.*)

Vol. VIII. Geology, Glaciology, Botany, Etc. (*In preparation.*)

Vol. IX. The Genus Diaporthe Nitschke and Its Segregates. By Lewis E. Wehmeyer. Pp. xii + 349. With 18 plates. $3.50.

Vol. X. The Distribution of the Currents of Action and of Injury Displayed by Heart Muscle and Other Excitable Tissues. By F. N. Wilson, A. G. Macleod, and P. S. Barker. Pp. viii + 59. $1.50.

University of Michigan Publications

General Editor: EUGENE S. McCARTNEY

HUMANISTIC PAPERS

Size, 22.7 × 15.2 cm. 8°.

The Life and Work of George Sylvester Morris: A Chapter in the History of American Thought in the Nineteenth Century. By Robert M. Wenley. Pp. xv + 332. $1.50.

Henry Philip Tappan: Philosopher and University President. By Charles M. Perry. Pp. xii + 475. $3.25.

Latin and Greek in American Education, with Symposia on the Value of Humanistic Studies. Revised edition. Edited by Francis W. Kelsey. Pp. xiii + 360. $2.00.

Orders should be addressed to The Librarian, University of Michigan, Ann Arbor, Michigan.

Size, 18 × 12 cm.

THE MENAECHMI OF PLAUTUS. The Latin Text, with a Translation by Joseph H. Drake, University of Michigan. Pp. xi + 130. Bound in paper. $0.60.

LANGUAGE AND LITERATURE

VOL. I. STUDIES IN SHAKESPEARE, MILTON AND DONNE. By Members of the English Department of the University of Michigan. Pp. viii + 232. $2.50.

VOL. II. ELIZABETHAN PROVERB LORE IN LYLY'S 'EUPHUES' AND IN PETTIE'S 'PETITE PALLACE,' WITH PARALLELS FROM SHAKESPEARE. By Morris P. Tilley. Pp. x + 461. $3.50.

VOL. III. THE SOCIAL MODE OF RESTORATION COMEDY. By Kathleen M. Lynch. Pp. x + 242. $2.50.

VOL. IV. STUART POLITICS IN CHAPMAN'S 'TRAGEDY OF CHABOT.' By Norma D. Solve. Pp. x + 176. $2.50.

VOLS. V–VI. EL LIBRO DEL CAUALLERO ZIFAR. By C. P. Wagner.
VOL. V. PART I. TEXT. Pp. xviii + 532. With 9 plates. $5.00.
VOL. VI. PART II. COMMENTARY. (*In preparation.*)

VOL. VII. STRINDBERG'S DRAMATIC EXPRESSIONISM. By C. E. W. L. Dahlström. Pp. xii + 242. $2.50.

VOL VIII. ESSAYS AND STUDIES IN ENGLISH AND COMPARATIVE LITERATURE. By Members of the English Department of the University of Michigan. Pp. viii + 231. $2.50.

VOL. IX. TOWARD THE UNDERSTANDING OF SHELLEY. By Bennett Weaver. Pp. xii + 258. $2.50.

VOL. X. ESSAYS AND STUDIES IN ENGLISH AND COMPARATIVE LITERATURE. By Members of the English Department of the University of Michigan. Pp. vi + 278. $2.50.

VOL. XI. FRENCH MODAL SYNTAX IN THE SIXTEENTH CENTURY. By Newton S. Bement. Pp. xviii + 168. $2.50.

VOL. XII. THE INTELLECTUAL MILIEU OF JOHN DRYDEN. By Louis I. Bredvold. Pp. viii + 189. $2.50.

VOL. XIII. ESSAYS AND STUDIES IN ENGLISH AND COMPARATIVE LITERATURE. By Members of the English Department of the University of Michigan. Pp. vi + 328. $3.00.

VOLS. XIV–XV. THREE CENTURIES OF FRENCH POETIC THEORY (1328–1630). By W. F. Patterson. (*In press.*)
VOL. XIV. PARTS I–II. Pp. xx + 978. $5.00.
VOL. XV. PARTS III–IV. Pp. vi + 523. $3.50.

HISTORY AND POLITICAL SCIENCE

The first three volumes of this series were published as "Historical Studies" under the direction of the Department of History. Volumes IV and V were published without numbers.

VOL. I. A HISTORY OF THE PRESIDENT'S CABINET. By Mary Louise Hinsdale. (*Out of print.*)

VOL. II. ENGLISH RULE IN GASCONY, 1199–1259, WITH SPECIAL REFERENCE TO THE TOWNS. By Frank Burr Marsh. Pp. xi + 178. $1.25.

VOL. III. THE COLOR LINE IN OHIO; A HISTORY OF RACE PREJUDICE IN A TYPICAL NORTHERN STATE. By Frank Uriah Quillan. Pp. xv + 178. $1.50.

VOL. IV. THE SENATE AND TREATIES, 1789–1817. THE DEVELOPMENT OF THE TREATY-MAKING FUNCTIONS OF THE UNITED STATES SENATE DURING THEIR FORMATIVE PERIOD. By Ralston Hayden. Pp. xvi + 237. $1.50.

VOL. V. WILLIAM PLUMER'S MEMORANDUM OF PROCEEDINGS IN THE UNITED STATES SENATE, 1803–1807. Edited by Everett Somerville Brown. Pp. xi + 873. $3.50.

VOL. VI. THE GRAIN SUPPLY OF ENGLAND DURING THE NAPOLEONIC PERIOD. By W. F. Galpin. Pp. xi + 305. $3.00.

VOL. VII. EIGHTEENTH CENTURY DOCUMENTS RELATING TO THE ROYAL FORESTS, THE SHERIFFS AND SMUGGLING: SELECTED FROM THE SHELBURNE MANUSCRIPTS IN THE WILLIAM L. CLEMENTS LIBRARY. By Arthur Lyon Cross. Pp. x + 328. With 4 plates. $3.00.

VOL. VIII. THE LOW COUNTRIES AND THE HUNDRED YEARS' WAR, 1326–1347. By Henry S. Lucas. Pp. xiv + 696. $4.00.

VOL. IX. THE ANGLO-FRENCH TREATY OF COMMERCE OF 1860 AND THE PROGRESS OF THE INDUSTRIAL REVOLUTION IN FRANCE. By A. L. Dunham. Pp. xiv + 409. $3.50.

VOL. X. THE YOUTH OF ERASMUS. By A. Hyma. Pp. xii + 350. $3.00.

CONTRIBUTIONS FROM THE MUSEUM OF PALEONTOLOGY

VOL. I. THE STRATIGRAPHY AND FAUNA OF THE HACKBERRY STAGE OF THE UPPER DEVONIAN. By Carroll Lane Fenton and Mildred Adams Fenton. Pp. xi + 260. With 45 plates, 9 text figures, and 1 map. $2.75.

VOL. II. Consisting of 14 miscellaneous papers. Pages ix + 240. With 41 plates, 39 text figures, and 1 map. $3.00.

VOL. III. Consisting of 13 miscellaneous papers. Pp. viii + 275. With 64 plates, 49 text figures, and 1 map. $3.50.

VOL. IV. Consisting of 18 miscellaneous papers. Pp. viii + 295. With 55 plates, 106 text figures, and 2 maps. $3.50.

Orders should be addressed to The Librarian, University of Michigan, Ann Arbor, Michigan.

ARCHAEOLOGICAL REPORTS

PRELIMINARY REPORT UPON THE EXCAVATIONS AT TEL UMAR, IRAQ, CONDUCTED BY THE UNIVERSITY OF MICHIGAN AND THE TOLEDO MUSEUM OF ART. Leroy Waterman, Director. Pp. x + 62. With 13 plates and 7 text figures. $1.50. Bound in paper.

SECOND PRELIMINARY REPORT UPON THE EXCAVATIONS AT TEL UMAR, IRAQ, CONDUCTED BY THE UNIVERSITY OF MICHIGAN, THE TOLEDO MUSEUM OF ART, AND THE CLEVELAND MUSEUM OF ART. Leroy Waterman, Director. Pp. xii + 78. With 26 plates and 12 text figures. $1.50. Bound in paper.

PAPERS OF THE MICHIGAN ACADEMY OF SCIENCE, ARTS AND LETTERS

(Containing papers submitted at annual meetings)

Editors: EUGENE S. McCARTNEY and ALFRED H. STOCKARD

Size, 24.2 × 16.5 cm. 8°. Bound in cloth.

VOL. I (1921). Pp. xi + 424. $2.00.

VOL. II (1922). Pp. xi + 226. $2.00. Bound in paper, $1.50.

VOL. III (1923). Pp. xii + 473. $3.00. Bound in paper, $2.25.

VOL. IV (1924), Part I. Pp. xii + 631. $3.00. Bound in paper, $2.25.

VOL. IV (1924), PART II. A KEY TO THE SNAKES OF THE UNITED STATES, CANADA AND LOWER CALIFORNIA. By Frank N. Blanchard. Pp. xiii + 65. $1.75.

VOL. V (1925). Pp. xii + 479. $3.00. Bound in paper, $2.25.

VOL. VI (1926). (Papers in botany only.) Pp. xii + 406. $3.00. Bound in paper, $2.25.

VOL. VII (1926). (No papers in botany.) Pp. xii + 435. $3.00. Bound in paper, $2.25.

VOL. VIII (1927). Pp. xiv + 456. $3.00. Bound in paper, $2.25.

VOL. IX (1928). (Papers in botany and forestry only.) Pp. xiv + 597. $4.00. Bound in paper, $2.25.

VOL. X (1928). (No papers in botany or forestry.) Pp. xiv + 620. $4.00. Bound in paper, $2.25.

VOL. XI (1929). (Papers in botany and zoölogy only.) Pp. xii + 494. $3.50. Bound in paper, $2.25.

Orders should be addressed to The Librarian, University of Michigan, Ann Arbor, Michigan.

Vol. XII (1929). (No papers in botany or zoölogy.) Pp. xii + 348. $3.00. Bound in paper, $2.25.

Vol. XIII (1930). (Papers in botany and zoölogy only.) Pp. xii + 603. $4.00. Bound in paper, $2.25.

Vol. XIV (1930). (No papers in botany or zoölogy.) Pp. xv + 650. $4.00. Bound in paper, $2.25.

Vol. XV (1931). (Papers in botany, forestry, and zoölogy only.) Pp. x + 511. $3.50. Bound in paper, $2.25.

Vol. XVI (1931). (No papers in botany, forestry, or zoölogy.) Pp. x + 521. $3.50. Bound in paper, $2.25.

Vol. XVII (1932). (Papers in botany, forestry, and zoölogy only.) Pp. x + 738. $4.00. Bound in paper, $2.25.

Vol. XVIII (1932). (No papers in botany, forestry, or zoölogy.) Pp. x + 623. $4.00. Bound in paper, $2.25.

Vol. XIX (1933). Pp. xii + 662. $4.00. Bound in paper, $2.25.

Vol. XX (1934). Pp. xvi + 755. $4.00. Bound in paper, $2.25.

Orders should be addressed to The Librarian, University of Michigan, Ann Arbor, Michigan.